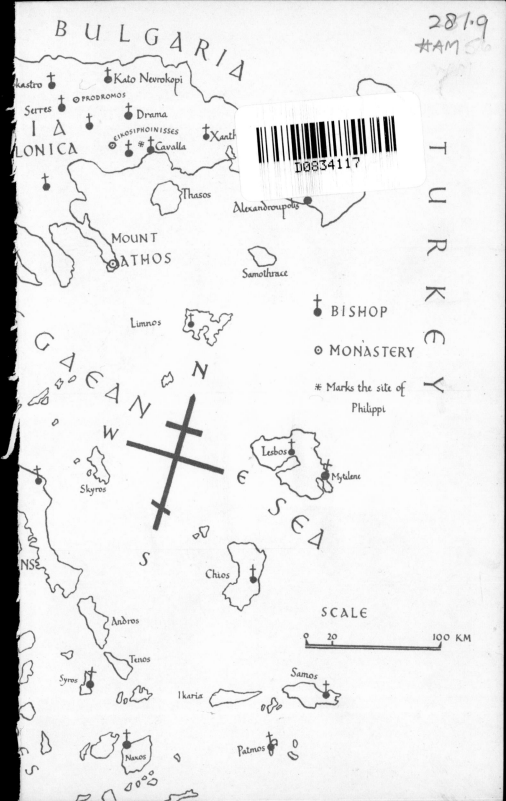

BULGARIA

kastro ✝●

●✝ Kato Nevrokopi

Serres ✝● ◉ PRODROMOS

I Δ

LONICA

✝● Drama

◉ EIKOSIPHOINISSES

⊙● ✳✝ Cavalla

●✝ Xanth

✝●

Thasos

Alexandroupolis ●✝

MOUNT

◉ ATHOS

Samothrace

Limnos

✝●

✝ BISHOP
●

◉ MONASTERY

✳ Marks the site of
   Philippi

AEAN

N

W

S

Lesbos ●✝

Mytilene ✝●

E

Skyros ✝●

SEA

Chios ✝●

Andros

SCALE

0   20   100 KM

Tenos

Samos ✝●

Syros ✝●

Ikaria

Naxos ✝●

Patmos ✝●

T
U
R
K
E
Y

THE WATERS OF MARAH

I   Search how it was in the beginning . . . return to the reverend Fathers

THE WATERS OF MARAH

THE PRESENT STATE
OF THE GREEK CHURCH

by

PETER HAMMOND

> And when they came to Marah, they could not drink of
> the waters of Marah, for they were bitter. . . . And he cried
> unto the Lord, and the Lord showed him a tree, and he
> cast it into the waters, and the waters were made sweet.
>
> *Exodus* XV, 23

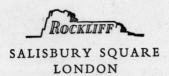

SALISBURY SQUARE
LONDON

PRINTED IN GREAT BRITAIN BY
THE CAMELOT PRESS LTD., LONDON AND SOUTHAMPTON

TO
THE CHURCH WHICH IS IN
THESSALONICA
AND TO ITS BISHOP
PANTELEIMON

ACKNOWLEDGEMENTS

I AM deeply grateful to Professor Basil Ioannides and the Rector and Senate of the University of Salonica for giving me an opportunity of spending two years in Greece, and to the many Greek friends, too numerous to mention individually, without whose unfailing kindness and *philoxenia* this book could never have been written. My thanks are due to Joan Ford, who read the book in manuscript; to Julitta Walker, for some notes on the history of the Anaplasis movement; and to Messrs. Hollis and Carter, for permission to quote from *The Greek Sedition* by F. A. Voigt. For much of the historical material used in Chapter XI I am indebted to the Archimandrite Seraphim Papakosta's biography of Eusebius Matthopoulos. I have also made use of Athanasius Papaevgeniou's *Martyres Klerikoi, Makedonias kai Thrakes*. I must also thank the trustees of the Burrows Memorial Prize and the Buxton Trust, and the Fellowship of St. Alban and St. Sergius, all of whom have helped to facilitate the publication of this essay; and Igor Vernik, in whose pleasant garden at Villemoisson sur Orge—though he may not have realised it at the time—the idea of the book first took shape.

P. H.

Stowe,
December 1955

CONTENTS

ILLUSTRATIONS

The engraving of the phelonion is reproduced from Dr. King's "Rites and Ceremonies of the Greek Church in Russia." The other illustrations are from photographs by the author.

I

PROLOGUE

> For these Reasons have I undertaken it, and if I have
> prevented any abler person, I beg pardon of him, and
> my Reader.
>
> ISAAK WALTON

IN the year of grace 1670, John Covel, master of arts and fellow of
Christ's College, Cambridge, being desirous, as he tells us, "of learning
some things abroad whereof I thought we had but a slight account at
home", went to Constantinople as chaplain to King Charles' ambassador at the Sublime Porte, Sir Daniel Harvey. Covel remained in
the Levant for nearly ten years and there became a diligent student of
the doctrine and practice of the Greek Church. The folio bearing the
title *Some Account of the Present Greek Church, with Reflections on their
Present Doctrine and Discipline etc.* which finally appeared in 1722 (the
year of its author's decease), as well as the travel journals and other
notes which are bound up in the two stout volumes of manuscripts
now in the library of the British Museum, bear witness to his unflagging
industry and curiosity.

Covel's *magnum opus*, it must be admitted, owes its origin primarily
to a singularly barren controversy which was at that time exercising
the minds of many French scholars and ecclesiastics, and which had
even aroused some interest on this side of the Channel, as to the
Greeks' attitude towards the scholastic doctrine of transubstantiation.
In the preface to his book he relates that "all Greeks who Travailed or
Stragled this way among the Europeans, were every where nicely
Catechised and Examin'd about this Point", and how in 1668 there
had come to Oxford a certain Jeremias Germanus, who "told every
Body that the Greeks believed no such thing". Covel also mentions the
fact that before leaving England he was asked by several scholars and
divines—Pearson, Gunning and Sancroft among them—"strictly to
enquire into this Matter after I arrived at Constantinople".

But the interest shown by these scholars in the Greek Church was not motivated by questions of controversy alone. While Covel was nicely catechising his Greek acquaintances in Constantinople, the British consul at Smyrna, Paul Rycaut, was writing his book on *The Present State of the Greek and Armenian Churches* which eventually appeared in 1679, and in the following year the English edition of the Reverend Thomas Smith's *Account of the Greek Church* was published in London.

The abortive Prayer Book revision of 1689 reflects this widespread interest in the Greek Church. It recommends that a note be annexed to the Nicene Creed "with relation to the Greek Church, in order to our maintaining Catholic Communion". During the last years of Dr. Covel's life the Non-Jurors embarked upon that remarkable correspondence with the eastern patriarchs which was only terminated by the intervention of the Archbishop of Canterbury, who assured the Patriarch of Jerusalem that "we, the true Bishops and Clergy of the Church of England, as, in every fundamental article, we profess the same Faith with you, we shall not cease, at least in spirit and effect (since otherwise, owing to our distance from you, we cannot), to hold communion with you, and to pray for your peace and happiness", and entreated him to remember him in his "prayers and sacrifices at the holy altar of God".

It would have been surprising had not the English reformers' reverence for primitive tradition and the ancient fathers of the Church led many scholars, from the seventeenth century onwards, to look eastwards towards a Church, little known indeed, but which claimed (as the patriarchs wrote to "the Remnant of the Primitive Orthodoxy in Britain" in 1718) "to preserve the Doctrine of the Lord uncorrupted, to adhere firmly to the Faith which He delivered to us, and to keep it free from blemish and diminutions, as a Royal Treasure, and a monument of great price, neither adding anything, nor taking anything from it". It was natural that such claims should awaken a response in those who, like Bishop Pearson, urged their fellow-churchmen to "search how it was in the beginning; go to the fountain head; look to antiquity; return to the reverend Fathers; have respect unto the primitive Church. . . ."

The English Church has never lacked scholars and theologians whose vision of historic Christendom has extended beyond the limits of the patriarchate of the west; who amidst the turmoil of controversy have not ceased to pray, like Bishop Andrewes, for the whole Church, eastern and western, in the very words of the Greek liturgies; or who, like Dr. Routh, while recognising that separation there unhappily is, have wished it were otherwise.

So far I have spoken only of professed scholars: men well-informed indeed but influencing only a small circle of their countrymen. But there is a further category of persons whose writings were not without a certain importance in preventing their contemporaries from wholly losing the consciousness of that more spacious Christendom which had all but faded from men's memory long before Jeremias Germanus strolled beside the pleasant fields which lie between Isis and Cherwell, or the most reverend and honourable the Metropolitan of Philippopolis, Exarch of all Thrace and Drogovia, had been made doctor of divinity in the Sheldonian, and had delighted a mighty concourse with "a very excellent speech, all in plain proper hellenistick Greek".

I refer to the travellers who in Greek waters, in Albania, in Turkey and elsewhere in the Levant, as well as in Russia, saw something of the Orthodox world at first hand and came home to write—often inaccurately enough—about the marvellous things they had seen. They are a motley crew: simple merchants and seafarers on the one hand, and, on the other, diplomatic officials and the *milordoi* whose memory still lingers about the classical sites of Old Greece: Master John Dallam, the organ-builder, who was commissioned by Queen Elizabeth to convey to the Sultan Mahomet III an ingenious instrument of his own making, and who has left us a diverting account of his wanderings; the Hon. Robert Curzon Jr., bibliophile, milord *par excellence* and indefatigable explorer of monasteries; the intrepid Urquhart and his mule Aristotle (a sagacious beast which had acquired so great a familiarity with ancient monuments that, so his master assures us, he came to a dead stop at every hewn stone); Thomas Alcock—another milord— who was so incensed by what he saw of the festival of St. Spyridon at Corfu in the year 1829 and who, far from admiring the traditional patterns of Orthodox asceticism, considered that "where the presence of females is wanting to command the suppression of that which is objectionable, and create an emulation in that which is agreeable, life is deprived of half its attractions"; ecclesiastics like the Abbé de St. Michon, ardent apostle of union and enthusiastic botanist, torn between the prospect of a visit to the Bishop of Syra and an expedition in search of rare flowers; or Père Robert de Dreux, chaplain to the French ambassador to the Porte from 1665 to 1669, and like his

3

contemporary, Dr. Covel, not "altogether a stranger to the Controversy between Claudius and Arnoldus about the great Dogma". They are an attractive company and one would willingly prolong the list.

A great deal that was written by these travellers was naïve and ill-informed to a degree. Dr. King says in the preface to his weighty quarto on the Greek Church in Russia, published in 1772, that "the many falsehoods and ridiculous stories repeated of this church, and spread over all countries, persuaded me that this is a subject hitherto little known: nor shall we wonder at the number of these falsehoods, if we reflect that the accounts we have had, for the most part, have been given by travellers who knew nothing either of the language or of the matter; but went into a church, stared about them, and then came home, and published an account of what they saw, according to their own imagination; frequently taking an accidental circumstance for an established custom, and not seldom totally misunderstanding whatever they beheld." Dr. King's strictures, it must be confessed, are not wholly unjust. Many of our travellers mislead as frequently as they enlighten, and, when all is said, the fact remains that for several centuries the Orthodox world has been little more than a half-effaced memory scarcely lingering in the consciousness of the western European; a *terra incognita* to the average Englishman; a world known only to a restricted circle of scholars, diplomats and seafarers.

During recent years there has indeed been a growing renewal of intercourse between eastern Christendom and the west. Not a little is due to the labours of such men as John Mason Neale, and, more recently, W. J. Birkbeck. Far the greatest factor, however, has been the Russian *diaspora*, and then, within the last decade, that widespread flight from the countries of eastern Europe of countless multitudes of ordinary people, which will surely go down to history as one of the characteristic marks of an age of displaced persons and refugees.

Now, for the first time since the day when what had formerly been different traditions bearing witness to the one faith hardened into division, there are large communities of Orthodox Christians living in our very midst, and the venerable liturgies deeply beloved of our Caroline forefathers are celebrated in our parish churches. Orthodox Christendom is no longer a world wholly apart, following the old paths in isolation from the theological strife which has rent the ancient patriarchate of Rome into warring fragments, and has effectually

4

obscured for the ordinary western Christian the vision of the organic body—one, holy, catholic and apostolic—in which (if indeed he ever enters his parish church) he professes his belief.

All this is, nevertheless, far too close at hand as yet to have had any widespread repercussions. Not only amongst ordinary people, but also in quarters where it would seem reasonable to look for greater enlightenment, it is still common to find the most abysmal ignorance in all that concerns the Orthodox world. Among the clergy of the Church of England one frequently encounters notions about the Greek or Russian Churches which are no less grotesque than the account of their own liturgical life which is attributed (with what truth, I must confess, I know not) to a certain Armenian cleric:

> You wish to know whether the English are Christians? They are Christians. They even have their eucharist—such as it is. Once a year the minister goes up into the pulpit with a large basket of loaves on his arm: he flings the loaves about among the people, who scramble for them in the church.
>
> The English Christians also have another religious ceremony called the National Debt. This consists in offering a large sum of money every year to the Emperor of the French: a ceremony much disliked and murmured at by the people!

It is, alas! still possible to meet with grave divines and scholars of Dr. Covel's own university, whose grasp of the rudiments of ecclesiastical polity beyond the Adriatic Sea is worthy of comparison with the classical statement of the Reverend Mr. Wortabet, missionary of the United Presbyterian Church at Aleppo, who observed that "If we understand the constitution and spirit and sympathies of the Greek Church, the Russian Emperor forms its head and soul", and added that "its compactness in this respect is unique".

Even in those circles where one can look for something more than ignorance and blind incomprehension—amongst those who through personal friendship, perhaps, or the patient spade-work of voluntary societies such as the Anglican and Eastern Churches Association or the Fellowship of St. Alban and St. Sergius, have come to know something of the life and worship of eastern Christendom—there frequently persists a stubborn if largely unformulated conviction that one has of course to remember that Orthodoxy is, after all, *eastern*, and, this being so, bears little relation to our own problems. A knowledge of the Orthodox Church—superficial though it be—can serve as a valuable weapon for polemical purposes: another stick with which to belabour the Bishop of Rome; and, even where such a controversial motive is lacking, a certain discreet dabbling in Orthodoxy is all too commonly looked upon as a delightful hobby, having an agreeable spice of novelty, but which it would be quite ridiculous to suppose had any urgent relevance to our own condition; an amiable eccentricity which may appropriately occupy the leisure hours of a few clergymen of a scholarly turn of mind, and which from time to time brings picturesque and exotic visitors to enliven for a few days the tranquil atmosphere of country parishes, but which is about as relevant to the conversion of our people to the catholic faith as astrology or the revival of the Cornish language.

Such an attitude is not difficult to comprehend if we bear in mind the fact that the religion of eastern Christendom has been re-presented to the west arrayed, more often than not, in a gorgeous vesture of Slavonic cut; a garment which the ordinary Englishman not unreasonably holds to be alien to his own outlook and tastes, albeit picturesque and not devoid of a certain exotic charm. Unfortunately it has all too frequently been precisely those elements in modern Russian Orthodoxy which bear the stamp of a particular age and setting (and which the Greek or Arab Christian, no less than the English or American churchman, feels to be wholly exotic) which have been widely, though none the less mistakenly, assumed to be peculiarly Orthodox by those whose knowledge of eastern Christendom is derived mainly, or even exclusively, from the Christians of the Russian diaspora.

An inevitable consequence has been that many western Christians, taking the accidents for the substance, have failed to penetrate the unfamiliar array to the common Christianity which lies veiled beneath it, and have built up for themselves a picture of the Orthodox Church in which flowing beards and imperfectly apprehended expositions of *sobornost* are elements of vastly greater importance than the faith once delivered to the saints.

There are those who seek the essential features of Orthodoxy in the works of nineteenth-century Russian writers such as Khomiakov and Solovyov when they might with greater profit turn to the writings of the fathers and the ancient liturgies: to the treasure house which belongs to catholic Christendom as a whole and not to any one people or age. I shall have occasion in the course of the present essay to speak of many things which to the western reader must needs appear strange and picturesque, and I can hardly insist too strongly that Orthodoxy does not stand in these things but in a life lived in the faith which is enshrined in the prayer of Christ in His Church: the faith that is summed up for all men and for all ages in the Nicene Creed and the tremendous paradoxes of Chalcedon.

During the last few years, thanks to the establishment of a Greek exarchate for western Europe with its metropolis in London, to the rapid growth of Orthodox communities in America, and to the various conferences held under the auspices of the World Council of Churches at which Orthodox delegates have been present, several Greek theologians and ecclesiastics have become well-known figures throughout western Christendom, and in England in particular. It is nevertheless a regrettable fact that apart from the extensive literature that has grown up around the holy mountain of Athos, and the researches of the late F. W. Hasluck, the later history of the Church of Greece has been almost wholly neglected by English writers and students.

Byzantine studies have at long last come into their own, but Covel and Rycaut have yet to find a successor; and this despite the fact that the last two or three generations have for the Greek Church been a period of momentous development and experiment. The only account yet to appear in English of the remarkable revival which has come about since the middle of the nineteenth century (save for a few articles in specialised journals enjoying an extremely limited circulation) is a translation of the brief biography of the Archimandrite Eusebius Matthopoulos by Father Seraphim Papakostas. Two or three slight and almost wholly factual introductions to the Greek Church by Greek authors writing in English, and our bibliography is complete.

Those who have been privileged to see something of the life of the Greek Church during recent years have long been conscious of the need for a book which should present a lively picture of what has been going on in Greece during the last generation or two, in terms which the English-speaking layman could understand; and it was the fact that nobody else, to my knowledge, was prepared to undertake a piece of work that badly needed tackling by somebody, that persuaded me to embark upon the present essay.

I would, however, stress the fact that I have set out to write a book which is rather in the nature of a personal impression of the present state of the Greek Church than a systematic handbook to her doctrine and practice. I have therefore felt free to omit, or to touch very briefly upon, many matters for which the reader might not unreasonably look in a work of a more formal character. Far be it from me to minimise the importance of such high matters as the process whereby a Greek prelate is elected, or the procedure of the Holy Synod; these and similar topics, however, will occupy our attention but slightly in the pages that follow. I have, nevertheless, sought to cast my net fairly wide, and if the mountain dioceses of Macedonia seem to occupy a more prominent place in the resulting picture than the terraces of Kolonaki, that, I would suggest, is as it should be. If I have succeeded in some measure in clothing with flesh and blood the dry bones of statistics and facile generalisations which, all too frequently, make up the sum total of my countrymen's knowledge of this Church, then I shall not consider my time ill spent.

I have introduced into my essay only so much in the way of historical and other background as seemed to be essential if the events of the last generation or two were to be seen in a true perspective, and if the full significance of certain elements in the contemporary scene were to be brought home to the uninitiated. I have indeed been at some pains to assume no more in the way of specialised knowledge than seemed reasonable to expect of that somewhat shadowy figure, the intelligent layman; and if, while scrupulously explaining the difference between an *Archimandrite* and a *Protopresbyter*, and nicely distinguishing between a *kalymmafchion* and a *skouphos*, I have failed to elucidate some no less recondite matter, I would plead that where so much is obscure it is difficult, with the best will in the world, to avoid leaving a patch of impenetrable shadow here and there, and refer the baffled reader to that systematic guide to the Greek Church which I hope some person better qualified for the task than the present writer will one day bring to completion.

I would only add, in conclusion, that the problem of the trans-literation of Greek words (with which one is inevitably faced if one decides, as a general rule, to eschew the use of Greek characters) fairly bristles with difficulties which I make no claim to have solved. Direct transliteration provides no easy way out and is liable to confront the perplexed reader with such obscurities as *mpar* and *Tsortsil*! I have taken refuge in compromise; and if any peevish pedant is so tiresome as to point out that since I have written of *Hieromonachoi* and *Hieratic* schools I should also have preferred *Hegoumenos* and *Haghios* to the forms which do in fact appear in the following pages, I will beseech his pardon and plead only that this essay is not for him but for those to whom all these high matters are but Greek.

II

SOME UNFAMILIAR PERSPECTIVES

> "And who", quoth the Patriarch . . . "Who is the Arch-
> bishop of Canterbury?"
> "What?" said I, a little astonished at the question.
> "Who", said he, "is this Archbishop?"
> "Why, the Archbishop of Canterbury."
> "Archbishop of *what*?" said the Patriarch.
> "Canterbury", said I.
> "Oh", said the Patriarch. "Ah! Yes! and who is he?"
>
> THE HON. ROBERT CURZON, JR.
> *Visits to Monasteries in*
> *the Levant*, London, 1849

THE western Christian who would enter with understanding into the
spirit of the Greek Church must be prepared to approach with a certain
childlike simplicity a strange world that will not be forced into the
mould of familiar categories; a world in which traditional western
controversies become meaningless, where the Pope is regarded as the
arch-Protestant and the Christian Scientist as an eccentric Roman
Catholic.

What is the western Christian to make of a Church, so manifestly
conservative and hierarchical in its whole ordering, which yet accords
to the laity so prominent—even, some might say, obtrusive—a place
in its public worship; in which laymen preach and teach while the
clergy meekly attend; a Church which detects in the western Protestant's
refusal to use incense a sign of popery; which honours the monastic
vocation and refuses to tolerate the unmarried parish priest? What of
the Greek country parson: a peasant-farmer, unlettered and, by western
standards, virtually untrained, administering the *mysteries* of initiation
and communion in his village church and labouring at his patch of
stony ground, the servant of the community?

Let the western Christian see something of the liturgical life of the
Greek Church, and he will tell you of gorgeous pageantry and ceremonial
and of services which never end; of bishops and metropolitans in

jewelled mitres and vestments of gold, assisted by priests and deacons whose "Garments and Accoutrements", in the words of a seventeenth-century divine, "are very Glorious and different"; of richly decorated churches where lamps burn day and night before the eikons of the saints. But let him go also to a house which stands beside the great basilica of St. Demetrius at Salonica and he will find himself in a gathering of students and professional men, the atmosphere of which recalls a nonconformist prayer-meeting; and to the adjoining hall where children shout the vernacular hymns of the catechetical schools, or where a young woman expounds a chapter of the Greek New Testament to an audience of housewives.

Christendom and the course of church history take on a very different aspect when one's vantage point lies to the eastward of the Adriatic: whether it be Constantinople or Jerusalem, Mount Athos or Alexandria. For the Greek Christian the visible fold of the Church is made up of the four ancient patriarchates of Jerusalem, Antioch, Alexandria and Constantinople, together with the patriarchate of Moscow and certain autocephalous churches. Beyond the frontiers of the Orthodox Church all is obscure and uncertain: to be committed to the boundless mercy of God, and approached (when circumstances require it) with wariness and circumspection. "As for the English Liturgy", runs the *Answer of the Orthodox of the East to the proposals sent from Britain for an union and agreement with the Oriental Church*, "we are unacquainted with it, having never either seen or read it; but we have some suspicion of it, because many and various Heresies, Schisms and Sects have arisen up in those parts, lest the hereticks should have introduced into it any corruption or deviation from the right Faith. Upon this account it is necessary we should both see and read it. . . ."

Within this outer darkness of heresy and schism the Greek is not given to nice distinctions, and strange confusions, baffling to the western mind, are common. A friend of mine was catechised at some length as to who it was who commemorated the Pope in the liturgy, by an old monk of Athos who was equally prepared to attribute this weighty offence to the Lutherans or to the Methodists! The persisting error of the patriarch of the west is seen in the same light as those of the reformers, as a hankering after innovation and new-fangled ways:

Some time since [write the eastern patriarchs to "the Remnant of Primitive Piety"] the Pope of Rome, being deceived by the malice of the Devil and falling into strange novel doctrines, revolted from the unity of the Holy Church, and was cut off; and is now like a tattered rag of the sail of the spiritual vessel of the Church, which formerly consisted and was made up of five parts, four of which continue in the same state of unity and concord, and by these we easily and calmly sail through the ocean of this life, and without difficulty pass over the waves of heresy till we arrive within the haven of salvation. But he who is the fifth part, being separated from the entire sail . . . is unable to perform his voyage, and therefore we behold him at a distance, tossed with constant waves and tempest till he return to our catholic, apostolic, oriental and immaculate faith, and be reinstated in the sail from whence he was torn off: for this will make him secure and able to weather the spiritual storms and tempests that beset him. . . .

Gregory, by the mercy of God Archbishop of Constantinople, New Rome and Oecumenical Patriarch, writes on September 26th, 1869, to "the most holy Archbishop, the Metropolitan of Canterbury, and Exarch of the Christians of the Anglican Confession in Great Britain, the Lord Archibald Campbell," to acknowledge the receipt of a copy of the English Book of Common Prayer which that dignitary had caused to be sent him. After having examined the said book to "ascertain how far it inclines to or diverges from genuine evangelical and catholic teaching" the Patriarch reluctantly confesses that it contains statements which appear "to savour too much of novelty"; these statements, he concludes, "throw us into suspense, so that we doubt what we are to judge of the rule of Anglican orthodoxy".

These passages are characteristic of the Greek view of Christendom. While the Orthodox Church faithfully preserves the tradition of the undivided Church—"neither adding anything, or taking anything from it"—the western world, encouraged by the evil example of its chief bishop, has confounded the faith once delivered to the saints with "strange, novel doctrines", the fruit of human reasoning; and when holy tradition has once been set at naught there can be no certainty and no "right worship": the saving truth of God is henceforth mingled with the vain imaginings of sinful men.

In the spring of 1950 I made an expedition to the westward of Siatista with a small escort of local militia. The leader of the party questioned me as to the state of Christianity in England.

"The English," he demanded, "are Catholics?"

"No," said I, "though there is in England a Catholic minority far larger than in Greece."

"The English are *diamartyromenoi* (Protestants), then?"

"Indeed, no," said I, knowing something of the associations of the term for the Greek mind; "the English are not Protestants."

The *kapetanios* was perplexed; and then, after a moment's reflection he suddenly exclaimed with enormous satisfaction:

"So, then, the English are simple Christians!"

Needless to say, where the prevailing ignorance is so abysmal much can depend—for good or ill—upon chance encounters and odd scraps of information. There are those whose knowledge of the *Ecclesia Anglicana* would seem to be limited to the fact that she is divided as irrevocably as Caesar's Gaul into three parts, high, low and broad: though the significance of these mysterious divisions eludes their comprehension. Others know her only through the widely publicised activities of certain of the more idiorrhythmic of her dignitaries. Occasionally, however, a happier encounter affords the suspicious Greek ecclesiastic a glimpse of something which he can recognise as familiar amid the obscurity in which the west is veiled: which may even prompt him to inform his wondering flock, when he preaches to them the following Sunday, that in the mysterious providence of the *Pantocrator*, though all the territories of the patriarch of the west have fallen into heresy, some remnant of primitive orthodoxy has been preserved in those islands whence came Byron and Codrington and the *Kyrios* Churchill.

It was my custom when travelling in Greece to carry with me several copies of a Greek translation of the Scottish Communion Office. The recipients of this work included the abbot of a certain monastery, whose hospitality I had enjoyed: a rigorist who regarded all that lay beyond the pale of Orthodox Christendom as unrelieved darkness and heresy. It was some months before I stayed at the monastery again, and my visit coincided with a festival. After the liturgy the abbot invited several of those who had been present in church to the guest-chamber, where coffee and cognac were served by a deacon. The inevitable catechism ensued:

"The *Kyrios* is not a Greek?"

"No, he is a stranger."

"From what country?"

"He comes from England."

"Ah! from England."

"Yes, he is a *theologos* from Oxford."

"He is Orthodox?"

At this point another of the visitors, a high-school teacher from Cyprus, rashly asserted in a loud voice that the English were all Luthero-Calvinists. "It is evident, Sir Professor," said the abbot, "that you are ill-informed in regard to the belief of the English Christians. *I*, however, have closely studied the liturgy of the British nation which, it is beyond doubt, is no other than that of St. James, the Lord's brother. The Christians who have such a liturgy are evidently orthodox in faith, even though their canonical status, owing to their remoteness and isolation, is somewhat irregular."

It is perhaps only fair to add that other travellers have on occasion met with a less encouraging response to their efforts to diffuse a more exact knowledge of our own liturgical life. Dr. Hunt, for example, who visited Mount Athos at the end of the eighteenth century, and who relates that: "In conversation with their prelates and well educated caloyers [from *kalogeros*—literally, 'good old man'—a common word for a monk], I so often found what I judged to be religious moderation, that I was once induced to show them a Greek version of the English liturgy; but when they saw that we kept Easter at the time fixed by the Gregorian or Romish calendar, and that we laid down no precise rules about the mode of fasting . . . I saw such a disposition for controversy arise, that I ever afterwards abstained from all allusion to similar subjects." Times have changed but little on the holy mountain, and the traveller may still encounter monks who, when topics such as fasting on Saturday are in question, will yield nothing in polemical ardour to the most celebrated patterns of orthodoxy who flourished in Byzantine days.

Now it is surely evident that the Greek Christian's conception of Christendom differs radically from any that prevails in the west: not least from that of the English churchman who, if he looks beyond the bounds of the *Ecclesia Anglicana*, finds his view blocked by the leviathan of Old Rome on the one hand and Protestant Nonconformity on the other. All that the Greek has in mind when he speaks of the Church lies unseen and forgotten beneath the horizon of this shrunken world. Vanished is that more spacious Christendom wherein the one faith was confessed and the one eucharist offered from Malabar to the misty shores of Albion and the territories of the "pope of another world". For the Greek, as for the western Christian, the horizon has contracted, and it is only by a considerable effort of the imagination that we can hope to comprehend an outlook that is unfamiliar to the point of fantasy.

One is sometimes asked what are the main points of difference between eastern and western Christendom, in terms which make it quite clear that one's questioner is thinking of particular doctrinal propositions. It can hardly be too strongly emphasised, however, that the manifest cleavage which now exists between the Orthodox and other Christians is less a matter of disagreement on specific issues than of two widely divergent attitudes and approaches. This is not to deny the reality and importance of certain dogmatic questions (such as that concerning the procession of the Holy Spirit, for example), but merely to assert that it is not there that the primary differences are to be sought. The truth of this contention is borne out by certain recent developments in western Europe, where the influence of what is commonly known as the liturgical movement has brought about in some very diverse quarters a radically changed attitude toward the Christian mystery: an attitude which—though there is nothing peculiarly *eastern* about it— has at times seemed to come very close to that which has ever been characteristic of the Orthodox world. Where this change of attitude has shown itself it has gone far towards creating a genuine *rapprochement* between theologians of east and west: much farther, I would add, than any amount of discussion of specific points of doctrine where no such common approach exists.

A generation of ecumenical conversation has revealed something of the difficulties of discussion amongst western Christians of different traditions: yet in the west, at least, most of the basic assumptions are held in common. Some affirm and some deny but all set out from the same premises—all speak what is virtually the same language. The crucial difficulty in relations between the Orthodox and western Christians lies in the decay of a common tongue. As the Russian lay theologian A. S. Khomiakov puts it: "All Protestants are crypto-papists . . . all the west knows but one datum *a*; whether it be preceded by the positive sign +, as with the Romanists, or with the negative — as with the Protestants, the *a* remains the same. . . . A passage to Orthodoxy is a rushing into a new and unknown world."

It is significant that it is the restoration of the liturgy to its rightful place in the Church's life which, more than anything else, has brought about a partial reassertion of orthodoxy in the west during recent years, for orthodoxy is not so much a matter of 'right opinion' as of 'right worship'. The surest path to a real understanding of the Orthodox Church is through her liturgical life. There is, with all its naïvety, much to be learned from the legend, which has come down to us in a mediaeval Russian chronicle, concerning the envoys of the Prince of Kiev. That monarch, so the story runs, wishing to make Christianity the religion of his people but doubtful as to which of its several forms was authentic, sent envoys to distant lands that they might judge for themselves. The envoys went first to the heretical Bulgars. They observed the way in which the people worshipped; how they bowed themselves to the ground and gazed hither and thither like men possessed. But, alas! "There is no joy among them," they reported upon their return to Kiev, "but only sadness and a frightful smell!" Next, they visited the Germans; but the worship of Latin Christendom left them unmoved. Thence, however, they journeyed to Byzantium, and were present at the divine liturgy of our father among the saints, John Chrysostom, in the great church of the holy wisdom; and there, they afterwards related, "we did not know if we were on earth or in heaven; for there is no such splendour to be found anywhere upon earth. Describe it we cannot: we know only that it is there that God dwells among men."

For the Greek Christian, as for the Russian, the humblest village church is always *heaven upon earth*: the place where men and women, according to their capacity and desire, are caught up into the adoring worship of the redeemed cosmos; where dogmas are no barren abstractions but hymns of exulting praise, and the saving acts of the divine compassion—the cross, the tomb, the resurrection on the third day and the ascension into the heavenly places—are made present and actual through the operation of the Holy Spirit who "ever was, and is and shall be; having neither beginning nor ending, but for ever joined to and numbered with the Father and the Son . . . through whom the Father is known, and the Son is glorified, and by all acknowledged, one power, one worship and one order of the Holy Trinity."

It is important to grasp this essentially liturgical approach, for it provides the key to much else; to the Greek Christian's understanding of scripture, to personal piety, and to the preservation of the faith during the centuries of oppression. Orthodox Christendom has never undergone an upheaval comparable to that which shattered the unity of the western world in the sixteenth century, not on account of the glacier of Turkish dominion which descended upon it a hundred years earlier, but because it had never known that separation of theology and mysticism, liturgy and personal devotion, which—when all is said as to the influence of political and economic factors—is required to explain the all-engulfing cataclysm of the Reformation.

In the next chapter I propose to consider certain features of the long history of the Greek Church in so far as they exercise a lively influence upon the contemporary scene; for in Greece it is peculiarly difficult to disentangle past and present, and historical memory is remarkably tenacious. In the remotest mountain villages of Epirus or the Peloponnese one may meet with small children who do not merely know far more about Lord Byron than one can reasonably expect of the majority of his countrymen—*that*, after a little time in Greece, one takes for granted—but who can sometimes relate strange apocryphal stories of Admiral Codrington or Sir Richard Church; and, in the imagination of the monks of Athos, Pope Innocent III occupies a position similar to that which Oliver Cromwell holds amongst the peasant farmers of Ireland.

III

THE PATTERN OF HISTORY

Therefore, brethren, stand fast, and hold the traditions
which ye have been taught.
                    ST. PAUL to the church in Thessalonica

IT IS no use beginning one's study of that in many ways anachronistic,
yet persistently lively institution, the Church of England, at the
sixteenth century: not so can one hope to comprehend the anomalies
of her parochial organisation and system of patronage, or to fathom
the element of uncertainty that attaches to every archdeacon's prospects
of eternal felicity. No more can the student of the Greek Church
expect to enter into the spirit of this venerable institution if he looks
no farther than the reading of the *Synodical Tome* whereby, in the year
1850, her autocephalous status was first accorded official recognition.

One cannot spend many hours in Greece without being struck by the
extraordinary continuity of her history. The girl who shepherds one
through the customs at the airport may well rejoice in the name of
Andromache or Ismene; it is startling to hear a ragged stevedore, one
of "that unpolished plebeian race always employed in the hardest
labours of the ports and which in every country represents the least
noble aspect of a people", being hailed by a passing boatman at the
Piraeus as Menelaus or Agamemnon. The traveller arriving at nightfall
in a mountain village of Thessaly or the Peloponnese is questioned in
terms which have scarcely altered since the prince of swineherds
examined the returned Odysseus: "Who are you and whence do you
come? What is your city and your family? Aboard what vessel came you
to Ithaca?" New Demetrius often proves to be but old Demeter, and
in the country dioceses there linger on observances of immemorial
antiquity: local rites connected with birth and death which carry one
back to an age infinitely remote from the Lord's coming in human
flesh.

Though the Greek that is heard to-day in the streets of Athens is
scarcely that of Aristotle or Pericles, the continuity of language is

18

nevertheless sufficiently striking. A Russian professor, a theologian of the diaspora, once described to me the overwhelming impression that this had made upon him when he first visited Greece in the 'twenties. He had travelled by train from Paris, and at the Greek frontier a *douanier* boarded the train to greet him and his companion with the very salutation wherewith the risen Lord had greeted His wondering disciples on the first Easter morning. Two days later the Metropolitan of Salonica had turned to him during the course of a conference with the invitation: "The *logos* is with the *kyrios!*"

The present Metropolitan of Salonica, the Lord Panteleimon, like his brethren at Corinth, Verroia and elsewhere, traces his succession in an unbroken line to the first *episkopos* of the church founded by the apostle of the Gentiles. Though the ancient Neapolis is now Cavalla, and Philippi has dwindled to a straggling line of cottages clinging to the hillside above the ruins of the Roman city, the local bishop retains the style of 'Metropolitan of Philippi and Neapolis'. There, as at Corinth, at Verroia and at Salonica, St. Paul's letters have been read in the churches for 1,900 years in their original Greek. To this day the Greek schoolboy hears the Gospels read at the liturgy in the language in which they were written.

The liturgy itself has undergone but little change for the best part of 1,500 years: the present Metropolitan of Salonica calls upon God to change the bread and wine at the eucharist in the very words used by his fifth-century predecessors in this apostolic see. The deacon who leads the prayers of the congregation in the basilica of St. Demetrius, and summons the catechumens to withdraw before the solemn recitation of the creed, employs formulas which were already traditional long before this great church was first erected.

The Greek Christian still stands to pray, and the ancient canons expressly prohibiting kneeling on the Lord's day (which is the day of the resurrection) and during the period from Easter to Pentecost are carefully observed (witness the controversy recently provoked by the custom, which has grown up within the new movements, of the laity kneeling at the invocation of the Holy Spirit). He still brings his bread and wine to church for the eucharistic offering. To this very day, between Easter and Pentecost, all other greetings give place to the triumphant *Christos anesti!* Christ is risen! and the reply, *Verily He is risen!* As recently as Dr. Covel's day this salutation was accompanied by a mutual embrace: "on meeting another," says the Doctor, "they

Embrace one another, and join mutually the side of the Mouth or Cheek to the other . . . and since the Resurrection of Christ is the Miracle of Miracles, and the main Pillar of our Christian Faith and Hope, I am much perswaded that this might be the very manner and way of giving the Holy Kiss amongst the Primitive Christians."

Nor is all this a matter of mere outward forms. Through all the vicissitudes of her history the Greek Church has been enabled to preserve something of the very spirit of the first age of Christianity. Her liturgy still enshrines that element of sheer joy in the resurrection of the Lord that we find in so many of the early Christian writings. The spirit of the ancient fathers of the Church lives on in the liturgy and in the piety of the ordinary Greek Christian. To enter into the spirit of the eastern liturgies is to comprehend as is possible in no other way the characteristic notes of Orthodox spirituality.

This is true above all of the liturgy of Holy Week and Eastertide; here one is perhaps most acutely conscious of the revolution that has been wrought in post-mediaeval western piety. It is a far cry from the Byzantine liturgy of the holy passion to that preoccupation with the sufferings of Christ with which we are familiar. Even in the darkness of the holy and great Friday the note of joy is sounded; the narrative of the passion is interspersed with the divine praises: it is the record of the triumph of the King, and Christ the Victor reigns in royal purple from His throne on Calvary.

> To-day is hanged upon the Tree
> He who hanged the earth free in the midst of the waters.
> A crown of thorns crowns Him who is King of the angels.
> He who wraps the heavens in clouds
>   is wrapt about with the purple of mockery;
> He who freed Adam in Jordan
>   is smote with hands;
> He who is the Bridegroom of the Church
>   is transfixed with nails;
> He who is the Son of the Virgin
>   is pierced with a spear.
> We worship Thy Passion, O Christ;
> Show us also Thy glorious Resurrection!

It is because her life is rooted so completely in the liturgy that the

Orthodox Church has been able to preserve in all its integrity the faith once delivered to the saints. Ecclesiastical organisation has never in eastern Christendom been looked upon as having an importance such as, at any rate from the eleventh century onwards, it assumed in the west. Provided only that he is free to participate fully in the liturgical life of his local church, the Greek or Russian Christian is prepared to sit curiously lightly to matters of jurisdiction and the machinery of ecclesiastical government and administration. Even when, as in the U.S.S.R. to-day, the Church is subject to every imaginable restriction save this bare permission to celebrate the divine mysteries, she can yet contrive to hold fast to her traditions with a tenacity which must often strike the western Christian as little short of miraculous: "the stable perseverance in these our days of the *Greek* Church", wrote Rycaut in the seventeenth century, "notwithstanding the Oppression and Contempt put upon it by the *Turk* . . . is a Confirmation no less convincing than the Miracles and Power which attended its first beginnings."

So, throughout the long centuries of Turkish domination, the Greek Church held fast the traditions which enshrined the saving truths of the divine economy. The Gospel was preached less by means of homilies and sermons than through the regular cycle of feast and fast; though Christian schools were maintained, often with great heroism in the face of overwhelming difficulties, the children of Hellas relied even more upon the visible catechism of the Church's liturgy. So it was that the faith was preserved as a royal treasure: the life of the mystical body burned on in secret, though the royal priesthood might be "expelled their Churches and those converted into Moschs; the Mysteries of the Altar conceal'd in secret and dark places . . ."

It is in remote townships like Kastoria that one can best enter into the spirit of the Greek Church under the Turkish yoke. To the traveller who approaches the ancient city of Diocletian from the southward there is little to suggest the presence of some seventy-two churches. Kastoria reveals its secrets only to those who are prepared to spend several days scrambling up and down the stony paths below the nineteenth-century metropolis, where tiny churches are set obscurely amidst the high, fortress-like domestic architecture of a later age. A great number of these churches date from Byzantine days, for from about the seventh century onwards this mountain township served as a place of exile for many whose presence at Constantinople was, for one reason or another, considered undesirable. Many more were built during the centuries of Turkish dominion. Outwardly they are scarcely distinguishable from the cottages which surround them: only the shallow apse at the east end proclaims the church.

Within, however, one finds oneself in another world. Walls unpierced by windows are covered with paintings which set forth the whole story of creation and redemption. Patriarchs and prophets mingle with the saints of the new dispensation; Elias is caught up to heaven in a chariot of fire and Jonah goes down to the bottoms of the mountains with the weeds wrapped about his head; those whose names are honoured throughout the length and breadth of Christendom, Athanasius, Basil and Gregory the Divine, rub shoulders with local saints like St. George of Iannina and the Neo-Martyrs; the Lord Christ is baptised in Jordan, He changes the water into wine and reigns in triumph from the tree of Calvary; the Holy Spirit descends in tongues of fire upon the apostles. Here in these little chapels—"rather like Vaults or Sepulchres than Churches, having their Roofs almost levelled with the Superficies of the Earth, lest the most ordinary exsurgency of structure should be accused for triumph of Religion, and to stand in competition with the lofty Spires of the *Mahometan* Moschs"—the mysterious life of the local church was nourished throughout the dark days of oppression; the saints which were in Kastoria, like their brethren at Thessalonica, obeyed the apostolic injunction to hold fast the traditions which they had been taught.

Not infrequently, it must be confessed, zeal for the preservation of the faith in the midst of an alien environment gave rise to a certain lack of discrimination. The pure gold of the apostolic tradition has not been handed down from generation to generation without gathering to itself certain accretions of doubtful worth, and the simple Christian is not always able to distinguish the one from the other or prepared even to admit the possibility of such intermingling.

This Reverence to the Church [observes one of the old writers] produces a firm belief and strict adherence to the Articles of it, and to all the Ceremonies and matters the most minute and indifferent, not suffering the least change or alteration in them. For although they are sensible (as many of their Priests have confessed to me) of the inconvenient length of their Liturgies . . . and of many superstitious Customs and Ceremonies derived to them from the times of *Gentilism*, which are now ingrafted into, and as it were grown up with their Religion, and many other Rites of which the wiser men are ashamed, and wish they were amended; yet they fear to correct and alter them . . . lest the People observing their Guides to vary in the least point from their ancient, and (as they imagine) their Canonical Profession, should begin to suspect the truth of all, and from a doubt dispute themselves into an indifference, and thence into an entire desertion of the Faith.

The dispute about the substitution of the Gregorian calendar for the Julian has shown that a substantial body of opinion (especially amongst the monks of Athos), is still violently opposed to change and reform even in matters which might to the detached observer seem to have little religious significance. With the solitary exception of 'modernist' Vatopedi, the whole monastic community of the holy mountain still insists on using the old reckoning. Elsewhere in Greece one finds scattered groups of Old Calendarists who have separated themselves from the local bishop rather than accept the reformed calendar. The *Palaioemerologitai*, as they are known, include clergy and monks and until recently were in possession of several small convents.

Though it may be that political motives have played a certain part in this curious controversy, it would be rash to deny the presence of a strong element of sincere religious feeling. Even the saints are liable to be involved in these disputes about the calendar. Witness the story of the 'modernist' *papas* who ventured to sing a hymn in honour of St. George before the eikon of the saint on the new-fangled day, and was not a little disconcerted when the saint fell flat on his face: what clearer testimony could there be to the detestation felt for the new calendar in the heavenly places?

The centuries of oppression did but strengthen the awareness (already more marked amongst eastern Christians than in the clerkly west), that the maintenance of holy tradition is the responsibility of the whole body of the faithful—not of the clergy alone. The English layman still feels himself more or less at the mercy of the parson—so far at least as what goes on in his parish church is concerned. Not so the Greek. A *papas* who ventured to deviate in the least particular from the forms prescribed by immemorial custom would suffer prompt correction from his congregation. If a bishop should fall into strange novel doctrines contrary to the traditions of the fathers, the holy people of God would rise up and denounce him. In this, as in other matters,

the effect of the Turkish dominion was to foster—perhaps to excess—
an attitude which was already discernible in Byzantine days and which
always made for a certain liveliness in ecclesiastical affairs.

*

During the last few years it has been becoming increasingly clear
that the episode which may, for the sake of brevity, be referred to as
'1054 and all that' has gained a far more important place in our text-
books of European history than it justly merits. No longer is it possible
to regard the schism of Cerularius as marking the decisive breach
between eastern Christendom and the west. A date which seemed to
hold out to the struggling schoolboy a refuge no less secure than that
of the Conqueror's triumph at Hastings has been swept away, to leave
him floundering in the troubled waters of speculation and surmise.
But whatever the immediate causes of the disastrous breach which was
to divide Christendom into warring factions, and which underlies all
our western divisions, there can be little question that far the greatest
factor in the hardening of the schism was the invasion of the Levant
by the crusading Franks, the sack of Constantinople and the establishment of a Latin hierarchy. These unhappy events made an impression
upon the Greek mind that the passing of eight centuries has not effaced.

The legend of Frankish aggression—unhistorical and confused though
it be—lives on in our own day especially amongst the monks. Pope
Innocent III, Michael Palaeologus, the Patriarch Bekkos, the Catalans
who established themselves in the Kassandra peninsula at the beginning
of the fourteenth century, and Pope Eugenius IV, who flourished more
than a century later, are all confounded in a wild farrago of monkish
imagination and prejudice. The Pope, attended by Frankish soldiers
and executioners, presides over the martyrdom of the twenty-six monks
of Zographou, and terrible stories are still to be heard on the holy
mountain of the gruesome fate that befell the renegade monks who took
part in the Latin mass at the Lavra. In a painting at the Serbian convent
of Chilandari the Pope appears in the company of Mahomet and the
arch-heretic Arius, and the earth opens and swallows them up together.

The traveller in monastic Greece must not, therefore, be surprised
to find that an unwary allusion to the Pope can still conjure up in the
imagination of a Greek monk a nightmare figure far surpassing the
inventions of the most rabid Protestant. I recall one such reference to

the servant of the servants of God which drew from a gentle old monk of the Great Meteoron the question: "The Pope is very *fanatikos*, is he not?" It is no light task to break down so vast a barrier of prejudice, especially when suspicion of the Frankish unbelievers (*apistoi*) has been confirmed by generations of bitterly resented proselytism.

Amongst the theologians, needless to say, more enlightened notions now prevail. One may indeed rejoice at the spread of a truly irenical outlook within the last few years, fostered, on the one hand, by the discovery of the recognisably 'evangelical' and patristic tendencies so richly manifest in recent French theology; and, on the other, by the conduct of the small Catholic minority during the fiery trial of the occupation, when many clergy and laity showed that (contrary to popular belief), it was possible to be an ardent patriot as well as a Catholic. To the great mass of Greek Christians outside Athens and the islands of the Aegean, nevertheless, the Church of Rome is still essentially a foreign body: a Frankish mission dimly associated with all manner of mediaeval atrocities: 'the Pope' is held responsible not only for the expulsion of the monks of Daphni by the Frankish Dukes of Athens and the excesses of the crusaders, but also for the errors of the *methodistai*, the Christian Scientists and other western 'innovators'.

The persistence of Greek national sentiment throughout the centuries of Turkish rule has been justly described as one of the most remarkable phenomena of modern history. It is from this epoch that there springs that identification of Church and nation which, despite certain fairly obvious dangers, is still an incomparable source of strength to the Greek people. During the dark days of oppression every national aspiration was fostered and preserved by the Church. The Patriarch of Constantinople was not merely chief hierarch of the Greek Church but also the recognised head of the whole Greek community, and as such he stood between his people and their overlords. In thousands of rural communities the parish priest and the schoolmaster kept alive the traditions of Christian Hellas, and when the day of liberation dawned it was an Archbishop of Patras who raised the standard of revolt: the national martyr, the Patriarch Gregory V, who was hanged by the Turks from the gateway of the patriarchate.

Religion and patriotism are still inextricably mingled in Greece. Hellas, when all is said as to the spread of secularism and indifference, remains a Christian nation in a sense of which we in the west can have but little conception. It was a Christian nation that performed miracles of valour, worthy of comparison with the greatest exploits of the heroes of antiquity, during that bitter winter when the Italian army was pushed steadily back towards the sea across the snowy heights of Albania. The war against the Communists partook of the nature of a conscious defence of a Christian civilisation against the "Accursed of God". Not least in the new movements, piety and patriotism are inseparably linked—even though I have never seen in a house of the Zoë Brotherhood paintings of the *Averoff* with her attendant ironclads steaming to the relief of the holy mountain, such as commonly adorn the guest-rooms of Greek monasteries.

This identity of Church and State has, it need hardly be said, certain weaknesses; the Church has not, for example, always enjoyed that measure of freedom in the election of her hierarchs that most people would consider desirable (there have been several deplorable examples of the intrusion of political considerations into episcopal appointments within the last generation). The decisions of the Holy Synod have to be ratified by the State, and a lay procurator sits with the bishops on the *hierarchia*. These, however, are but trifling disadvantages as compared with the opportunities afforded by the profound associations that bind the Church to every department of Greek life, and which give to the nation-wide revival of the last few years such boundless potentialities for good.

Though the Greek Church has held fast the traditions committed to her charge, the guardians of these traditions have been as men only dimly aware of the nature of the treasure entrusted to their keeping: conscious only of its infinite worth and of the duty of passing it on intact and undiminished to those who followed in their steps. Now, it seems, the guardians are beginning to realise something of the true character of the royal treasure that they have watched over so faithfully these many centuries. The younger Greek theologians, like their brethren of the diaspora, are rediscovering their proper tradition and are filled with wonder at its richness and splendour. The possibilities latent in this reawakening are infinite. As yet (so far as Greece is concerned), it has scarcely begun. There can, however, be little question that the growing self-awareness found to-day amongst Orthodox theologians, the first fruits of which have already been gathered in Paris, is of incalculable importance not for the Orthodox world alone, but for Christendom as a whole.

IV

THE ORGANIC BODY

Jerusalem which now is, and is in bondage with her children.

THERE is an old story, still to be heard in the mountain villages, which tells how God fashioned the dry land; how He put all the earth through the mesh of His sieve: here a pile of fine rich soil, the granary of Africa, and there another which was Sicily. When all was done there remained within the sieve a heap of stones and dross: God threw them over His shoulder, and there was Greece. *Tout ce païs,* remarks an old traveller, *est plein de hautes montagnes.*

It is important to bear in mind the physical characteristics of the setting within which the Greek Church carries out her work of reconciliation and renewal. Greece is a land of high mountains and narrow coastal plains; of few towns and wretched communications. The majority of her people live, as they have lived from time immemorial, in small rural communities widely dispersed among the mountains, winning a laborious subsistence from the parched and stony soil which scarcely covers her rocky skeleton. More than half of the whole area of Greece is utterly barren; much of what remains consists of forest and poor pasture; less than one-fifth is under cultivation. Greece and poverty, the saying runs, have ever been sisters.

At the time of the last census approximately one-seventh of the total population of Greece dwelt in the Athens-Piraeus region, the phenomenal growth of which during the last 100 years has set it strangely apart from the rest of the country—even though "the equipages of Athens", as the Abbé de St. Michon observed, "have not quite the freshness nor the elegance of those seen in the Champs Elysées". Salonica had a population which was approaching 300,000; the next largest town, however, was Patras with less than 80,000 inhabitants. Most of the remaining towns, a large proportion of which are situated in the fertile plains of Macedonia and Thrace, are market towns and centres of rural industries but little more.

Thus, despite a certain drift from the villages to the towns during the last few years, the average Greek is still a countryman. Even the Athenian, if one delves into his personal history, is generally found to have his roots in some mountain village of the Peloponnese or in one of the islands. The generality of the Greek bishops are charged with the pastoral care of a flock dispersed in village communities among the mountains; a single market town or *comopolis* forming the centre of the ecclesiastical as of the civil administration.

The Church of Greece, from the point of view of outward organisation, consists of sixty-seven dioceses: thirty-four belonging to Old Greece and the remainder to the territories annexed to the Greek kingdom after the Balkan wars of 1912-13 and the first world war. These latter dioceses, though formally subject to the jurisdiction of the Patriarch of Constantinople, are at present placed under that of the Holy Synod of the Hierarchy, which is presided over by the Archbishop of Athens and of all Greece. This body, which is made up of the metropolitans of the sixty-seven dioceses, assembles every three years and may be summoned on other occasions if need arise. Extraordinary business apart, however, the affairs of the Church are administered by the Holy Synod of the Church of Greece, which is composed of twelve bishops under the presidency of the Archbishop. All the bishops are called in turn to serve on this body, and during the greater part of their year as *synodikoi* (which normally recurs about once every five years), they reside in Athens, going home to their dioceses only during the heat of the summer and for the great festivals.

In Greece the one, holy, catholic and apostolic Church has not been replaced by 'the Churches'. According to the figures of the 1940 census, out of a total population of 7,344,860 persons, no less than 7,090,192 were Orthodox, while the non-Orthodox Christians amounted to a bare 51,851. This small minority consists of Roman Catholics and a few so-called 'evangelicals' who came to Greece in the early 'twenties from Asia Minor and owe their origin to the proselytising zeal of American missionaries. All of them are confined to the islands and to a few towns on the mainland: in the country districts a Dissenter would be a curiosity indeed.

The Greek diocese is, by English standards, very small and sparsely populated; in some respects more akin to a rural deanery than to our overgrown dioceses. Its average population—if we leave on one side the

Athens-Piraeus region—is no more than about 85,000 souls. In terms of parishes there is considerable disparity between different dioceses: that of Ioannina, in Epirus, one of the largest, includes 230 parishes—many of them mere hamlets of forty or fifty families—while that of Nevrokopi, on the frontier of eastern Macedonia, has only fifteen. The average number is rather less than 100. If we take the twenty-four dioceses of Macedonia and Thrace, for example, we find that the average works out at seventy-eight parishes to the diocese, while the metropolitans of Philippi and Neapolis, Xanthi, Nevrokopi, Eleftheroupolis, Nea Zichni, Alexandroupolis and Hierissos all have less than sixty communities committed to their care, and only five bishops—the metropolitans of Salonica, Drama, Kilkis, Serres and Florina—more than 100.

As against this comparatively low average population and number of parishes one has, of course, to set in the balance the extremely primitive nature of the communications which the Greek bishop can command. To this day the majority of the villages of northern Greece are inaccessible to wheeled transport, at any rate during the winter months; and while the truly remarkable achievements of the last few years—the repair of the shattered railways, and the construction of roads and air-strips—have given Greece a very fair system of long-distance communications, the facilities which most bishops enjoy for travel within their own dioceses remain much as they have been since apostolic days. The metropolitan of a country diocese will think nothing of long journeys by mule or mountain pony across appallingly difficult terrain, his episcopal vestments slung from the high wooden saddle; of fording torrents swollen by the melting snows, and negotiating precipitous slopes where the path seems scarcely to afford adequate foothold for a goat—much less for an elderly ecclesiastic. It is little wonder that many mountain villages saw their father in God but seldom, even in the days before the natural hazards which confronted the traveller had been supplemented by mines and wandering bands of *katsapliades*, as the Communists were styled in the villages.

When we turn to the internal organisation of the dioceses we find many features which cannot but seem strange to most western Christians. We have come to take for granted the fact that a bishop, charged with the pastoral care of a vast and unmanageable diocese, inevitably delegates most of his priestly functions to his parish clergy. In the small country dioceses of Greece, however, the bishop retains a far greater measure of direct personal responsibility, and delegates comparatively little to his curates. The ministry of the word, for example, is always the work of the bishop: the most that the parish priest is permitted to do is to read a homily sent him by his diocesan. In some dioceses the metropolitan alone preaches, and the country people hear sermons only when he is able to visit their villages. As a rule, however, the bishop will be assisted by a *hierokeryx* or 'sacred herald'—'preacher' seems a miserably inadequate translation of such a splendid word—who is normally a priest-monk (though he may sometimes be a lay theologian), and lives in the metropolis. Often, too, the bishop and his *hierokeryx* will be assisted by several lay preachers who go out into the villages Sunday by Sunday to preach at the liturgy.

Thus, at Siderokastro (the 'Iron Castle'), close to the Bulgarian frontier, the Metropolitan, the Lord Basil, finding himself, when the refugees began to return to their villages in the summer of 1949, with only one priest qualified to assist him in the ministry of the word, formed a little society of lay preachers known as the Guardians of Spiritual Enlightenment, which included the headmaster of the local high school and one of his assistant masters, as well as the doctor and the dentist of the town and two or three other educated laymen, several of whom now go out to preach in the surrounding villages every Sunday.

A friend who visited the diocese of Chalkis during the 'thirties has told me of the ancient Fiat which used to leave the metropolis at daybreak every Sunday and scatter monkish theologians among the hamlets of Euboea. At Kozani, in western Macedonia, no sooner were the roads reasonably clear of mines in the summer of 1949 than the Metropolitan started to send out every Saturday afternoon an army truck laden with young catechists who would spend the week-end preaching and teaching in remote villages of the diocese and return to their work or their school on Monday morning.

What is true of preaching applies also to the sacrament of penance; it is to the bishop, not to his parish priest, that the villager who is oppressed with the consciousness of grave sin will turn for the benefits of absolution and ghostly counsel. The Greek priest is not allowed to act as a confessor without the express authorisation of his bishop. "As for Confession", says Covel, "it is not to be made to every ordinary Priest, but only to such Confessors . . . who are chosen out of monasteries, and are solemnly appointed and authorised to this Office . . . so that a regular or secular Priest not thus qualified, durst not attempt to take it." In the *Great Euchologion*, or Prayer Book, of the Greek Church the order for confession is in fact immediately preceded by a short office for the making of a *pneumatikos*, or spiritual father, in which the bishop, after he has read the Gospel containing our Lord's words: "Whose soever sins ye remit, they are remitted unto them; and whose soever sins ye retain, they are retained", addresses the would-be *pneumatikos* (who must, needless to say, be in priests' orders) as follows:

"Our mediocrity, through the grace of the all-holy and divine Spirit, promotes thee, the most pious N. *Pneumatikos*, to the ministry of spiritual fatherhood, etc."

Covel quotes ancient canons to the effect that "if any one without the Mandate of the Bishop of the place shall dare to receive . . . spiritual accounts and Confessions, such a one shall be Canonically punished as a Transgressor of the Divine Canons; because he hath not only destroy'd himself, but all they also who have been Confessed by him are still unconfessed, and whatever things he hath Bound or Loosed, are yet uncorrected". And again: "Let all the Priest-Monks, who take Confessions, or Bind and Loose know that our Holy Fathers will not suffer any Priests to reconcile Penitents without the Archbishop's Order". According to an old canonist "a Bishop may . . . according to his Judgment, give this Right or Power of receiving Confessions to a secular Priest, but this is to be done discreetly, to some choice or well approved Persons only, and upon some extraordinary occasions".

Professor Bratsiotes, in the introduction which he contributed to the English translation of the life of the Archimandrite Eusebius Matthopoulos, observed that "unhappily there are very few confessors, because it is much more difficult to develop confessors than to train preachers; and it requires much individual genius and great maturity in virtue and experience to be a proper confessor". At the time when these words were written only eight members of the Zoë Confraternity—all trained theologians as they are—were licensed as confessors. In the country dioceses to-day the only clergy who are permitted to assist the bishop as *pneumatikoi* are the priest-monks attached to the metropolis; married priests who are authorised to hear confessions are rare indeed.

What then of the parish clergy? There is no parallel in Greece to the country parson who has "read the Fathers also and the Schoolmen and the later writers", and who has been one of the fairest ornaments of the English Church these many centuries. The Greek country parson is a peasant farmer who cultivates his land like all his parishioners, and who exercises a ministry which is almost wholly liturgical in character. His ecclesiastical duties are limited in practice to administering the mysteries of baptism and the holy chrism; to marrying and burying, and offering week by week the unbloody sacrifice; to singing the divine office; to memorial services, blessings of homes and crops and sundry other objects, and to an occasional exorcism.

The parish priest *must* be married and at least thirty years of age, and the most that he can hope for in the way of preferment is a slight increase in his basic stipend if he is able to spend a year or two at one of the seminaries (*phrontisteria*) for parish clergy. This basic wage— which is supplemented by fees and offerings in kind, as well as by the fruit of the country parson's agricultural and other labours—is miserable enough. It was only in 1949 raised to 250,000 drachmas (the equivalent of less than six pounds sterling) a month: a pair of boots then cost about 70,000 drachmas and a pig perhaps 300,000. In such circumstances the support of a large family leaves little margin for luxuries, even when harvests are good and life runs smoothly and securely. Unsatisfactory as the economic position of the village *papas* remains, it is considerably better than it was fifty years ago. Until 1909 the parish priest was entirely dependent upon the fees of his parishioners and the labour of his own hands. The provision of a regular stipend—inadequate as this may seem—was only made possible by the creation of a General Ecclesiastical Fund deriving its income from confiscated monastic property and lands; and while the anti-monastic legislation of recent years has aroused considerable resentment among the monks themselves, there can be little doubt that the redistribution of wealth which it has involved has been of incalculable benefit to the Church as a whole.

Even in the towns the scope of the activities of the married clergy is strictly limited. There are a few married priests in Athens engaged in work of a type generally reserved for the monastic clergy; one of them, who presides over the press and information office of the *Apostoliki Diakonia* (the Home Mission of the Church of Greece) and has a son and a daughter who are both students of the theological faculty of the university, bears the title of *protopresbyter*—though this is rare in Greece. There are certain indications that the number of educated married clergy may before very long increase considerably; this has already happened among the Russians of the diaspora and elsewhere in the Orthodox world. It is, of course, from the celibate clergy that the bishops are chosen. Before presenting himself to a bishop the candidate for ordination must decide finally and irrevocably to what state of life he is called, since marriage is not permitted after ordination. This rule, as will appear when we come to consider the training of the Greek clergy, gives rise to many grave practical problems.

Such then, very briefly, is the framework of the diocesan and parochial organisation. The married clergy, "in parishes, residing on their cures", form a distinct class with well-defined duties and limitations peculiar to their condition; while the general administration of the diocese, the ministries of preaching and confessing, together with the organisation of the catechetical schools and Christian Unions which have become so important an element in the pattern of Greek church life within the last few years, are the immediate responsibility of the metropolitan assisted by his headquarters staff of monks and lay theologians.

The Greek bishop is still in a very real sense the *persona* of his diocese: the natural leader of the whole community in matters temporal as well as spiritual. Not for nothing is he commonly referred to as ὁ Δεσπότης, 'the Despot'. During the Turkish occupation the power of the bishop within his own diocese was all but unbounded, and as he had formerly mediated between his people and the Turkish authorities so, more recently, it was he who commonly bore the heaviest burden of responsibility during the occupation of Greece by the Axis troops. Archbishop Damaskinos was called to play, on a wider stage and before a larger audience, it is true, a part which was being sustained no less faithfully, albeit more obscurely, by many of his brethren in the provincial towns of Greece during the years from 1941 to 1945. Though times have changed since the day when the people of Salonica overthrew the minarets of the fleeing oppressor with such patriotic and religious ardour that many casualties were caused by the falling masonry, the Greek bishop still maintains a style befitting his position. The metropolis (where it has survived the destruction of the war years) is generally amongst the most impressive and substantial structures of a provincial town, and though the bishop is readily accessible to all and sundry, he nevertheless bears himself with considerable dignity. When he walks abroad, carrying a silver-headed staff and accompanied by a deacon, the people draw aside to let him pass, bowing their heads and putting off their caps. The faithful who come to the metropolis—whether they be peasants from some nearby hamlet or senior army officers from the garrison, it makes no difference—bow to kiss the hand of their father in God and greet him with the word *proskyno*, 'I worship': with that same *proskynesis* which is offered to the eikons of the saints, and which is not to be confounded with the *latreia* which we accord to the Three Persons of the consubstantial Trinity alone.

For the Greek bishop is not merely 'the Despot'. He is moreover 'the Saint'. Thus, one may frequently hear the country people refer to their metropolitan as ὁ ἅγιος ᾿Εδέσσης, ὁ ἅγιος ᾿Ελευθερουπόλεως, 'the Saint of Edessa, the Saint of Eleftheroupolis', etc., in recognition of the objective sanctity which attaches to the episcopal office, quite independently of the moral character of him who occupies it. If the bishop is the despot, tracing his ancestry back to those local potentates who flourished during the last days of the Byzantine Empire, he is also the successor of the apostles, the bearer of more than temporal power; binding and loosing and wielding an anathema which can arrest the normal processes of dissolution to which the body is subject after death; a father in God to whom the humblest member of his scattered flock can turn in need or perplexity, for ghostly counsel or for material aid.

For all the dignity attaching to his high office the Greek bishop is commonly the most approachable of men; the sheer accessibility of the generality of the bishops of the country dioceses is a matter for wonder and rejoicing in a world fallen beneath the curse of an impersonal and irresponsible bureaucracy. Every morning, his liturgy fulfilled, the metropolitan takes his seat in his office and all the world comes to see him: Papa Iannis, who needs a new cassock, and Papa Athanasi who wants to go to the recently established seminary, although he forsook the scholars' bench to look after his father's sheep while he was yet in the second class of his village school; an elderly widow whose son requires medical attention comes to ask for help from the Fund for the Poor.

Go almost any forenoon to the metropolis at Salonica, a few yards from the windy quays where gaily painted caiques discharge their cargoes of charcoal and resinated wine, timber from the slopes of Athos, and lemons and pottery from the islands of the Aegean, and observe the crowds who throng the steps awaiting an opportunity to dart into the office of 'the Saint of Myra', who sits at his desk beneath an eikon of the Pantocrator, questioning, counselling, reproving and writing letters of commendation, while a stalwart archimandrite leans against the door with outstretched arm to keep the multitude without at bay.

Dr. Holland, who was travelling about Greece in the year of Napoleon's retreat from Moscow, relates that when he visited the Archbishop of Larissa the metropolis was filled, both in the morning and also after dinner, with people approaching the Archbishop, either as petitioners or to obtain an adjustment of differences; and describes how "on entering the apartment, each person knelt before him, kissed his hand, and frequently after rising repeated this ceremony a second time". The Archbishop's manner, in fulfilling this part of his pastoral office, was, he says, "mild and ingratiating, without any loss of dignity proper to his station".

The bishop, though he must be unmarried, need never have lived as a member of a religious community in the technical sense. The great majority of the Greek metropolitans are chosen from the archimandrites attached, in one capacity or another, to episcopal households. The title of archimandrite was originally confined to the superior of a monastery—the literal meaning of the word is 'ruler of a fold' (*mandra*)—nowadays, however, it is commonly conferred upon any priest-theologian. The Greek archimandrite is almost invariably a graduate either of the theological faculty of the University of Athens or of the Academy at Halki (the theological school at Salonica has been in existence only a few years). He may have taken the monastic habit on Mount Athos, or elsewhere, when scarcely more than a boy, and, showing promise of more than the average ability, have been sent to the university by his monastic superiors as a young deacon. Alternatively, he may have come to the theological faculty after completing the ordinary course at a *gymnasium* or hieratic school, in which case he will not, in all probability, be ordained deacon until he has finished his studies.

After taking his degree he will normally pass to the household of a bishop, whom he will serve either as personal deacon or as chaplain and *hierokeryx* of the metropolis. He will doubtless become an archimandrite and will be addressed not merely as 'Reverend Sir' but as 'Altogether-most-blessed'! (*Panosiologiotate!*) In due course he may be called to take charge of a large parish in Athens, to undertake administrative work of some kind, or to serve as a secretary to the Holy Synod. It is from this category of the clergy that most of the bishops are chosen —though a monk may be summoned from his community to be consecrated, and an unmarried lay theologian or professor is also eligible for election to the episcopate.

A small minority of the present metropolitans of the Church of

Greece have studied in western Europe or America after completing their course at Athens or at the Academy of Halki, near Constantinople. Of those who go abroad for post-graduate theological studies far the greater number marry and become lay theologians, and it is to the latter rather than the episcopate that the Greek layman looks for academic learning. The metropolitan of scholarly interests, though far from unknown, is somewhat exceptional in these days. Happily, however, it is not necessary to burn midnight oil at Halle or Tübingen in order to learn to love our Lord with great fervour and simplicity and to feed His flock, and among the bishops of the Church of Greece there are many devoted pastors and fathers in God tending their scattered flocks in the obscurity of the war-ravaged mountain dioceses with a zeal not unworthy of the successor of the apostles.

The office of deacon has, so far as the west is concerned, long since ceased to be a reality. In Greece, however, it is otherwise. The diaconate is not, as in this country, a mere step to the priesthood; a kind of noviciate which the ordinand must needs serve before being admitted into priests' orders. In the Greek Church a man who has been ordained deacon may well remain in the diaconate for the rest of his days. The function of the deacon is essentially different from that of the presbyter. His liturgical rôle is of the utmost importance, and one of the chief qualifications in the candidate for the diaconate is the possession of a powerful and resonant voice. It is the deacon who leads the prayers of the congregation from the space before the royal doors—"a body standing before men, but a mind knocking at the gates of heaven through prayer"—in the vivid image of the sixth-century ascetic and master of the spiritual life, St. John of the Ladder; it is he who sings the Gospel from the *ambon*, or pulpit, high on the north side of the church.

In the monasteries the deacons are responsible for baking the *prosphora*, the loaves used at the eucharist. Thus Covel remarks somewhere in his Athonite journals that: "The priests and deacons do no work but what is in ye church or immediately belonging to it . . . ye deacons bake ye προσφορά, and may sometimes be sent of an errand, but nothing else. Ye priests do nothing at all. All laborious work wtever out of ye church else is done by καλόγ. or hired labourers." And elsewhere: "The προσφορά is baked by ye deacons, ye other bread by ye καλόγ. aforesaid."

In Athens and its suburbs, and in Salonica, there are a few married deacons attached to parish churches. More often, however, the deacon is a monk and belongs to the *familia* of a bishop, whom he serves as personal attendant and factotum. Outside the larger towns one never finds a deacon attached to a parish but always on the staff of the metropolis and retaining his close connexion with the bishop. In the two university towns there is always a sprinkling of young deacons who have been sent by their monastic superiors to study at the theological schools and who are attached to a parish church during their four years at the university. Many of these student-deacons are also permitted to preach. It may be noted in passing that in the Orthodox world an archdeacon is in fact, and not merely in name, a deacon, and is, moreover, a person of some consequence.

*

The English churchman, even when faced with the present acute and continuing shortage of clergy, is with difficulty persuaded that the laity are called to play an active part in the evangelistic work of the Church. Everywhere in the west the lay theologian is something of a phenomenon. A young man does not read theology at Oxford or Cambridge unless he intends to be a parson: theology is surely the concern of the clergy? It is well, therefore, that we should realise that in Greece (and throughout Orthodox Christendom for that matter), very different notions as to the active ministry of the laity prevail. The lay catechist, theologian and preacher fulfil a ministry that is scarcely less essential to the life of the Greek Church than that proper to bishop, priest and deacon respectively. How varied and important this lay ministry can be, will, I hope, become clearer when we come to consider the work of a movement such as the Brotherhood of Theologians, Zoë and the organisations connected with it. A very large share of the responsibility for the great spiritual upheaval of recent years must be assigned to lay men and women: the majority of the voluntary movements and associations are predominantly lay in character.

If I may venture upon a generalisation, I would assert that among ordinary Orthodox Christians one commonly finds a greater sense of responsibility for the Church than can be looked for in western Christendom to-day. The Church does not tend, as it does so often in the west, to be identified in the thought of ordinary men and women with the clergy; nor is it said of a young man who offers himself for ordination that he is 'going into the Church'. For the Orthodox, every Christian is in some sense called to be a theologian: to verify in his own life and experience the truths which are set forth in scripture and tradition; and although the bishop has, in virtue of his office, a peculiar responsibility for bearing witness to the *paradosis* which enshrines the saving truth of the Gospel, it is a responsibility that is shared by every lively member of the Church—by the laity no less than by the ordained ministry which is called to perform a particular function within the one body. In this connexion it may be remarked that monasticism, among the Orthodox, has never developed into a predominantly clerical institution. As in the early days of Benedictine monachism, the majority of Greek monks are peasants of little education; very few are in orders —a community of forty or fifty *kalogeroi* may well include only two or three priests or deacons.

From about 1936 onwards the voluntary religious movements, which had already obtained widespread recognition in the Athens-Piraeus region, as well as in several provincial centres of Old Greece, began to take an important place within the normal diocesan and parochial system but in some measure as supplementary to it. To-day their influence has spread to the remotest corners of the Kingdom of the Hellenes, and no balanced account of the organisation of the Church of Greece can fail to give a prominent place to these predominantly lay movements which (under the general supervision of the hierarchy and with full episcopal approval) now play so vital a part in almost every aspect of the Church's life and evangelistic work.

The more one sees of these movements and of their widespread influence, the more one realises how different might have been the present condition of the Church of England had the Methodists not been forced to go into schism at the end of the eighteenth century. There is indeed a striking analogy between the situation in Greece to-day and that of the *Ecclesia Anglicana* as it might have been had the Methodists remained within her fold and continued to receive the sacraments of the one body at the hands of their parish clergy while exercising, under the general control and supervision of the episcopate, a lay apostolate of their own. The tragic character of that schism cannot but be brought home to anyone who has lived and worshipped among Greek Christians during recent years, has seen the apostolic labours of lay men and women as theologians, preachers and catechists, and has realised that this Church—at first sight so rigidly hierarchical—is in fact in no merely superficial sense the Church of the laity: a Church whose every member, whether clerk or layman, is called to exercise an active apostolate appropriate to his status and vocation—"for the perfecting of the saints, for the work of the ministry, for the edifying of the body of Christ".

V

A VILLAGE FESTIVAL

If any Art or Polity can be said to have place over the
affection of the People, none seems more efficacious than
the strict observation of the Fasts and Feasts of their
Church, by which the people are taught as in a visible
Catechism . . . more (I dare say) than by their ill-composed
Sermons, or repetition of the Scripture in the Vulgar
Tongue; for being severely imposed, and observed with
much solemnity, they affect the Vulgar with an awe of
something divine and extraordinary in them.

PAUL RYCAUT

A FEW years after the restoration of the house of Stuart to the English
throne, the Archbishop of Larissa, in Thessaly, received an unexpected
visitor: a certain Père Robert, *Capucin de Saint-Jaques à Paris, et Aumonier
de l'Ambassadeur de France*. This reverend personage chancing to be in
Larissa during Holy Week (according to the western reckoning), he
attended a celebration of what, despite a certain confusedness in his
account, was manifestly the liturgy of the Presanctified Gifts. Describing
this in the journal which was his constant travelling companion during
the period 1665-69, he observes that the Archbishop, when he had
delivered his sermon, "went in procession about the church, accompanied
by nine bishops, his suffragans". To-day, though the traveller may but
rarely and with great good fortune chance upon such a mitred assembly
as that which Père Robert describes, the divine liturgy is still celebrated,
even in the smallest and poorest village of the Greek mountain dioceses,
with something of its traditional splendour, and in such fashion as to
impress upon the mind of the least sensitive of worshippers that he is a
participant in no work of man's devising but in the very worship of
heaven; in the praises of those who sing without ceasing to the glory
of the holy and consubstantial and life-giving and undivided Trinity.

The festival which is observed on August 15th is described in the
service-books as that of the Dormition, or Falling Asleep (*Koimesis*),
"of our most holy, glorious Lady, the Mother of God and Ever-Virgin

Mary". To the simple Greek, however, it is *the* feast of the *Panaghia*, which not the Marys only but also the men and boys named Panaghiotis keep as their name-day: a very much more important occasion in Greece than the mere commemoration of one's birth after the flesh. The importance of the festival is emphasised by a fast of two weeks' duration immediately preceding it. The other liturgical commemorations of the *Theotokos* centre on particular events. March 25th, for example, apart from the national associations which have made it one of the greatest days of the year among Greeks, is essentially the memorial of the Annunciation: "To-day," runs the dismissal hymn, "is the chapter-head of our salvation and the revelation of the eternal mystery. The Son of God becomes the Son of the Virgin, and Gabriel brings the good news of grace". So with the other evangelical commemorations. The liturgy of August 15th, on the other hand, seems to sum up the whole work in the pattern of man's redemption of her who contained Him whom the heavens cannot contain, and who, through the mysterious operation of the life-giving Spirit, herself became the dwelling of the infinite Creator.

> All creation rejoices in thee, thou who art highly favoured;
> Both the assembly of the angels and the race of men.
> O hallowed temple and logical paradise, the boast of virgins,
> From whom God took flesh and became a little child,
> Who is from all eternity our God.
> For He made thy womb His throne
> And fashioned thy body broader than the heavens.
> All creation rejoices in thee, thou who art highly favoured:
> Glory to thee!

★

On August 13th, 1949, furnished with a document wherein the officer commanding the Drama gendarmerie called upon all whom I should encounter in my travels to give me all conceivable manner of assistance, I embarked in the antique vehicle which then connected the village of Kato Nevrokopi with the rest of Christendom (it was blown up by a Communist mine a few months later). During the early stages of our somewhat wayward progress through the narrow streets of Drama it became evident, from the sounds which came from overhead that, in addition to the forty-four Greek passengers who occupied the interior of the vehicle, there were others who had with less formality installed themselves amidst the multitudinous array of baggage, live-stock and firearms which renders every Greek bus incapable of passing beneath what used, in England at least, to be described as 'a low bridge'. To the north of Drama the road crosses a dusty plain for several kilometres and then turns sharply to the right between two high peaks and winds laboriously up a rocky defile. Every few hundred yards there was a bridge: either guarded by a block-house, manned by men of the mobile section of the home-guard, or else lying in ruins and necessitating a perilous descent into a dried-up water course. These occasional outposts apart, we saw no human habitation for the best part of another twenty kilometres, when we reached the head of the pass. Here we halted for a few minutes and refreshed ourselves with cold mountain water from a stream by the roadside. Shortly after three o'clock we began the descent into the well-watered plateau, within sight of the Bulgarian frontier, on the northern fringe of which lies the village of Kato Nevrokopi, and which had been the scene of bitter fighting when the Germans poured into Greece in April, 1941. A few minutes later we were among the houses of Nevrokopi and my fellow-passengers pointed out to me the cottage, in no way distinguishable from its neighbours save by the board bearing the Byzantine eagles and the inscription *ΙΕΡΑ ΜΗΤΡΟΠΟΛΙΣ ΝΕΥΡΟΚΟΠΙΟΥ* beside the door, which, *faute de mieux*, has served as the bishop's headquarters since 1945: the old metropolis having been destroyed during the Bulgarian occupation of eastern Macedonia.

Half-past three on a warm August afternoon not being a discreet hour at which to call on a Greek bishop, I retired to the green shade of a vine beside the *plateia* to sip coffee and discuss such varied topics as the Bishop of Birmingham, Schiller and the Scottish liturgy (and, inevitably, the incredible folly of the British electorate in banishing Mr. Churchill to the opposition benches), with the commanding officer of the gen-darmerie and other local celebrities. Meanwhile, a troop of small boys was despatched at regular intervals to reconnoitre in the vicinity of the metropolis. At half-past four it was reported that the windows were open (all true Greeks sleep with windows and shutters firmly closed), and I was thereupon escorted to the metropolis where I was warmly welcomed by the Bishop. We talked until a little after six o'clock, when the *ephemerios*, or curate, of the parish arrived to lead the way to church for evensong.

When the Metropolitan was suitably attired he took his silver-headed stick and we set out in a little procession towards the cathedral church of St. Demetrius, which towers above the wretched cottages that surround it like some great vessel among her attendant tugs. The Metropolitan and myself were preceded by the parish priest, while well ahead there danced a certain Anargyri, whose daily joy and responsibility it is to remove straying cattle and goats from the Bishop's path, to wave to their feet the loungers on doorsteps, the coffee drinkers and those who play *trictrac* in their leafy retreats; finally, to silence the village's solitary gramophone and other profane noises. As our little procession hove in sight, the bell-ringer, stationed among his charges at the summit of the campanile, shattered the slumbers of all who had immoderately prolonged their siesta, and we made our way up the steps into the narthex of a surprisingly lofty church.

After evensong we returned, somewhat less formally, to the Bishop's cottage for supper—a simple meal of potatoes and fruit (by reason of the fast) which was shared by his two nephews, both of them orphans. I slept that night at an inn adjoining the cottage-metropolis.

The following morning, it being Sunday, we were in church from a quarter to seven until a little after ten. The liturgy ended, the colonel in charge of the local garrison drove us out in his jeep to the village of Granitsi, high on the wooded hills above the plateau, where we sat under a great oak while the villagers came to greet their father in God and brought little gifts of fruit and honey.

At evensong in the cathedral that evening, while the cantors sang of:

> Things creeping innumerable,
> Both small and great beasts,

a dormouse appeared from behind the cupboard where the liturgical books were stored, and sat most devoutly before the beautiful doors for a considerable space. The Bishop told me afterwards that it was the first mouse—the colloquial *pontikos*, with a twinkle at my use of the classical word—he had seen in the church during the four years that had elapsed since his consecration as Metropolitan of the smallest and poorest see of Greece.

The old diocese of Nevrokopi had included 120 communities. After the first Balkan war, however, it had been partitioned, and ninety of its villages as well as the town of Nevrokopi now lie within Bulgarian territory. Kato Nevrokopi, where the Greek Metropolitan has his throne, is a large village, or *comopolis* (it had a pre-war population of about 2,000 souls), about twelve kilometres from the frontier. The whole of this region was evacuated by the civilian population in March, 1941, when invasion seemed imminent, most of the refugees taking shelter in Drama, some forty-five kilometres to the southward. When the Germans abandoned eastern Macedonia to the Bulgars, all who were able to do so fled to Salonica, Verroia and other towns beyond the river Strymon. It was only after the withdrawal of the Bulgars in the autumn of 1944 that the Greek population began to trickle back. In 1949 no less than twelve of the thirty villages of the diocese were in ruins and uninhabited, and the number of the orphans was said to approach 900. Kato Nevrokopi itself, though it still bore traces of the great battle which had raged about the forts of the Metaxas line and their heroic defenders, had come through the years of occupation and the more recent troubles almost unscathed, save for the deliberate destruction of the metropolis and the school.

It had been arranged that the Metropolitan should celebrate the liturgy next morning at the village of Dasoto, four or five miles away, which would be keeping its patronal festival. The day was ushered in by bugle-calls and a great beating of drums, revealing shortly after five o'clock that the newly-formed scout troop was already abroad. These martial noises were soon mingled with the soft ringing of a multitude of bells, as the cattle were driven out through the narrow paths between the cottages to the dusty river bed where they assemble each morning before moving off to the pastures. By a little before seven it had become evident that others besides ourselves were keeping the feast at Dasoto, as a few carts drawn by oxen or buffaloes, together with some solitary riders, rattled across the bridge and headed westwards. We followed in a jeep. Our path lay through fields of maize and tall sunflowers, above which occasional glimpses of a blue and white flag of vast dimensions indicated the scouts' line of march, along tracks which a heavy shower would render impassable to anything on wheels. Dasoto came into view after a quarter of an hour; a cluster of lime-washed cottages, the church prominent amongst them, on the lower slopes of the heavily wooded heights that surround the plateau.

The parish priest and some thirty or forty men and boys had come as far as the outskirts of the village to welcome us. The Bishop's vestments, and his mitre in its brass box, were borne away to the church on a flood of ragged boys, and we followed rather more sedately while the bells jangled in the tower. The Metropolitan went straight to his throne on the south side of the church after vesting in the open narthex, and I was led to the stall on his right, immediately beneath the great eikon of the Pantocrator in the dome. The church had been recently re-decorated and a gay diaper pattern now covered every part of the interior that was not frescoed. Not for the first time I was struck by the contrast between the comeliness and colour of the village church and the squalid dwellings which surrounded it. The little groups of people who had followed us up the stony path from the *mesochori*, or village-square, crowded into the church, setting up their candles before the eikons of our Lord and His Mother, bringing loaves bearing the seal "Jesus Christ conquers" and wine for the offering, oil for the lamps and lists of relatives and friends, both living and departed, to be commemorated at the liturgy that morning. The parish priest came with the singers and the verger to ask the Bishop's blessing, and the morning office (the first part of which had been sung before our arrival) was taken up again.

While the Magnificat was being sung, the parish priest went all about the building censing the holy things and the holy people with a proper indiscrimination, and when the great doxology was reached the sacristan ran down the church and set the three chandeliers swinging in alarming fashion while the belfry again resounded to the clash of metal. Mattins gave place to the divine liturgy; the church became more and more crowded till the people filled the narthex and over-flowed down the steps into the path outside. The scouts arrived; the chandeliers swung more slowly, scattering drops of molten wax upon the heads of the congregation and splashing the strip of brightly coloured carpet which extended from the holy table down into the midst of the church; the incense and the venerable prayers rose to heaven, and the children scrambled up the stair leading to the high pulpit or balanced on the backs of the stalls occupied by their grandfathers.

The Epistle (from St. Paul's letter to the Philippians), was read by the chief singer, or *psaltes*, a soldier from the garrison at Nevrokopi who had learned the traditional chant in some village church on Pangaion, overlooking the ruined basilica where "the saints in Christ Jesus which were in Philippi" celebrated in their day that same holy offering in which we at Dasoto were taking part. There, like the ragged boys who now pressed upon him from all sides, he had joined with slowly growing

confidence in the familiar chants, had had a hand clapped precisely
to his mouth when he rashly ventured upon the uncharted depths of one
less familiar, and little by little had attained to his present mastery of
his art. This is the universal method for training singers: the Greeks
know nothing of the prolonged agony of choir-practices. As a boy gains
confidence he will occasionally be permitted to sing the Epistle at the
liturgy: it is by no means unusual, even in a big urban parish, to see
such a 'reader'—perhaps not more than twelve or thirteen years of age.

The Gospel was sung from the throne—not from the pulpit—by the
parish priest, and, as is customary, was followed immediately by the
sermon. The men and boys parted to allow the Bishop to reach his
throne, and then closed in solidly around him: a sea of intent faces
stretching from the doors of the sanctuary out through the shadowed
narthex into the fierce glare of sunlight beyond. The sermon, as befitted
the occasion, was homely both in language and illustration. The Bishop
took his text from the Gospel appointed for the feast: "Yea rather,
blessed are they that hear the word of God and keep it". He pictured
the two sisters: Martha, "cumbered about much serving" (a pungent
sipasng reference to certain absent members of his flock who were so
preoccupied with their chaffering that they could ill spare an hour or
two to come to church), and Mary, who "sat at Jesus' feet and heard
His word". It was well that we should hearken to the divine word;
that we should come to church and hear the holy Gospels read Sunday
by Sunday. It was still more to the point, however, that we should
be not mere hearers of the word but doers also; that we should not only
hear the word of God but *keep* it. Therein lay the true holiness of that
other Mary, the Mother of the Word. It was on account of her entire
conformity to the divine will that we venerated her, the fiery chariot
of the word, the bush burning and yet unconsumed, above every
creature: above the bodiless powers and the choirs of archangels, above
the cherubim and seraphim who veil their faces before the un-
approachable glory.

"For us too, my children", the Bishop went on, "this is the sure way
of salvation. There are no bounds to the creative energy of the word
in the life of the Christian who surrenders himself in simplicity to its
power". A series of illustrations followed: the eunuch of Queen
Candace, hearing the divine word and straightway being baptised; the
converting power of the word as revealed in the life of St. Augustine
—a father who figures so infrequently in the discourses of Greek prelates

as to lead me to suspect the offering of a discreet compliment to western Christendom; the fruits of the word, love, joy and peace, made manifest in the life and death of the blessed Polycarp.

"And you boys", said the Bishop, with 'a diligent and busy cast of his eye' toward certain of the more youthful of his auditors; "you who steal eggs and fruit and take other people's food out of the communal oven: there is no reason why you—if you keep the word of God faithfully—should not be as great as St. Peter or St. Paul, or why at the end of your lives you should not be able to echo those ever-memorable words of Polycarp: 'These eighty and six years have I been His servant' . . ."

Looking round that crowded church, my mind went to the Whitsuntide hymn: "Blessed art thou, O Christ our God, who hast made the fishermen wise by the sending down upon them of the Holy Spirit, and through them hast drawn the world into thy net."

The sermon ended, the singers took up the solemn chant of the Hymn of the Cherubim, and a hush fell upon the congregation as the ministers with their attendants emerged from the prothesis chapel and made their slow circuit of the church, the veiled oblations borne aloft, to the accompaniment of that all-embracing appeal:

> May the Lord God be mindful of us all
> in His kingdom, always, now and for ever,
> and unto the ages of ages.

The holy gifts were carried up within the sanctuary and laid upon the altar. The singers resumed their interrupted hymn; the atmosphere was heavy with incense—which, say the commentators, is here an emblem of the mixture of myrrh and aloes which Nicodemus brought for the entombment of the Lord:

> Lo, Christ is crucified, the Life is buried,
> the tomb is made fast, the stone is sealed.

Two shallow alms-baskets piled high with tattered notes were passed slowly round the church, while the sacristan sprinkled perfume from a pewter vessel into the outstretched hands of the more accessible among the male members of the congregation.

The long drawn-out alleluias died away into silence as the parish priest resumed his place before the doors and took up anew the litanies which properly pertain to the deacon's liturgy:

> For the precious gifts which have been offered,
> For this holy temple, and for those who enter it in
> faith, reverence and the fear of God . . .

while the reiterated *Kyrie eleison* of the singers rose and fell and we commended "ourselves and one another and all our life to Christ our God". At the cry: "The doors, the doors!" all became suddenly alert, and a young girl—one of those celebrating their name-day—pushed through the crowd of women and children who filled the space between the lectern of the singers and the eikonostasis on the north side of the church and, standing before the eikon of the Mother of God, read the Nicene Creed. The Bishop commenced the great eucharistic prayer and the climax of the liturgy drew near. After the loaves that remained over from the consecrated bread had been blessed, the Bishop sent me, by the hand of his assistant, a portion bearing the seal IC . XC . NI . KA: how many a holy custom have we forfeited in exchanging the *artos* of scripture and primitive tradition for the *azymes* which bear no evident relation to the common bread which one bakes and breaks at home, or to the daily toil of ordinary men and women. In Greece the bread and the wine that are brought to the altar are the very same as those which are eaten and drunk at home, and such loaves as remain over after the distribution of the blessed bread—the *antidoron* (literally, 'instead of the gift')—go to the parish priest; so, we may recall, the English Prayer Book requires that: "the Bread be such as is usual to be eaten. . . . And if any of the Bread and Wine remain unconsecrated the Curate shall have it to his own use."

Came the solemn pronouncement of the Lord's words: "This is my body. . . . This is my blood", and the great cry "Thine of thine own we offer to thee . . ." and then the Bishop knelt before the holy table and called upon God to "send down thy Holy Spirit upon us and upon these thy gifts, and make this bread the precious body of thy Christ, and that which is in this cup the precious blood of thy Christ, changing them by thy Holy Spirit", while the singers softly intoned their hymn of adoring praise, and the holy people of God stood with bowed heads in the pools of sunlight, veiled by the slowly spiralling haze of incense.

In some parts of Greece where movements such as the Brotherhood of Life have been most active, there have, as we shall see in a later chapter, been certain changes in liturgical practice during recent years: very often now the celebrant reads in an audible voice the whole of the *anaphora*, or great eucharistic prayer, which the rubric directs him to say *mystikos*—mystically, or secretly—and the whole congregation kneels at the invocation of the Holy Spirit. None of these influences had as yet reached this remote corner of New Greece, however, and the liturgy was still celebrated at Dasoto after the fashion which caused Robert de Dreux, in the seventeenth century, to observe that "it is not easy to see all that they do when they say mass, because the celebrant is hidden by a screen which shuts off the altar, and only shows himself three or four times". This, however, is a topic to which we shall have occasion to return.

The Lord's Prayer (like the Creed) was recited by a girl, and there were some thirty communicants including several children borne in the arms of their mothers—a familiar sight this in every Greek parish church. When the liturgy was ended, and the Bishop had distributed the blessed bread to the whole congregation, I observed some twenty of those who had communicated kneel before the royal doors while their father in God read a brief prayer of absolution. I have referred elsewhere to contemporary Greek practice in regard to the use of the mystery of confession. In the country districts at least, where confessors are rare, this is by no means as uniform as some are apt to suppose, or as might be inferred from the customs which obtain among the Russians of the diaspora, in Paris and elsewhere, with whom the sacrament has tended in recent times to become an obligatory part of the preparation for holy communion.

When one has fasted as a Christian one feasts as a Christian—in Greece at least.

> Then for their Festivals [says Dr. Covel] . . . there is not one that appears there but will contribute something, as his share, towards the providing of victuals and drink in abundance, (as at our old Whitsun-Ales, or setting up May-poles and the like in England) there is hardly one Greek so poor, but he will borrow, or pawn, or sell his very Cloaths, or something else, to get Money for Wine, to Celebrate the Festival; and it is the same Practice amongst them upon the Holydays set apart for the Virgin Mary, or any other

peculiar Saint, especially those to whom they are particularly devoted. These jolly Easterlings, when they hear . . . that the Christians pretending to be Reformed in the West, do utterly hate and abjure all such Practices as *Heathenish* and *Prophane*, must think them all the vilest Miscreants living.

When the last of the *antidoron* had been distributed, Anargyri had replaced the mitre in its brass box, and the Metropolitan had concluded a long conversation with the churchwardens about the best method of shoring up the roof—a section of which was sagging ominously—we left the church and made our way to the dwelling of the parish priest where a vast table had been erected in the shade of a vine. There we feasted until it was high afternoon: the Lord Agathangellos, the president of the community, the *kapetanios* of the militia, the *papas*, the schoolmaster, Anargyri, the churchwardens, the singers and several officers from the garrison of Nevrokopi who had accompanied us to Dasoto that morning.

It was not by any means my first experience of a village festival: a few months earlier I might well have been deceived into thinking that the bowls of eggs, goat's milk cheese, olives, and finely-shredded vegetables soaked in oil and lemon which appeared with the *ouzo* constituted the substance of the feast and not a mere *hors d'oeuvre*. Now I knew better, and I was not surprised when the clearing of the table by the *papadia* and her daughters after forty minutes proved to be no more than a prelude to a banquet of an altogether more serious character.

As the dishes came and went and the dark wine flowed freely, I recalled Dr. Covel's description of another such festival at the great Athonite house of Iveron: "The best monkish fare that could be gotten was provided, excellent fish (severall ways), oyl, salet, beanes, hortechockes, beets . . . chees, onions, garlick, olives, caveor, Pyes of herbs, $\phi\alpha\kappa\alpha\grave{\iota}\varsigma$, $\kappa\tau\omega\pi\acute{o}\delta\iota$; pepper, salt, saffron in all. At last conserved little oranges, most exquisite, good wine (a sort of small claret), and we always drank most plentifully. . . . He is no Greek that cannot drink twenty or thirty plump glasses at a setting."

After the feast there was dancing, and the sun was low in the west when we drove back to Nevrokopi. The day drew to a close amongst the eikons of those who had finished their course, with those yet in the way of salvation joining with one voice in the ancient canticle, *Hail! Gladdening Light*, to the praise and glory of the Holy Trinity.

VI

HEAVEN UPON EARTH

Let the Christian consider well when he enters the church
that he is entering into another heaven. That same majesty
of God which is in heaven is also in His church, and on
this account the Christian must needs enter with reverence
and fear.

From a *Synopsis* printed at Venice in 1857

DR. COVEL, it must be confessed, looked with a somewhat jaundiced
eye upon the liturgical performances of the Greeks of Constantinople—
the "jolly Easterlings," as he styles them. Not for him the wondering
awe of the emissaries of the Prince of Kiev who, seven centuries before
his advent as chaplain to King Charles' ambassador at the Sublime
Porte, had been present at a celebration of the divine liturgy of our
father among the saints, John Chrysostom, in the great church of the
Emperor Justinian, and had not known whether they were yet on
earth or in heaven by reason of its surpassing splendour.

"A miserable Jumble, or patcht Piece of Service", says Covel, "so
confused and so tedious, as it takes away all Devotion"; not to be compared with the chaste dignity of that incomparable liturgy whose
compilers "with wonderful Prudence and sound Judgment did distinguish, or rather . . . garble the Offices of Greeks and Latins: and
retaining and adding only such things as might promote true Piety and
primitive Devotion, did cast away all the rest."

The good Doctor was plainly subject to the prejudices which are
characteristic of most Frankish divines and travellers of his generation;
and yet, making due allowance for a certain lack of sympathy in the
face of an unfamiliar liturgical tradition, we must admit the substantial truth of his assertion that "the greatest part of the Easterlings'
Oeconomy and discipline, especially of the Greeks, consist first in their
Pomp and amusing Ceremonies at their Liturgies and other Offices . . .
and in celebrating their Fasts and Feasts."

Nobody who has lived and worshipped amongst Greek Christians
for any length of time but has sensed in some measure the extraordinary
hold which the recurring cycle of the Church's liturgy has upon the
piety of the common people. Nobody who has kept the great lent with

the Greek Church, who has shared in the fast which lies heavy upon the whole nation for forty days; who had stood for long hours, one of an innumerable multitude who crowd the tiny Byzantine churches of Athens and overflow into the streets, while the familiar pattern of God's saving economy towards man is re-presented in psalm and prophecy, in lections from the Gospel, and the matchless poetry of the canons; who has known the desolation of the holy and great Friday, when every bell in Greece tolls its lament and the body of the Saviour lies shrouded in flowers in all the village churches throughout the land; who has been present at the kindling of the new fire and tasted of the joy of a world released from the bondage of sin and death—none can have lived through all this and not have realised that for the Greek Christian the Gospel is inseparably linked with the liturgy that is unfolded week by week in his parish church. Not among the Greeks only but throughout Orthodox Christendom the liturgy has remained at the very heart of the Church's life.

What the west knows as the liturgical movement bears witness to a very different state of affairs. Throughout western Christendom we can trace the growth of a spirit profoundly alien to that which characterises the Orthodox Christian's approach to the mysteries of the faith. The prayer of the Church no longer shapes and controls the piety of ordinary men and women as it did in former days. Liturgy has as it were become separated from dogma and then, inevitably, from spirituality also. The holy eucharist—the corporate action wherein every member of the organic body has its appropriate *liturgy* to perform—has become clericalised; has come to be thought of as the act of one member acting on behalf of the whole body.

Many who reverence the Bible as the word of God forget that the treasures of the divine scriptures are fully revealed only to the worshipping *ekklesia*, in whose liturgy they are embedded as in a precious frame. Every fragment of a shattered Christendom has its private *lex orandi*, born of isolation and bearing the marks of controversies which are in their turn the legacy of schism and partial vision; while personal devotion—no longer fully subject to the control of the liturgy—has brought forth strange fruit; and a theology divorced from worship and banished to the schools has come to be regarded as a barren science of the intellect: a necessary discipline for scholars and specialists, but utterly irrelevant to the life of the ordinary Christian doing daily battle against the threefold enemy.

The liturgical movement in the west is nothing less than a reassertion of the true nature of the liturgy and of its place in the life of the Church, springing from a recovered vision of the nature of the Christian mystery, and from the realisation that dogma and scripture can never be isolated from the living liturgical tradition of the worshipping community without serious impoverishment and distortion. Its scope embraces a far wider field than the province of the liturgiologist, and though it is commonly associated with such 'ecclesiastical' matters as the purifying of the traditional chant and the reform of ceremonial, it is ultimately concerned with fundamental theological realities. Herein lies the secret of the widespread influence of the movement— an influence which although it has been most profound within the bounds of the Roman communion has yet extended in some measure to German Lutherans, French and Scottish Calvinists and others scarcely less remote from Old Rome. The movement is inextricably bound up with the return, now manifest in many different quarters, to a truly theological approach to biblical exegesis, and a recovered awareness that the ancient fathers are not so dead as some would have them be.

Dom Olivier Rousseau (whose *Histoire du Mouvement liturgique* affords an admirable survey of the origins and later development of the movement throughout western Christendom) has justly observed that so far as the Orthodox Church is concerned there can be no question of a liturgical movement, for her piety has never deviated from her worship.

I have already had occasion to refer to certain reforming tendencies which are exercising a growing influence upon the liturgical life of the Greek Church at the present time. Father Eusebius Matthopoulos never wearied of expounding the significance of the divine liturgy to the multitudes who flocked to hear him in every city of Old Greece, and one of the primary aims of the Brotherhood which this great preacher and evangelist founded at the beginning of the present century has always been the reverent celebration of the holy mysteries. One has but to compare the manner in which the holy eucharist is celebrated at the Metropolis in Athens, or the little chapel dedicated to St. Catherine above the outer harbour at the Piraeus, with the use which still obtains in the average Macedonian village church, to realise something of the progress that has been made within a generation.

While, however, one may in a certain sense speak of a liturgical movement within the Greek Church to-day, it is important to recognise how restricted is its scope when compared with recent developments in western Christendom. The very limitations of this Greek 'liturgical movement' illustrate the Roman Catholic historian's contention that the Orthodox Church has never lost her hold upon certain important truths which we in the west are only now, after long centuries of neglect, beginning to recover and make our own.

The word *leitourgia* had in classical Greek the meaning of a public service or duty—it might be building a wall or fitting out a hollow ship for a naval expedition. Despite the specifically religious associations which the word has acquired through later usage, it is still sometimes employed in this quite general sense. I remember, for example, being told on one occasion in a small provincial town of northern Greece that the municipal school was not *liturgising* that morning: was not performing its liturgy, or service.

For the Christian, likewise, the liturgy which he fulfils every Sunday in his parish church is a public service; an action performed on behalf not of any terrestrial *polis* but of that city which, as Augustine puts it, is Christ's body of which Christ is the head. The holy eucharist in particular, the service to which the Greek Christian commonly refers as 'the divine liturgy', and upon which the whole of the liturgy, in the wider sense of that word, centres, is supremely the characteristic act of the Church: a corporate action in which every member of the one body takes part. Nor is it those now on earth who alone participate in the eucharistic liturgy. It is not merely the bishop, priest, deacon and reader who, with the remainder of the *laos*—the holy people of God—have their peculiar service to offer within the setting of the one oblation. The saints and the angels, the many-eyed cherubim and the six-winged seraphim, no less than the earthly ministers of Christ's body have each their several liturgy to perform; the whole company of the heavenly Sion is present and active in every village church or hilltop chapel where the holy and ineffable mysteries are fulfilled and where the King of kings and Lord of lords comes forth to be sacrificed and given for food to the faithful.

For many centuries now, so far as the west is concerned, this aspect of the eucharist as the characteristic action of the whole Christian community has tended to be obscured. The passing of the austere Latin of the ancient liturgies as a language "understanded of the people" and the banishing of theology to the schools gradually brought about the virtual exclusion of the laity from any active participation in the celebration of the divine mysteries. The liturgy was no longer thought of as a corporate action in which the whole congregation—the laity no less than the clerks—had an essential part to play. Slowly but surely the mass came to be regarded rather in the light of a marvellous rite, fraught indeed with inexpressible wonder and mystery, performed by the sacred ministers: as something *said* rather than *done*. The common people, capable no longer of entering into the full meaning of the prayer of the Church, came to church to hear the mass and to occupy themselves with 'private' devotions bearing little relation to the action which was taking place within the sanctuary, where the sacred ministers performed their liturgy on behalf of the whole body. The ceremonies which from about the thirteenth century onwards gathered about the elevation of the holy gifts belong to an age which had already acquiesced in the growth of a popular piety no longer effectively subject to the control of the prayer of the Church.

The English Prayer Book attempted to restore to the laity their rightful liturgy. The mass was again sung that the people might hear it and in a language which they could understand. But the reformers themselves were too much subject to mediaeval assumptions: the real roots of the trouble still lay hid. An emphasis on audibility was not enough and congregational worship was not necessarily *corporate* worship. For the common people the new vernacular mass was still something said rather than done; metrical psalms and the congregational hymns which gradually superseded them, had no more organic connexion with the eucharistic action than the older vernacular devotions wherewith our forefathers had occupied themselves while the priest, aloof and apart, performed his mysterious acts at God's board.

The expression 'to hear mass' has no parallel in Greek. The Greek Christian goes to his parish church not so much to *hear* a service as to play his part in a corporate action in which all the different orders of the Church are actively involved. The very arrangement of the church emphasises this fact; the sacred ministers are not, as is now usual in the west, separated from the people by a long quire or chancel. The holy table stands not against the east wall of the apse but clear in the midst of the *altar*, or sanctuary as we should say. The average Greek church, it should also be borne in mind, is by western standards very tiny— even the great basilicas of Salonica are dwarfed by the cathedrals of the gothic north—and since the space which separates the holy table from the eikonostasis is commonly no greater than suffices to permit of the prostrations of the celebrant, and, in a parish church, the laity occupy the greater part of the space beneath the dome, and press against the great screen which bears the eikons, many of the congregation are thus within two or three yards of the holy table itself.

But what, the reader may ask, of the eikonostasis? Does not this solid screen, pierced only by three doors, extending right across the whole width of the church, cut off the laity from all effective participation in the action taking place within the sanctuary quite as much as mere physical remoteness? Does it not tend, as has been asserted by Dom Gregory Dix, to force "upon the eastern liturgies the character of two simultaneous services, the one proceeding outside the screen for the people, conducted chiefly by the deacon; the other—the real liturgical action—proceeding inside the screen conducted by the celebrant"?

That there is an element of truth in such contentions may be admitted: witness a tendency which is steadily gaining ground in Greece to-day. In many town churches (with the exception of a few provincial cathedrals liturgical reform has as yet made little headway in the country districts), the curtain which could be drawn across the space above the double doors in the centre of the eikonostasis has now fallen into disuse—at any rate so far as the eucharistic liturgy is concerned. The doors themselves are as a rule only about three feet in height, and it has long been customary to draw these curtains (thus screening the sanctuary completely from the view of the people) at two points during the divine liturgy, at both of which there is much coming and going about the holy table; at the placing of the holy gifts upon the altar immediately after the Great Entrance; and again during the communion of the ministers. This custom has now been abandoned in many places. In a few churches the doors themselves have been removed as, for instance, at Aghia Katerini, Piraeus (where the liturgy is celebrated with a reverence and propriety unsurpassed in all Greece), and, I am told, in the chapel of the Oecumenical Patriarchate at Constantinople.

When all is said, however, the effects of the eikonostasis have been grossly exaggerated by western writers, too many of whom have been content to reiterate *ad nauseam* the strictures of their predecessors in the field of controversy: strictures grounded not infrequently upon the most superficial acquaintance with the liturgical practice of eastern Christendom. The divisive properties of the eikonostasis are most marked in a large church when the space before the royal doors normally occupied by the laity is railed off and reserved for the singers and distinguished visitors. Such an arrangement, so far as Greece is concerned, will be found only in certain churches of Athens and Salonica. It would, I fancy, be generally acknowledged by all who have worshipped among Greek Christians as well as in the churches of the Latins that as an instrument for creating a sense of separation between ministers and people the eikonostasis of the Easterlings is vastly inferior to the Frankish quire or chancel. An Orthodox priest who has celebrated the liturgy in more than 200 western churches (most of them Anglican) has remarked that he finds himself far more cut off from his congregation in an English parish church—without an eikonostasis of course, but with a long chancel, often having a screen at its *western* end—than in an Orthodox church where the screen is never further away than four feet from the altar.

It needs also to be borne in mind how great a part of the eucharistic action is enacted *outside* the eikonostasis in the midst of the congregation. Thus the deacon, whose normal place is immediately beneath the eikon of the Pantocrator in the dome, acts as a constant link between all the various orders of the church. The bishop's throne, which forms part of the ordinary furnishing of every Greek church—a constant reminder that the parish priest 'liturgises' only as the deputy of the diocesan—also stands outside the screen, on the south side of the space beneath the dome, so that the bishop is often completely surrounded by his flock. At the solemn entries which occur during the course of the divine liturgy —the lesser, with the book of the Gospels, the greater, with the holy gifts veiled and borne aloft—the sacred ministers descend into the body of the church and make a slow circuit of the whole building. Outside the eucharistic liturgy itself, some of the most memorable events of the liturgical year—the great blessing of the waters at Epiphany (the Feast of Lights, as it is popularly known), the solemn kneeling at the second vespers of Whit-Sunday and the adoration of the holy cross on September 14th, as well as many of the profoundly moving ceremonies of Holy Week and Eastertide—are celebrated not within the sanctuary but in the midst of the congregation.

This would naturally be impossible if the Greek church were encumbered with chairs or pews. In fact, the only seating consists of a few stalls, with crutch-like supports for the arms, against the walls of the church. Standing—not kneeling—is, as it has always been, the normal attitude for prayer. At one of the great festivals the people will stand for hours wedged so tightly together that it is impossible even to cross oneself. All other considerations apart, such a setting is hardly favourable to the growth of certain individualistic types of piety which flourish amongst the Franks, who worship their Creator in strange and novel ways, each isolated from his fellow and entrenched within the citadel of his own pew.

In Greece there is but one celebration of the liturgy on a Sunday or holy day in any one church. This is a rule which is waived only in cases of extreme necessity and then only when a *parekklesion*, or side-chapel, is available so that it is not necessary to use the same altar twice (most Greek churches have only one altar). A priest may celebrate only once on any given day.

In Greece the times of services are never announced and questions on this score are invariably met with evasive if not actually misleading replies. Services commence earlier in summer than in winter. An hour or two after sunrise the bells will be rung and the priest and a couple of readers will begin to sing the morning offices—*mesonyktikon* (which should, as the name indicates, be read at midnight, as it is in the monastic use), and *orthros*, or lauds, the office of the dawn. Towards the end of the latter service—perhaps an hour or more after the village's first awakening—the bells will be rung a second time. Still the church is comparatively empty. The holy eucharist follows *orthros* without a break about nine o'clock, and by the time that the thrice-holy hymn is sung (when the bells summon the faithful for the third and last time) the congregation will have begun to swell, until, at the great entry with the holy gifts, the greater part of the village will be packed within the walls of the church, the men to the right, the women to the left, the air by this time heavy with incense.

The whole service is invariably sung. What the west knows as a low mass, the 'early service' or 'eight o'clock', dear to so many English churchmen, is unknown to the Greeks. The traditional Byzantine chant is still more or less universal and is always sung without instrumental accompaniment; only in certain urban parishes has it been partially displaced of recent years by that bastard child of strangely-matched parents, the so-called European chant. In its pure form the traditional plainsong can be quite ravishing in its unearthly beauty. Never shall I forget the singing of the monks of Moni Petraki who gather morning by morning in their tiny church, while Athens lies in darkness and before the first tramcar has gone clanging down the tree-lined avenue of the *Basilissa* Sophia towards the outer suburbs.

"Nowhere, either in Greece or the East," observes the Abbé de St. Michon, "do men sing as loud as we do. It is an usage that we owe to the barbarism of our fathers. The oriental psalmody is sweet, low and without effort." Alas! it is not always so. "Their singing", says Thomas Smith, "is very mean and pitifull, without figure and the relishes of art, and is at best but a kind of harsh Plain-song." "We heard the Greek Vespers", wrote Sir George Wheler in 1675, "worse sung than *Hopkins* Psalms used to be in some of our Country Churches." All too frequently the beauty of the traditional chant has been overlaid by accretions and adornment from alien sources; and its delivery, as the Abbé justly remarks, "with nasal sounds which weary European ears". Much of the "tedious and indiscreet length of liturgies" whereof so many Frankish travellers have complained, is due not to any inner necessity of the rite itself but solely to the elaboration of the chant. The restoration of the oriental plainchant to something of its earlier simplicity and directness has therefore become an imperative need in circles where the holy mysteries are celebrated frequently: one cannot expect the laity to spend the greater part of every morning in church. There are churches in Greece to-day where the liturgy is celebrated with great reverence in an hour and a quarter, even when many of the secret prayers are read aloud.

Concelebration—which has all but disappeared from the west—is still very much a reality in Greece, and is an important factor in enabling the Greek Church to retain the ancient rule of a single eucharist attended by the whole church in each several locality. On a Sunday morning at an important parish church, such as St. Panteleimon, Acharnon (in the suburbs of Athens), one may see five or six priests attended by a deacon concelebrating at the great square altar, often with a bishop (one of the suffragans of the Archbishop, or a provincial metropolitan serving his term of duty as a member of the synod) presiding over the whole assembly. The Greek bishop or priest who finds himself away from his own diocese on the Lord's day does not take his place amongst the laity in the body of the church but joins the other ministers gathered around the holy table and there fulfils his proper liturgy.

Now there are those who, while recognising that the Orthodox Church has in many respects faithfully preserved the liturgical tradition of the first centuries of our era, would yet ask whether the liturgy of the laity has not—within the bounds of the *oikoumene* no less than in the west—been reduced to a mere shadow of its former self. Is not the Greek Christian for all practical purposes a mere passive onlooker at a gorgeous spectacle performed by the resplendent ministers: even though the sacred participants in the divine drama sometimes descend from their apron stage and mingle with the audience?

It must be admitted that the average Greek layman communicates very rarely, often only once or twice a year; outside the immediate sphere of influence of the movements, hardly ever more than four times. This reluctance of the laity to communicate frequently is a phenomenon which has been common to east and west from a very early period— though in the west (among Orthodox of the diaspora as well as amongst western Christians) there has been a widespread return to something more nearly approaching primitive practice. Its causes are complex and, to a great extent, a matter for speculation. One factor which is peculiar to the east is the place which the *antidoron* has come to occupy. It would be an over-simplification to say that the blessed bread which the Greek Christian is accustomed to receive at the end of every liturgy is consciously looked upon as a substitute for the holy communion; nevertheless, the *antidoron* has a deep significance for the Greek layman —more, perhaps, than in other parts of the Orthodox world.

The reluctance to communicate frequently does not, as we can see from the history of certain movements within western Christendom, necessarily spring from carelessness and sloth; often it is due to a sense of unworthiness which is none the less real though it be considered misguided. Even in reforming circles in Greece to-day one discovers great wariness on the part of the clergy in recommending frequent, let alone daily, communion to their people. This is not, it is held, a matter to be undertaken lightly, or without the advice and approval of an experienced confessor; and few priests will permit their penitents to communicate as often as once a month unless they are satisfied that the desire goes hand in hand with a real determination to follow Christ in their daily life. To communicate every Sunday is regarded as an inestimable privilege, but one which is hardly for all men.

Then we must not ignore the part played by the ordinary Christian in the offertory. In the country districts of Greece the housewife who bakes her bread on Saturday will set aside one loaf upon which she has stamped with a wooden seal a traditional design wherein the words "Jesus Christ conquers"—abbreviated to I(HCOY)C . X(PICTO)C . NI . KA—constitute the most prominent feature. Early on Sunday morning she will set out for the parish church with her loaf, and arriving whilst the singers are still chanting the morning psalms, and taking it to the door of the chapel where the elements are prepared, she will hand it to the priest together with a vessel of wine, the family diptychs —or lists of relatives and friends, both living and departed, to be commemorated by name at the holy eucharist—and perhaps a flask of oil for the lamps and a few grains of incense. Even in an urban parish church the faithful may purchase a sealed loaf at the counter in the narthex where candles are sold, and send it to the celebrant with their diptychs.

It is frequently asserted that the offering of the people disappeared from the eastern liturgies at an early date. One can only marvel at the number of eminent scholars who have been led astray in this matter through failure to distinguish clearly between the offertory procession of the Roman rite and the offering itself. The procession never found a place in the Byzantine rite, which retained the older practice of presenting the bread and wine informally before the commencement of the eucharistic liturgy. So widely-used a liturgical handbook as the late Dr. Srawley's *Early History of the Liturgy* asserts that "the offerings of the people, which consisted partly of bread and wine, out of which the elements of the eucharist were taken, and partly of alms . . . continued in the west longer than in the east".[1] In actual fact the offering of the people has never disappeared from the Byzantine liturgy and may still be witnessed in any Greek village church on the Lord's day.

But even though it be admitted that the offering of the bread and wine makes the ordinary people something more than mere passive spectators at a gorgeous pageant, it may yet be said that from very early times the rightful liturgy of the laity has in practice been transferred to the choir: the common people hardly open their mouths from one end of the eucharistic liturgy to the other. Now it is true that congregational singing as practised in the west is so rare among the Greeks as to be almost unknown. Only on one of the great festivals of the Church's year will the whole congregation take up the melody of some ancient hymn: the paschal anthem *Christ is risen from the dead*, for example, or the dismissal hymn at the Epiphany. Normally those parts of the liturgy which properly belong to the laity are in fact sung by the *psaltai* or trained singers —and this applies even to the responses to the petitions of the litanies.

[1] 2nd edition, Cambridge, 1949, p. 127. Dom Gregory Dix and Professor Burkitt have already been taken to task on this issue by the Archimandrite Alexis van der Mensbrugghe.

What, on the other hand, is very common is for the laity to repeat, almost inaudibly, the words of the prayers and hymns of the liturgy as they are chanted by the singers. Not only is this practice very widespread among Greek Christians, it is also officially encouraged, while from very early times only the canonically appointed *psaltai* have been allowed to sing aloud in church. Thus, in a modern Greek catechism, the question:

"Does not the whole of the *laos* take part in public worship?" receives the following answer:

"Yes, it does and should take part; not only by standing reverently and following in spirit what is being done, but also by joining in and softly singing ... thus to show that it is a lively member of the body of the Church."

In other words, the excellent practice commonly known to the western world as 'praying the mass' is one with which the ordinary Greek Christian is thoroughly familiar. He has never been accustomed to occupy the long hours that he spends in church with 'private' devotions—indeed the expression would be unintelligible to him. It is not only "pious Russians of the middle classes" who (in the words of John Mason Neale) "feel a repugnance to use any devotions but those of the Church".

It is necessary, moreover, to bear in mind that the separation between the Greek *psaltai* and the whole body of the faithful is much less marked than in western Christendom, with its surpliced choirs. The singers are quite plainly members of the congregation: the spokesmen of the whole body of the *laos* amongst whom they stand. They normally wear lay dress; only in an urban parish church will one normally see an *anagnostes*, or reader, wearing a simple black gown. The ordinary singers are indistinguishable from the rest of the people. Indeed, one of the things which commonly strikes the visitor to Greece who finds his way for the first time to a parish church is the unexpectedly prominent (some would say obtrusive) part played by the laity in the church services. Very often long stretches of incomprehensible offices seem to be conducted entirely by laymen; the parish priest only occasionally emerging from the sanctuary, and disappearing as quickly after a brief *ekphonesis*, to leave matters wholly in the hands of two middle-aged gentlemen in double-breasted suits, supported by a nondescript collection of young men and boys.

This, to the western mind, curiously prominent liturgical rôle of the lay-singers has occasioned comment in other ages than our own. On the feast of St. Thomas of Canterbury in the year of our Lord 1400, King Henry IV rode out to Blackheath at the head of an imposing array, to welcome to his dominions the Emperor Manuel II Palaeologus with a following which included several Greek ecclesiastics, both bishops and priests.[1] These unwonted guests remained in London until the end of February following. The Greek services were celebrated daily, many English churchmen being present, and several contemporary accounts of the impression created by these unfamiliar rites have been preserved. More than one chronicler notes with surprise that laymen as well as clerks took an active part in the services which, to quote Adam of Usk, "were joined in as well by soldiers as by priests; for they chanted them without distinction in their native tongue".

One last word in connexion with the liturgy of the laity. A contemporary of King Henry IV relates that the Emperor's chaplains were catechised by certain English churchmen who had been present at the Greeks' services as to whether "the common people and the ignorant in their country did indeed understand the scriptures and the divine words which they recited together with the learned." Is the 'old school-Greek' whereof Covel and others speak, sufficiently understanded of the people?

Let us hear another voice from the fifteenth century: "The Grekis", says John Purvey, "wiche ben nobel men, han al this in ther owne langage. But yet adversaries of trewith seien, wane men rehersen that Grekis . . . han al in ther owne langage, the clerkis of hem speiken grammaticalliche and the puple understondith it not."

It should be remarked that the Orthodox Church has never opposed the translation of the scriptures or the liturgy into new tongues when such translation has been necessary for the furtherance of her missionary and pastoral work. On the contrary, the liturgy of St. John Chrysostom is probably celebrated in more languages than any other of the historic rites of Christendom. I have myself been present at celebrations at which old Slavonic, Greek, English, French and Arabic have all been used during the course of the liturgy, and W. J. Birkbeck mentions a committee he encountered at St. Petersburg in 1889 which was engaged in translating the liturgy for a small tribe in the north-east of Siberia, numbering less than 5,000 souls and whose language contained scarcely

[1] The story of this Byzantine Emperor's fruitless expedition to the west in quest of military aid against the Turk, and of his sojourn in Paris and London—one of the most diverting episodes in fifteenth-century history—is related in some detail in Schlumberger's *Byzance et Croisades* (Paris, 1927), pp. 87-147: "Un Empereur de Byzance à Paris et à Londres."

more than 200 words in all. Amongst the second and third generations of Orthodox *emigrés* in America to-day English is being widely used as a liturgical language.

This being so, it is reasonable to presume that where an ancient liturgical language is retained (as in Greece, for example) it is still tolerably intelligible to the ordinary people. It may indeed be questioned whether, except for brief epochs of the Church's history, her common prayer has ever been cast in a language wholly familiar to the unlearned. This is not the place to embark upon a description of the present condition of the Greek language: the subject is peculiarly complex and, in certain of its aspects, highly controversial. Suffice it to say that the *katharevousa*, or 'purified' language, which is still, despite many violent assaults, the normal medium of literary expression, differs comparatively little from the formal Greek of the Byzantine writers. The leading articles of a newspaper such as *Kathimerini* (the Greek equivalent of *The Times*) can be read with fair comprehension by an average classical scholar. The *demotiki*, or popular language, on the other hand, has undergone a far greater transformation since the days when the liturgies were composed, so that a comparison of the two forms of Greek will reveal very wide differences both in grammar and vocabulary.

Both *katharevousa* and *demotiki* are current to-day, and an educated Greek will be familiar with either. A Greek bishop, for example, will normally use, within the privacy of his own metropolis and in everyday conversation with his people, a Greek which he would never dream of employing when writing to a fellow *despotes* or to the Holy Synod. Amongst the ordinary people, however, at any rate since the popular language ousted the *katharevousa* from the primary schools, the latter is never used; the average shepherd or grocer would be hard put to it to compose a letter in the sort of Greek that may be heard in the lecture rooms of the national university.

This does not mean, however, that the Greek of the liturgies is more or less incomprehensible to the common people. Far from it. It is often quite startling to find how much of the Psalter, the New Testament and the Church's prayers the Greek peasant has made his own. The fact is that in the ordinary Greek village the children spend so much time in church from earliest infancy onwards that they inevitably become familiar with the language that is used there. By the time they grow up they will commonly know much of the liturgy and the scriptures almost by heart. If anyone should doubt this let him consider the family prayers and personal devotions of the Greek laity. These are made up wholly of prayers, psalms and hymns drawn from the liturgy: scarcely ever (save in certain circles influenced by the new movements) do they include vernacular prayers. The *Hiera Synopsis*— the laity's manual of prayers—consists entirely of extracts from the Church's liturgy. The form of evening prayer commonly used in a Greek household is simply a shortened version of the Little Compline which closes the day in every monastery.

The 'liturgical' approach to the Bible has, it must be confessed, certain limitations. If the laity were present at *all* the services of the Church they would indeed acquire a working knowledge of the greater part of the holy scriptures. In practice, however, they will normally hear only those portions of the Old and New Testaments which are read on Sundays and holy days at the eucharistic liturgy and (depending on the regularity of their attendance) at mattins and evensong. Since 'Bible-reading' is little practised outside the new movements (where, indeed, it is universal) this inevitably means that the majority of the Greek laity, being wholly dependent upon the lections which occur in the course of the regular liturgical cycle, are unfamiliar with considerable portions of the Bible, particularly of the Old Testament.

It is, moreover, almost certainly true that the common people understand very imperfectly some of the elaborate 'canons' which recur only once every year (and then generally at mattins when few of the laity are present in church). But, as W. J. Birkbeck remarks not in-appositely of the Russian muzhiks of his day: "I myself have heard a great many more quotations (and intelligent quotations too) made from the canons . . . of St. Cosmas and St. John Damascene than I have ever heard from the Norfolk peasantry, amongst whom I have lived all my life, from the Hebrew prophets, which are read, or ought to be read, in all our churches throughout the months of September and October!"

While many a Greek Christian's familiarity with the Bible will extend only to those passages which are read during the course of the liturgy, his *theological* understanding of the scriptures is commonly far deeper than that of the, often better-informed, English churchman. Unlike so many an earnest student of the Bible, he realises—however obscurely—that the divine history is related at every point to what goes on week by week in his parish church: that it is only to those who are baptised into Christ's saving death, who are living in the mystery revealed in the Church, that the full meaning of the scriptures is laid bare.

VII

A THESSALIAN THEBAID

It seems a place of such stupendious solitude, as if the
situation thereof had been designed for the retirement of
Monks or the Cells of Anchorites.

PAUL RYCAUT

For the Quiet and innocency of their Life, the natural
Beauty of the Place, the Rocks, Mountains, Streams,
Woods, and curious Plants, joyn'd with the Harmonious
Notes of Nightingales, and other Birds, in whole Quires,
celebrating, and as it were, welcoming the forward Spring,
to speak the truth, so charmed my melancholick Fancy for
a time, that I had almost made a Resolution never to part
with so great a Happiness, for whatever the rest of the
World could present me with. But, in conclusion, it prov'd
too hard a Task for me, so soon to wean myself from the
World.

GEORGE WHELER
A Journey into Greece, 1682.

THE traveller who follows the shallow streams of Peneios beyond
Trikkala, with its Byzantine citadel, towards Kalambaka at the head of
the Thessalian plain, will observe, long before the ruined cottages and
hastily improvised dwellings of that oft-destroyed township come into
view, a singular group of fantastically shaped rocks rising abruptly
from the plain. As he draws nearer and the mountains close in on
either hand he will distinguish what appear to be human habitations
occupying seemingly inaccessible sites among these monstrous crags and
pinnacles. Above Kalambaka itself the limestone cliffs tower toward
heaven, "asperous, craggy, and barren"; a few monasteries and hermitages clinging as it seems miraculously to the very brink of the abyss,
in defiance alike of the violence of the elements and of the laws of
gravity. These are the Meteora monasteries, so extraordinary in their
situation that one is disposed to accept the local belief that God formed

these strange rocks for the peculiar benefit of the communities of stylites who, in the fulness of time, were to build their chapels and hermitages upon their barren summits. Assuredly, there are few places on earth so admirably fitted to serve as a refuge for those who are called to the solitary life and to the labour of the angels as this rocky wilderness above Kalambaka.

The early history of the monasteries is lost in obscurity. We cannot say at what period the first solitaries found their way to this remote corner of Thessaly. It seems clear, however, that certainly before the end of the thirteenth century, and perhaps considerably earlier, there were many hermits scattered about this wild region. *Staghi* (as Kalambaka, the ancient Aeginion, was known in the Middle Ages), seems to be a contraction of *eis tous aghious*—the name is still preserved in the official title of the Metropolitan of Trikka and Staghi. It may have been many years before the unorganised eremitical life crystallised into anything in the nature of regular communities. Many of the monasteries trace their origins to the troubled epoch during the latter part of the fourteenth century when the Emperor of the Serbs carried on an intermittent campaign against the successors of Constantine from his base at Trikkala, a few miles further down the valley of the Peneios, and the desert of the solitaries was invaded by armed bands and by men whose warfare was not with principalities and powers. The hermits took refuge among the high rocks. How they first succeeded in establishing themselves on some of the apparently unscalable heights which are now surmounted by the crumbling ruins of their cells is one of the unfathomed mysteries of monastic history—though there are explanations to be heard in the mountain villages of Pindos.

Between 1356 and 1372 there came to Staghi a monk trained in the great coenobia of Mount Athos, Athanasius by name, who founded on the summit of the Platys Lithos—the vast mass of rock which towers to a height of more than 1,800 feet to the north of Kastraki—the monastery dedicated in honour of the Transfiguration of our Lord and Saviour which has ever since been known as the Great Meteoron. As darkness descended upon the glories of New Rome, and the church of the Holy Wisdom—"the most fayr Chirche and the most noble of alle the world"—fell into the hands of the infidel, the desert blossomed and a flourishing group of monasteries sprang up among the barren rocks. The Great Meteoron prospered and served as a model for other foundations, thanks to the wisdom of its founder and to the benefactions of the wife of the Despot of Ioannina, whose brother, Ioasaph, had come to Staghi as a postulant in 1388. By the sixteenth century there would seem to have been as many as twenty-four communities scattered about the rocks.

The convent of St. Stephen, built on the site of a hermitage founded in 1312, lies on the farther side of a chasm spanned by a drawbridge. In order to gain access to most of the monasteries, however, it was necessary to be hoisted in a net lowered from the gate-house of the monastery (commonly situated some 150 feet above the farthest point to which the traveller could attain by his own unaided efforts), or to clamber up ladders somewhat imperfectly secured by long wooden pegs to the face of the precipice. Travellers' accounts abound in references to the perils of either means of ascent: to frayed ropes which were replaced only after a catastrophe had actually occurred, and to the horrors of ladders hung perpendicularly upon the face of the cliff, below which, as Curzon relates: "the precipice went sheer down to so tremendous a depth, that my head turned when I surveyed the distant valley over which I was hanging in the air like a fly on a wall." It was not until 1925 that, as the result of the construction of some rough tunnels and steps, it became possible to reach the four monasteries then inhabited without considerable hazard to life and limb. The alterations then effected are bitterly lamented by the present *Igoumenos* of the Great Meteoron, the Archimandrite Callinicos, as a misguided concession to episcopal infirmity on the part of his predecessor. It seemed very doubtful, however, whether the combined energies of the few remaining monks would suffice to operate their ancient windlass at all effectively. Curzon (who visited the Meteora in 1834) speaks of the ten or twelve monks at Aghia Trias who pulled him up to their monastery with a rope thirty-two fathoms long, and of the like number of reverend stevedores who assembled at the bars of the capstan at St. Barlaam, and whose efforts had the somewhat disconcerting effect of lifting him off the floor in his net and launching him "out of the door right into the sky, with an impetus which kept me swinging backwards and forwards at a fearful rate". To-day, the largest community can muster no more than half a dozen monks, of whom two are well advanced in years.

A great transformation has indeed come about since the days of prosperity vividly depicted in an old print which hangs in the sadly dilapidated guest-chamber of the Great Meteoron. More than twenty monasteries are there represented, each one inaccessible on its rock. Wayfarers seeking hospitality strive to attract the notice of monastic porters, remote and unheeding in their aerial gate-houses. Venerable bearded figures in flowing black robes dangle in nets above the abyss, or swing with grave and solemn motion upon rope-ladders; while their brethren labour unceasingly at windlasses and capstans high above the earth, and hoist provisions, firewood and travellers to their fastnesses among the rocks.

The Thebaid of Staghi to-day presents a very different picture: no more than four of the original twenty-four foundations are now inhabited. The history of the monasteries from the sixteenth century onwards is one long record of steadily declining numbers. There were interminable struggles for supremacy between the abbots of the Great Meteoron and the superiors of the hermitage of Panaghia Doupiani, who strove to retain their ancient title of 'Father of the ascetics of Staghi'. Discord rent the communities, there were disputes concerning the lands belonging to the monasteries, and before long the number of those inhabited was reduced to fourteen. The English travellers Holland and Hughes, who paid brief visits to the Meteora during the early part of the nineteenth century, found only ten remaining. During the further twenty years that elapsed before the advent of the Hon. Robert Curzon with his escort of brigands three more convents were abandoned.

As late as 1830 many of the caves which mark the perpendicular rock face were apparently inhabited: though whether by hermits or, as seems more probable, by refugees, is not entirely clear. Urquhart describes these cave-dwellings: some "like handsome houses, with regular landing-places, windows and projecting balconies", others, the smaller and meaner ones, "shut in with basket work, with a hole to enter by", and reached by curious ladders hanging like chains, some of which were drawn up when their lord and master was installed in his aerial dwelling; while those which were longer and gave access to the more elevated among the caves were pulled up fifteen or twenty feet from the ground and let down with "a strange clattering noise". All have been swept away and only the dark holes in the face of the cliff remain. By 1911 only thirty-eight monks were left, dispersed among four communities: the Great Meteoron, Aghios Barlaam, Aghios Stephanos and Aghia Trias. A monk from the Belgian monastery of Amay, who visited the Meteora in 1931, found the number of the monks still further reduced to twenty-one. A decade of war has added a catastrophic chapter to this melancholy tale of gradual decline, for it was not possible that the monks should remain aloof from the calamities which have befallen their native land during those terrible years. The day was long since flown when the monks could look down from the security of their rocky retreats upon scenes of slaughter and pillage as armies came and went on the plain below; and, turning away with the sign of the cross and a *Kyrie eleison*, go back to their labours. The unscalable heights were impregnable no longer.

I spent several days at the monasteries in January 1950, accompanied by a young theologian from the Russian Academy in Paris. Heavy falls of snow had blocked the Metsovo pass—the one road that leads north-westwards from Kalambaka across the heights of Pindos, connecting the plain of Thessaly with Ioannina and Epirus—and the cold was intense. We had slept the previous night at Trikkala, where the Metropolitan had shown us a number of charred manuscripts which had been salvaged from the monasteries. Our first concern upon reaching Kalambaka the following morning was to seek out the curate of the place, Father Christos Benda, whom we discovered wrapped in a blanket at his fireside. He was not a little startled at the sudden apparition of two Frankish visitors in the doorway of his cottage, and regarded somewhat gloomily our proposal to sleep at the monasteries for the duration of our stay, assuring us (not without reason, as we subsequently discovered), that the monks had little enough bedding to protect their own persons from the bitter winds which swept the exposed summits. He promised, nevertheless, to come with us to look for the *Igoumenos* of the Great Meteoron who was said to have descended from his airy retreat that morning in order to deal with some piece of monastic business. First, however, we were taken to see the fourteenth-century basilica with its remarkable marble *ambon*, and to visit the school, where we found classes of 150 children overflowing the one available building (which had perforce to serve as primary school in the forenoon and as high school for the rest of the day), and packed into two small chapels which had been furnished with desks. The children were delighted at the diversion caused by the appearance of the *xenoi*. Papa Christos carried us off in search of the abbot who was finally run to earth in a tavern where, monastic business satisfactorily des-patched, he was disposing of a dish of vegetables.

An hour or so later we were scrambling up the chasm which separates the Platys Lithos from the adjacent massif of Drakospelaia. Hundreds of feet above us the walls of the monastery of St. Barlaam stood out, a ragged fringe of ivory, against the sky. The *Igoumenos* reined in his pony and pointed out to us the site of the monastic prisons, high in the towering cliffs above Kastraki.

"Your names once again, that I may remember them?"

"Boris and Petros."

"Boris and Petros", repeated Father Callinicos, readjusting the bundles of leeks which festooned his saddle, "*na eisthe kala!*"

"The *Kyrios* Boris", he went on, as we relapsed into single file, "is from Paris, and yet, you say is Orthodox?"

"He is indeed Orthodox, O *Igoumenos*."

"But the Christians of Paris are of another dogma, are they not? Are they not Catholics?"

My exposition of the state of the Christians of Paris and of the condition of the erring patriarch of the west was cut short as the gatehouse of the Great Meteoron came into view in breath-taking perspective. We gained the narrow platform of rock at the head of the gully, immediately below the monastery, and Gregorios threw back his head and sent cries of *Agathangelle!* echoing and re-echoing among the high rocks.

Having reached the foot of the precipice, says Curzon, we stopped in the middle of this dark chasm and fired a gun . . . which was intended to answer the same purpose as knocking at the door in more civilised places; and we all strained our necks in looking up at the monastery to see whether any answer would be made to our call. Presently we were hailed by some one in the sky, whose voice came down to us like the cry of a bird; and we saw the face and grey beard of an old monk some hundred feet above us peering out of a kind of window or door. . . . Presently, after a careful reconnoitring from several long-bearded monks, a rope with a net at the end of it came slowly down to us, a distance of about twenty-five fathoms; and being bundled into the net, I was slowly drawn up into the monastery, where I was lugged in at the window by two of the strongest of the brethren, and after having been dragged along the floor and unpacked, I was presented to the admiring gaze of the whole reverend community, who were assembled round the capstan.

Autres temps, autres moeurs. "Unhappily", said Father Callinicos, as we waited at the foot of the precipice and Gregorios unsaddled the pony, "there have been regrettable changes; formerly there was great security." The windlass, it appeared, was now used only for hauling up firewood and victuals. We took a last look at the leeks, now 100 feet above our heads, and entered the dark passage which gives access to the steps leading to the monastery. Agathangellos was awaiting us outside the now disused refectory: a youngish monk, clad in a tattered grey cassock and soft cap, who had come to the Meteora, we subsequently discovered, in 1939. He carried us off to the guest-chamber (little used in these days) and left us among the faded memorials of former splendour while he went in search of refreshment. A few minutes later the insistent clamour of the *semandron* summoned us to vespers in the fine *catholicon*, dating from the middle of the sixteenth century, where Athanasius the Athonite, clad in the habit of a western monk, looks down from the apse—a fragment of an earlier church on the same site, built by Ioasaph in 1388. A frugal supper of vegetables, goats' milk cheese and bread followed, and afterwards we sat on wooden stools round a fire of brushwood and talked to the *Igoumenos* and the other members of his little family, while Agathangellos busied himself in the kitchens, where cats as lean as the stylite saints depicted in the frescoes of the narthex lurked in the shadows. Father Callinicos, we discovered, had been at the Great Meteoron for nearly forty years. There was one other priest in the community: a Father Theophylaktos who had lived in the Athonite house of Xeropotamou for several years as a simple monk before he was ordained and came to Thessaly in 1935. Another monk—also named Callinicos—had been carried off by the Italians and had died in exile. Apart from Father Agathangellos, the only remaining member of the community was a very ancient personage named Paul who appeared to lead the life of a solitary, and whom we but dimly discerned amidst the shadows of the church. Gregorios, who had accompanied us from Kalambaka, was no monk but a married man with a wife and several children, lately returned to their village in the mountains to the west of Trikkala. We encountered him again some ten days later, breasting a snow-covered ridge among the foothills of Pindos with a couple of heavily-laden pack-animals, and accompanied by a little troop of refugees on their way home after three years in Kalambaka.

Shortly after eight o'clock Father Agathangellos reappeared with a huge iron lantern, to lead the way along rickety galleries and past rows of long-abandoned cells to the church. We shivered in our stalls while compline was shrilly chanted, without book and by the light of a single guttering candle, in the narthex. "They are so expert and ready therein", says Rycaut, "that they can run from the beginning to the ending without stop or hesitation, and gallop it over at that rate, that one must have a good ear and some skill in the Greek language, to distinguish the different sound of the words which they utter." As the monastic day ended, the monks emerged from the shadows of the narthex, and, one by one, filed past the *Igoumenos* to ask his forgiveness and blessing, and he theirs:

"Your blessing, holy father, and forgive me, a sinner."

"May God forgive you, holy father."

At the Great Meteoron, despite the gloomy prophecies of those who had tried to dissuade us from staying at the monasteries, there were plenty of blankets, and we slept soundly till, long before the dawn, the *semandron* recalled us to church for mattins and lauds. We groped our way towards the door of the narthex, slipping and stumbling on the ice-bound rocks and mindful of Father Agathangellos' parting exhortation to "avoid the edge of the abyss". The whole world seemed wrapt in an unfathomable silence—infinitely remote there floated up out of the vast emptiness at our feet the faint clink of a chain, where a mule moved restlessly in the camp at Kalambaka. We crept into the church with the unearthly chant rising and falling in our ears. Agathangellos, a candle held between his fingers, swayed back and forth at his lectern, a solitary pool of yellow light in the universal blackness; an occasional movement from the remoter recesses of the darkened church betrayed the presence of other members of the community. With the first pale light of dawn mattins gave place to lauds, and as a shaft of dusty sunlight pierced the darkness, picking out the gold and crimson of antique frescoes and bringing new life to limbs rigid with the cold, Father Callinicos, from within the sanctuary, took up the ancient hymn: "Glory to Thee who hast shown us the light . . ."

When the office was ended and we had drunk a cup of coffee and a thimbleful of *ouzo*, we spent a little time exploring the monastery, now stripped of all its movable treasures. Then, after taking leave of our kind hosts, we made our way to Aghios Barlaam where we were welcomed by the Archimandrite Ambrose and a young deacon named Bessarion. The *Igoumenos* was below in Kalambaka but would be back later in the day. There was, alas! no bedding at the monastery, said Father Ambrose: everything had been carried off by the Communists, to equip a field-hospital which they had established in the mountains to the northward; "What is to be done? But we will find something for you when you return this evening."

We spent the rest of the day scrambling about the rocks and visiting long-abandoned monasteries and hermitages. At St. Nicolas—fast falling into ruin, and where one must tread with circumspection—we found a few paintings remaining in the two chapels and the refectory, as well as an iron chest containing liturgical books and an eikon of the Forerunner; elsewhere, nothing save slowly crumbling masonry and the all-enveloping silence. We paid a fleeting visit to Kalambaka and returned to St. Barlaam a little before sunset laden with cognac and cigarettes. Like the Great Meteoron, this monastery, which crowns the towering cliffs of Drakospelaia, was until quite recent times inaccessible save by net and windlass. It is a sixteenth-century foundation, having been built about 1517 by two brothers from Ioannina—Nektarios and Theophanes—on the site of the fourteenth-century hermitage founded by the solitary from whom the monastery takes its name. In 1950 it was inhabited by six monks. The *Igoumenos*, Father Christopher, told us he had been at the monastery for twenty-one years, and for another twenty years at a convent to the westward of Trikkala. He was seventy-seven—twelve years older than Father Ambrose, an Athenian who was ordained many years ago at Moni Petraki in the shadow of Lykavettos. This was the only one of the monasteries where we came across any novices. Father Bessarion (who came from a village near Larissa and who had seen service with the British army in the Middle East), had been received only five months earlier, as had another young deacon, a native of Chios. There were in addition two simple monks, one of them more than ninety years old.

That night it snowed heavily. Father Bessarion produced a threadbare carpet which, folded double, afforded us a little protection against the bitter cold; and he and a shepherd from Kalambaka, who was living at the monastery, kindled a huge fire which blazed on the open hearth of our cell until morning, while the wind howled along the deserted galleries, the ancient timbers groaned and shivered, and it seemed that an exceptionally heavy squall would send the whole monastery with its domed chapels and its frail scaffolding of cells and domestic buildings spinning off into the abyss. When daylight came we seemed to be suspended in the void, without visible contact with the world which we had revisited the previous afternoon. We returned to the *Igoumenos'* cell and sat and talked around a brazier filled with glowing charcoal, while we waited for the weather to moderate. Father Christopher told us of his own experiences during the troubled years of war; how he had been thrown into prison at Trikkala by the Italians and had escaped by jumping from a window; how several years later he had been carried off by the Communists in company with some 300 men, women and children from Kalambaka, and had been in the mountains for six days before his release; he told us too of the great monastery where he had taken the monastic habit, and of its 366 cells. Father Ambrose joined our little circle and catechised us as to our age, our families, were our parents living, were we married or *agamos*: "Certainly marriage is of God; a soldier from England and a *koritsi* from Piraeus, and God joins them. Truly, this is a great mystery, as says the apostle."

So the morning passed and at midday Father Bessarion reappeared with bean soup and bread for our lunch. By one o'clock the snow had somewhat abated, and since the visibility had increased sufficiently to enable us to see the monastery of Rosani, 500 yards distant, we decided to set out for St. Stephen where we were expected that evening. The *Igoumenos* and Father Ambrose advised us to take the easier, though less direct, path by way of Kalambaka; but being reluctant to add two miles or more to our journey in such weather we insisted on following the path which keeps to the high ground. Father Bessarion accompanied us a little way, and then, since the weather seemed to be improving, he left us after giving us precise directions as to our route.

All went well for a time, despite the fact that the path was entirely obscured beneath the drifting snow, and Rosani (formerly the dwelling of an aged female solitary) gradually faded from our view. Shortly afterwards, however, the mist thickened until visibility was but a few yards, and it was not long before we were in difficulties. For a time we crept along the edge of the abyss, edging our way cautiously across expanses of bare rock scoured by the wind, a thin coating of ice affording none save the most precarious foothold, until it seemed that we must be within a stone's throw of Aghia Trias. Alas! there were no monks left to answer our shouts; no slight thinning of the mist afforded us a momentary glimpse of the encompassing heights such as would have sufficed to give us our bearings. For three hours we wandered in an unfamiliar world until, an hour before dark, the mist lifted somewhat, and we found ourselves clear of the rocky wilderness, among low hills covered with dwarf oaks, and detected the distant barking of a dog. We struck down the bed of a torrent in the direction of the sound and came, after some forty minutes, upon a fold of muddy sheep guarded by two shepherd-lads, who, startled though they were at our sudden appearance, directed us to the nearby hamlet of Kopraina. In the gathering darkness, and as men with long-barrelled guns converged upon us from all sides, we entered the village, and bursting in upon an astonished assembly in the tavern called for the president. Ten minutes later, elated by several draughts of raw spirits, we were reclining on the presidential hearth, while the maidens of the household unlaced our boots, and our sodden outer garments steamed before a huge fire. The parish priest arrived in breathless haste to welcome the strangers, and the whole village buzzed with the news of our unlooked-for advent.

That night we enjoyed the hospitality of the village president, who had fought with Zervas in the mountains of Epirus, and who slept like a good soldier with a greatcoat for pillow and a loaded rifle beside him on the hearth. Earlier that evening he had told us of the English officer who had once come to the village, during the long years of the occupation, and who had snatched a few hours sleep in that same room where we supped, before slipping away to the mountains at daybreak. Our own visit to Kopraina was more prolonged: we were taken to see the church, the chapel in the cemetery on the hillside above the village, and the school, where a geography lesson was in progress.

The parish priest excused himself and retired to supervise the preparations which, we gathered, were even then in hand for a festal lunch. At high noon the *kapetanios* reappeared and led the way to the half-finished parsonage, where we found the parish priest drawing water from the well, his flocks and herds all about him, while his two sturdy daughters laboured excitedly in the kitchen and clattered to and fro in their wooden shoes. "*Kalos orisete*, welcome!" exclaimed Father Apostolos, setting down his bucket in great haste and rubbing his hands on the skirt of his cassock; "Come, all is ready, let us eat! Some wine, O *Papadia!*" He led the way indoors and we took our places at the festal board—a section sawn from the trunk of a great oak. It was a merry gathering, and as we feasted in this country parsonage and the children listened wide-eyed to our tales of the strange and marvellous ways of the Franks, that other world from which we had so lately descended took on a curious, dream-like quality. It was hard to realise that before nightfall we should be back on the windswept heights above Kalambaka and amongst the ascetics of the Thebaid of Staghi.

A little before three o'clock Father Apostolos and the village president bade us *kalo taxeidi*, after accompanying us as far as the outskirts of the village, and we set out for Aghios Stephanos with a guide. The sun had vanished beneath the jagged rim of Pindos when we at last worked our way gingerly across the icy rocks above the deserted monastery of the Holy Trinity and came suddenly upon Aghios Stephanos, four-square upon its rock like the heavenly Jerusalem, and found the whole of Thessaly lying at our feet.

Vespers was drawing to a close in the church of St. Charalambos, which stands so close to the brink of the precipice that one could, it seemed, empty the contents of a thurible into Father Christos' chicken-run below in Kalambaka. We spent two nights at this monastery before setting out for the mountain villages of Pindos, and I returned alone for a final visit some ten days later.

Of all the monasteries now inhabited St. Stephen had, it seemed evident, sustained far the greatest calamities as the result of war. Sacked first by the Italians and later by the Communists, it was a mere shell of a building, its unglazed windows affording little protection— as we learned by bitter experience—against wind or snow. Its former guest-rooms were crammed with wrecked furniture and empty ammunition boxes, while the eikons in the smaller of the two churches (the chapel dedicated to St. Stephen) had been wantonly defaced. Almost everything of value had been carried off when the monastery was pillaged: vestments and plate, an ancient gold cross from Mount Athos, five horses and mules, 130 sheep, provisions and fodder, beds and bedding, pots and pans, crockery and cutlery, carpets, even the bee hives, and—needless to add—the excellent wine for which the monastery was renowned in former days. The few surviving monks lacked the barest necessities of life and it was hardly surprising that sickness should have taken a heavy toll of this and the other communities during the winter months. The *Igoumenos* of St. Stephen's was the Deacon Anthimos, who came to the Meteora between the wars from the great Athonite house of Vatopedi—"a good house and garden . . . snakes very big and long in it", notes Dr. Covel. There were also living at St. Stephen three simple monks—lay-brothers, as they would be called in the west—Ephrem, who had been a monk for twenty years, Eusebius, who was formerly a policeman, and Cyril. Whilst we were staying at the monastery there arrived from Trikkala a certain Papa Iannis, an octogenarian with three married daughters. He had obtained his bishop's permission to come and share the life of the monks (there being no other priest in the community). Finally, there was Basil, a layman of sixty-five, who, after spending his boyhood in America, had returned to his native Thessaly to serve more than one monastery as a resourceful factotum; and there were the inevitable stylite cats. The *Igoumenos* was plainly a sick man—it was little wonder, considering what he had been through during the last few years and the rigours of the life at St. Stephen's—and the morning we left the monastery there was not a monk capable of getting to his place in church for *mesonyktikon* and *orthros*.

Life at the Meteora to-day is hard indeed, and under such conditions as prevail it is hardly astonishing that the liturgical life of the monasteries should exhibit but little of the dignity and splendour which one rightly looks for in a large and well-ordered community. We were none the less deeply impressed by the efforts which are made to maintain the regular course of the *opus Dei*. Night after night, while Kalambaka sleeps, the few remaining ascetics of the Thebaid of Staghi gather in the dimly-lighted chapels among the high rocks to perform what for the monk must always be his primary liturgy; morning by morning as the sun touches the heights of Pindos with new fire and the flickering candles grow pale in the first light of dawn, the great trinitarian doxology banishes the shades of night and unites heaven and earth, angels and archangels, sinful men and those whose warfare is accomplished, in a single bond of adoration:

> Glory to God in the highest,
> And on earth peace, goodwill towards men.
>> We praise Thee,
>> We bless Thee,
>> We worship Thee,
>> We glorify Thee,
> We give thanks to Thee for Thy great glory.
>> O Lord King,
>> O God of Heaven,
>> Father Almighty;
> O Lord, Only-begotten Son, Jesus Christ,
> And O Holy Spirit.

VIII

NEW WINE AND OLD BOTTLES

There is no village or city . . . which is not surrounded by
monasteries as if by walls, and the inhabitants are supported by their prayers as if resting upon God.

Historia Monachorum

THE importance of the monastic life for the whole of the Orthodox
world can scarcely be exaggerated. From the days when rumour of the
heroic exploits of the hermits of the Egyptian deserts first moved men
to forsake home and family and friends, and to go forth to do battle
with the demons in those very regions which were held to be peculiarly
their own, the ascetic life has never ceased to exercise its compelling
attraction. The Orthodox Christian has always had the greatest veneration for the monastic ideal: it is only in quite recent times that the
traditional view of the function of the monk and of his importance for
the life and health of the whole body of the Church has been widely
challenged. The great historic centres of Orthodox monasticism—the
deserts of Egypt and the Judaean wilderness, the holy mountains of
Sinai and Athos, the monastery of Studium, at the very heart of
oikoumene, and the great *lavras* of Kiev and Moscow beyond its farthest
confines—all these have exercised an incalculable influence upon the
life of eastern Christendom.

Orthodox monasticism, though it has many different forms, does
not consist of a multiplicity of distinct orders and congregations, each
with its peculiar characteristics and sphere of activity. The western
Christian who feels the call to the religious life may decide to test his
vocation as a Carthusian, as a Benedictine, or as a member of an 'active'
order such as the Jesuits or the Franciscans. The Greek simply becomes
a monk. There are no 'orders' in eastern Christendom: no Order of St.
Basil, as so many writers have mistakenly supposed. Thus Père Robert
de Dreux remarks that all the Greek metropolitans and patriarchs "are
chosen from among the religious of St. Basil, of whom there are a great
number in that country", and speaks of Mount Athos as "inhabited

by a great number of the monks of St. Basil, who dwell there in great austerity". So too (to quote a more recent instance of the same error) Bardenhewer asserts that "the Basilians are the one great Order of the East", while the reverend author of *Eighteen Centuries of the Orthodox Greek Church* speaks of "the ancient unity of the Order of St. Basil, which has subsisted since his time with its original simplicity".

Such expressions as these rest upon a fundamental misunderstanding of the nature of eastern monachism. Antony, the hermit of the Egyptian desert—not Basil—is the patriarch of eastern monks. Western writers have all too frequently been led astray by the supposition that the rules of St. Basil have exercised, within the context of eastern monachism, an influence comparable to that of the *Regula Sancti Benedicti* in the west.

In actual fact this supposed analogy is without foundation. The writings of the great Cappadocian have, it is true, exercised a considerable influence upon the development of coenobitic monachism in the east: though for the working out of much that was latent in the original rules we have to look to the work of Theodore of Studium (759-826). There is, however, no one document which has moulded the growth of eastern monachism as the Rule of St. Benedict has shaped the religious life of the west. The essential character of eastern monachism does not depend upon the writings attributed to St. Basil, nor indeed upon any written rule, but upon a traditional observance which was slowly hammered out in the great centres of eastern spirituality and which was spread abroad throughout the Orthodox world from Sinai to Siberia.

The Basilian monk is a Frankish invention. The Orthodox Church knows no *Order of St. Basil*—only the order of monks: the whole company of those who have sought to follow the Lord Christ in poverty and nakedness and in the spirit of the evangelical counsels; those who wage war incessantly on the ramparts of the city to guard the Christian polity against the assaults of the enemy without.

In a certain sense one may say that all Orthodox monks and nuns are contemplatives: though it has to be recognised that western categories such as 'contemplative', 'active', 'mixed', etc., are not really applicable to eastern monachism, which knows of only one *activity* proper to the monk—the unremitting struggle of prayer and the ascetic life. The Orthodox Christian who takes the monastic habit does so that he may renounce the life of this present world and abandon himself to the

labour of the angels. A great part of the day and night he will henceforth devote to the *opus Dei*: the chanting of the divine office. For the
rest, he will practise the prayer of Jesus and will be nourished upon the
Gospels and the Psalter, the *Philokalia* (a collection of the writings of
many of the great ascetics and fathers of the Church), and certain
classic works of monastic spirituality—notably the *Ladder of Perfection*
of St. John the Scholastic, Abbot of Sinai, which is read in every
Orthodox monastery during the great lent.

Within this traditional framework there exist considerable variations
suited to differences of personal vocation. Though the *coenobium*, or
monastery of the common life (that form of eastern monachism which
owes the greatest debt to the legislation of St. Basil and St. Theodore
of Studium), has commanded the greatest influence, the coenobitic
life is only one among several traditional patterns of asceticism which
lie open to the Orthodox monk. Side by side with the regular discipline
of the community there exist other forms of the monastic life which
trace their origin not to Cappadocia but to the primitive hermits of the
desert; and despite St. Basil's admiration for the coenobitic life it can
scarcely be questioned that, amongst the generality of Orthodox
Christians, it has commonly been the solitary who has been accorded
the greatest veneration and respect.

To this day, a large coenobium (such as one finds on Mount Athos,
for example) will as a rule possess several small, dependent *sketai*, where
two or three monks pursue a manner of life that has seen but little
change during the course of 1,500 years, and may have in addition one
or two anchorites nesting in inaccessible caves amongst the rocks
and following an observance of incredible austerity; these are the
μεγαλόσχημοι—monks of the great or angelic habit—of whom Covel
observes that they "never eat at most above three times in a week;
whence they are emaciated to meer Skin and Bones before they quite
leave this world; this extravagant Fasting being counted the very heighth
of an Aschetick Life."

Such extremes of asceticism, needless to say, are not for all men.
Towards the end of the fourteenth century there made its appearance
on the holy mountain a somewhat relaxed form of the monastic life
known as the idiorrhythmic. The idiorrhythmic monk is literally one who
follows his own rhythm. He owns personal property and takes his
meals (prepared, if he be well-to-do, in his own kitchen by a monkish
servant), not in the refectory but in the privacy of his own rooms. The

government of the idiorrhythmic convent is normally vested in an assembly of senior monks presided over by two *epitropoi*. Such a system as this, although in certain of its features it recalls the loosely organised settlements of hermits of pre-coenobitic monachism, has in practice prospered chiefly in times of decadence. The true contemporary parallel to the settlements of the desert is not the idiorrhythmic monastery but the *skete*, or group of ascetic cottages, where the living traditions of Orthodox spirituality are preserved in all their integrity.

The great age of the idiorrhythmic monastery extended from the end of the fourteenth century to the middle of the sixteenth and was followed by a widespread reversion to the coenobitic pattern. Nine of the twenty ruling monasteries of Athos are now idiorrhythmic. There are, moreover, many Athonite monks who, though wearing the monastic habit, live after a fashion differing but little from that of the ordinary Greek peasant or fisherman. Many of them own their *kellia*, or 'cells'. A Greek prelate who wishes to retire to the holy mountain may purchase the lease of a cottage (commonly known as a *kathisma*, or 'seat') where he will pass the last years of his life with a monk or two to minister to his needs.

Between these two extremes lies the coenobium, the life and organisation of which differ but little in substance from the pattern laid down by St. Benedict. It should, however, be remarked that the Orthodox convent has never become a community of clerks: the overwhelming majority of Orthodox monks are to this day what we should call lay brothers; it is not even essential that the abbot should be in orders—though if he is not a *hieromonachos* he cannot claim the title of archimandrite but only of *hegoumenos*.

There can be little question that the ordinary regimen of the Orthodox coenobium, to say nothing of that which obtains in the *sketai*, is of a rigour which the average Frankish monk would find insupportable. A visitor from the Belgian priory of Chevetogne remarked, after a short stay at the celebrated convent of Mar Sabbas, that the diet was such that that of La Trappe would seem quite relaxed by comparison. Much, however, that western Christendom would now consider intolerably rigorous, the Greek peasant-monk takes for granted. "The contempt of food and drink and of a soft bed", as Chrysostom observes, "is a matter of no effort to many persons, especially if they have led a rustic life, and been brought up to these hardships from their infancy."

As of Orthodox Christendom in general, so of the Church of Greece in particular, it may be said that the monastic life has been of quite unique importance in shaping her life and piety. This is no less true of the long centuries of the captivity than of the earlier and more formative ages of her history. Even to-day, when the monasteries are subject to widespread criticism, the ancient traditions of monastic spirituality persist and sometimes reveal themselves most unmistakably in precisely those circles where hostility toward the existing institutions—especially in their more idiorrhythmic forms—is most evident and outspoken. It needs to be remembered that the first stirrings of the new missionary spirit, which has had so notable an effect upon the Greek Church within the space of the last 100 years, centre upon the great monastery of Megaspelaion in the Peloponnese, and that Eusebius Matthopoulos, the founder of the Brotherhood of Life, was himself a monk of this convent, steeped in the ascetic traditions of his Church.

"There is no place where the *Greek* Religion is professed", says Rycaut, "so famous for Monasteries as that of Mount *Athos*; and indeed if we consider the number of them, and of the Religious belonging thereunto, it is not to be parallel'd in all the world . . . the grand Conservatory of the Christian Religion in *Greece*, and ancient austerity of living, and therefore not unaptly stiled by them Ἅγιον ὄρος, or the *Holy Mountain* . . . the high Pique or Peer whereof . . . is uneven, craggy, and as horrid as Caucasus."

Athos remains, after more than 1,000 years, the heart of Greek monasticism. Isolated and aloof, the life of the holy mountain moves to a slow rhythm which is as little susceptible of change or alteration as the constant surge of the waters about the rocky promontory, in whose narrow clefts and ledges the anchorites roost like wild sea fowl. In Greece one can never wholly escape from the all-pervading influence of Athos. One is always dimly aware of the holy mountain, brooding over the dark waters of the Aegean, its head wrapped in the clouds. At the very heart of fashionable Athens one may encounter a student-deacon from the *sketai* of St. Anne, or a stately *epitropos* in silken gown bound for the offices of the Holy Synod.

Thanks to its isolation, Athos suffered comparatively little from the ravages of war—though many monks endured imprisonment and ill-treatment, and considerable damage was done to monastic properties scattered about the mainland of northern Greece. The Communist revolution in Russia and the subsequent division of Europe into two

83

hostile camps have, however, already gone far towards transforming the holy mountain into a purely Hellenic preserve, and threaten wholly to deprive it of the pan-Orthodox character which it yet retains, despite the fact that for many years now every monk has been required to adopt Greek nationality. Three of the twenty ruling monasteries—St. Panteleimon, Zographou and Chilandari—are non-Hellenic convents, being Russian, Bulgarian and Serbian respectively. In former days these monasteries were amongst the wealthiest on the mountain; St. Panteleimon, in particular, with its numerous dependencies—some of the latter far larger than any other ruling monastery—could boast of more monks than were to be found in all the other convents together. All these alien monasteries, however, were dependent mainly upon the produce of lands which now lie behind the iron curtain, and to-day, cut off as they are from their sources both of supply and of recruitment, they are in a most melancholy condition.

Of all the thousands of Russian monks who once inhabited the holy mountain scarcely 300 remain. The majority of these are aged and infirm: many of them physically incapable of cultivating the vegetables, olives and vineyards which now form the monastery's only means of support. It is now more than thirty-five years since the monks have been cut off from their own land. A certain amount of assistance continued to reach Athos from the Russian community in Jerusalem, but this also has ceased since the property became subject to the jurisdiction of the Moscow patriarchate. With the passing of the years the position of the alien monasteries becomes more and more desperate, as the list of invalids grows longer, and fewer and fewer hands are available for the support of those who can no longer work; and greatly as one may regret the fact, the day seems not far distant when Athos will become a purely Hellenic community.

Mount Athos apart, the organised religious life has come very near to complete suppression in northern and central Greece during the last few years. I have already said something of the sufferings of the ascetics of the Thebaid of Staghi. The fortunes of two or three other important monasteries are not without a certain melancholy interest.

Take, for example, the ancient convent of Eikosiphoinisses, which traces its foundation to the second decade of the sixth century: a vast walled enclosure on the wooded slopes of Mount Pangaion, accessible only by mule-tracks winding high above the marshes of Philippi. It is said that there were some fifty monks inhabiting the convent at the beginning of this century. Eikosiphoinisses suffered grievously at the hands of the Bulgars in 1913 and again five years later. All its flocks and herds were driven off and the monastery was looted of most of its treasures—precious manuscripts, vestments, holy vessels and reliquaries. There could, therefore, be little room for doubt as to the fate in store for it when the Bulgars again swarmed into Greece in the wake of the German forces in the summer of 1941.

The history of the convent from this time down till its destruction three years later is obscure. The pillage of its remaining property seems to have commenced about two months after the Bulgars had descended upon Drama and expelled the Greek clergy; a certain Botseph, Bulgarian *protosyngellos* of the metropolis, celebrated the festival of the Dormition of the Mother of God by stealing from the monastery a mitre, an ancient chalice, six silver crosses such as are used for the blessing of the waters at Epiphany, sundry liturgical vestments and ten manuscripts on parchment from the library. Some six weeks later several Bulgarian officers were moved to emulate the pious labours of this worthy ecclesiastic. They returned from their expedition to the heights of Pangaion driving before them a train of asses laden with clothing, furniture and other tangible fruits of their pilgrimage.

Another Bulgar, Sophronios Natseph, the *epitropos*, makes a fleeting and discreditable appearance upon the stage of Greek history on June 20th, 1943, on which day he despoiled Eikosiphoinisses of seventeen carpets, ninety-eight goats and as much bedding as he and his accomplices were able to bear away with them down the rocky paths.

The final chapter in this catalogue of infamy was written a little more than a year after this episode when, on July 13th, 1944—a few months before they fled from the scene of their barbarous crimes—the Bulgars set fire to the monastery and destroyed it utterly. Only the *catholicon* (which stood somewhat apart in the centre of the great courtyard) and a single block of cells survived the conflagration; the rest of the convent, including a three-storied edifice said to contain 300 cells, the bakery and the refectory (dating from the eleventh century), and all the stables and outbuildings were gutted. Before setting fire to the monastery the Bulgars looted it of everything of value and drove off all the live-stock. The library, which contained some 1,500 volumes, was reduced to ashes.

All the monks of this monastery endured great hardship and privation. One was executed by the Bulgars; another died as the result of the treatment which he suffered at their hands. The former was the *monachos*

Daniel—a native of Thasos, who had taken refuge in the village of Palaiochori, on the lower slopes of Pangaion, when the district was invaded by the Bulgars. He was tortured before being put to death. The other monk who perished was the *hieromonachos* Sophronios, carried off as a hostage to Bulgaria. The *igoumenos* of the monastery, Gregorios Katsivakes, fled with several other monks to the village of Nikesiani, a few miles to the northward. There he fell into the hands of the Bulgars and was carried off into exile in northern Bulgaria. After six terrible months he was allowed to return, broken in health, to Nikesiani where he remained supported by the alms of the people.

When the occupation was over, Mount Pangaion—together with the heights of Chalkidiki (with which it enjoys easy communications)— became a stronghold of the *katsapliades*. The coastal road between Cavalla and Salonica was closed to traffic after it had been mined repeatedly, and all vehicles had to make a long detour to the north of Pangaion by way of Drama and Serres. The ruins of Eikosiphoinisses remained uninhabited. Only recently have a handful of monks gone back to the monastery which lies desolate like the city of the Philippians amidst the marshes far below.

A few miles to the north-west of Eikosiphoinisses and close to the town of Serres stands another historic convent, that of St. John the Forerunner. This, too, has fallen a prey on more than one occasion to the rapacity of the Bulgars. In 1918 the conventual library was looted and its chief treasures carried off to the Bulgarian monastery of Rila. Thence, in due course, they were returned to the Greek government, and (with a view to their greater security), distributed amongst the libraries of Athens. The cataloguing of the library of this Macedonian convent had, incidentally, been carried out some years before this calamity by one who was subsequently to become a well-known figure throughout western Christendom: the late Metropolitan of Thyateira, Germanos.

In 1941 the monastery was sacked by the Bulgars. The monks joined the innumerable host of refugees. Several are said to have died of starvation in the streets of occupied Serres. Others escaped to Nigrita, Salonica and Athens. Seven of them came back in 1945 and were joined by two novices. It was not long, however, before the monastery was again attacked and pillaged—this time by the Communists. Every scrap of food and clothing was carried off to sustain the democratic warriors of the mountains. In view of the constant threat of further raids, the Metropolitan of Serres arranged for rations to be sent daily to the monastery, and this state of affairs endured down till the summer of 1949, when it was considered safe to lay in stores once again. In the spring of 1950 only three monks were living in the convent: one of them a priest who could celebrate the divine mysteries. The other monks had been sent by the Metropolitan to serve in parishes of the diocese, where (owing to the very high proportion of casualties amongst the village clergy), the shortage of clergy was peculiarly grave.

All over northern Greece the same tragic history has been re-enacted time and time again. The monastery of Aghios Nikanor, Zavordas, lies at the heart of a barren and desolate region to the southward of Kozani, and within the jurisdiction of the Metropolitan of Grevena. Like so many Greek monasteries its situation is remarkable: the summit of a high rock set amidst the swirling waters of the Aliakmon. The remoteness of its site, far from the lines of communication, brought this convent through the years of occupation unscathed; isolation, however, afforded little protection against the Communists. The monastery was attacked and looted; everything of the slightest value was borne off to the mountains together with the convent's pack-animals and its 300 sheep and goats. The abbot, Father Gabriel Balayiannes, and an older monk named Gerasimos Stathopoulos were murdered, and the survivors fled to the village of Palaiochori (some four hours' journey from the monastery) where they were still living when I visited this region in the spring of 1950.

Southwards, over the pass which skirts snow-capped Olympus and connects western Macedonia with the broad plains of Thessaly, stands the ancient monastery of Panaghia Olympiotissa at Elassona. This, too, was pillaged, the monks driven out, the abbot severely beaten, imprisoned and sent into exile. In almost every diocese of Macedonia, Thrace and Epirus the few surviving monasteries and their inhabitants have suffered a like fate.

The Abbé de St. Michon observes that in his day the Greek monk was a patriot who fought for the independence of his country, and who was loved for virtues which belong more to the soldier than to the man of prayer. The cannon of Megaspelaion were indeed used to some purpose against the Turk during the war of independence, and Urquhart gives a vivid description of his arrival at the monastery of Lezini, in the guise of a "goul or spirit of the marsh", with twenty muskets and a nine-pounder full of grape trained upon him. Alas! the monkish batteries have been allowed to rust these many years, and armed resistance, however effective it may have been a century ago against a lightly armed assailant, could have availed the monks but little in the face of an enemy equipped with modern artillery. The monasteries lay at the mercy of the *barbaroi*: an easy prey, holding out a tempting prospect of plunder.

Elsewhere in Greece the destruction and pillage of religious houses has been less universal than in the isolated dioceses of the north. The ascetic life still flourishes in many communities scattered amongst the islands and in the Peloponnese; one may still find convents where the unrelenting battle with the powers of darkness is waged with something of its ancient ardour and where the monk is still manifestly the guardian of the walls; but such houses, it must be confessed, are now few and far between.

It must not, however, be supposed that the present decline of Greek monasticism is wholly attributable to the effects of a decade of war. Long before the storm burst upon them in 1940 the Greek monasteries had, with few exceptions, been reduced to a sorry plight. At the beginning of the nineteenth century many convents were very wealthy. Since then the foundations of their economy have been undermined by the loss of their properties situated in Rumania, the Caucasus and elsewhere, and as the result of a series of confiscations by the Hellenic government dating from 1833 onwards. Although a portion of the wealth made available by these confiscations has gone to swell the General Ecclesiastical Fund, and so to benefit the work of the Church, this anti-monastic legislation continues to arouse acrimonious controversy not only among the monks but (for rather different reasons) among churchmen in general.

There are, nevertheless, few laymen who would oppose the diversion of monastic property to the furtherance of social and educational projects and the improvement of the condition of the parochial ministry. The contemplative life has few champions outside the *sketai* of the holy mountain. There are many who value the monasteries for their former contribution to the life of the nation, for their traditions of hospitality, and for their archaeological interest, but few indeed who now regard them as centres of spiritual power. The traditional monasticism has come to be looked upon—at any rate in the towns—as an out-of-date phenomenon, quite irrelevant to the needs of the present time.

This is true not least of many of the leaders of the new movements, many of whom are outspoken critics of the monks. Everywhere the demand is for *activity* (in the western sense of that word): for training preachers, confessors and catechists, and for raising the standards of clerical education. The monks are looked upon as idle drones who make no contribution to the life of the whole body. Inevitably, such views (which are widespread to-day) have had a marked effect upon monastic recruitment, and postulants are but few. All over Greece the monasteries lie abandoned and falling into ruin; rambling buildings in remote mountain sites visited only by shepherds, or inhabited by a solitary *kalogeros*, more farmer than monk, tending his vineyards and his olive groves and watching over his flocks and herds.

It would, nevertheless, be rash to assert that the new movements which have sprung up and taken root within the last two generations are anti-monastic in character, however hostile they may seem to be towards the traditional forms of the monastic life. It is tempting to compare a society such as the Brotherhood of Theologians, Zoë, for example, to the friars who made their appearance in western Europe more than seven centuries ago and who were frequently no more sympathetic towards the old monasticism than is the Greek theologian of the present time. I shall have occasion to describe this brotherhood in some detail in a later chapter; here I would but remind my reader of the fact that its founder was himself a monk of Megaspelaion, grounded in the traditional observance of that monastery, and that its members (though they do not bind themselves by permanent vows) are celibate priests or laymen, living under a common rule. Despite its novel constitution and organisation the movement retains much of the spirit of the old asceticism, and, in some respects at least, has more of the nature of a reassertion of the fundamental demands of the ascetic life in a form appropriate to the needs of the present time than a denial of their abiding value.

Soon after my arrival in Salonica in 1948, I was warned of the errors of the Zoë brothers and their sympathisers by a *very* idiorrhythmic monk, who assured me that these unhappy innovators were seeking to persuade men that the path that led to salvation was strait and the gateway narrow: such language seemed to have a familiar ring!

If we confine our view to the relics of the old monasticism it must be confessed that the prospect for the future is melancholy in the extreme. Everywhere the old order is passing away; amidst the crumbling walls a few survivors linger on as aliens in an unfamiliar world. But what of the new wine that is to be found in abundance within the religious societies? Is a new monasticism seeking forms appropriate to a changed environment? It is too early as yet to speak with any confidence, and yet there are signs that out of the present ferment may come something not so very far removed from the traditional patterns of the ascetic life.

Assuredly the passion for activity will have an end. It is but one aspect of that fascination which the feverish culture of the west holds for the modern Greek. Even now there are close personal links between the Zoë Brotherhood and certain convents in Old Greece and the islands where the ancient warfare is still waged with something of its first fiery ardour, and these may well prove to be of great importance for the future of Greek monasticism. We may be certain that the apostolic zeal and devotion which is so abundantly manifest within the religious societies will in time bring about a new awakening to the continuing need for men and women who will give themselves wholly to prayer. Then, indeed, we may hope to see a widespread revival of the monastic life that will people the ancient convents which now lie desolate and abandoned, and bring again the anchorites to the barren heights of Staghi.

IX

A DAY OF WASTENESS AND DESOLATION

It is not enough to understand the extremity of the affliction that has been endured, although if this is not understood, nothing has been understood.

F. A. VOIGT
The Greek Sedition

SINCE a measure of security was restored to Greece, the ecclesiastical authorities have had little respite from urgent practical problems clamouring for solution. To the most cursory reader of a periodical such as *Ekklesia* (the official journal of the Greek Church), it must have been apparent that during the years which followed the collapse of the Communist sedition the bishops were constantly preoccupied with questions of material welfare and relief. Scarcely an issue but contained some reference to the resettlement of refugees, plans for the rebuilding of destroyed churches or the provision of clothing for the clergy; while the *Paidoupolis*, the *Paidikos Stathmos* and the P.I.K.P.A. clinic and food-distribution centre had, it would seem, become permanent features of the diocesan organisation in many parts of Greece.

It would, nevertheless, be a mistake to assume that the Church of Greece was forced by her preoccupation with these overwhelming material needs to neglect what must always be her primary task. Quite the contrary is true. That concern for the poor, the prisoners, the homeless and the oppressed which one looks for in a Church which pays peculiar reverence to St. John Chrysostom, went hand in hand with a missionary activity which, all else apart, would have sufficed to make the decade from 1940 to 1950 a memorable one in the annals of the Greek Church. Greece, as a theologian of the Zoë Brotherhood wrote to me in 1949, "issued from the war completely ruined—materially. Nothing was left to her of her national wealth. Her houses, villages, fields, factories, communications, and economy were all utterly destroyed. Spiritually, nevertheless, she emerged from the chaos of war reborn."

It is only against this background of suffering and devastation, of foreign occupation and armed sedition, that it is possible to grasp the full significance of the spiritual ferment which marked these ten years, or to understand the magnitude of the task which the Church faces at the present time. For this reason I make no apology for dwelling at some length on the extent of the all-engulfing catastrophe which overwhelmed the Greek nation from the time of the Italian invasion of 1940 down to the decisive defeat of the Communists in the campaigns of 1949.

Much has already been written concerning the sufferings of the people of Greece during these terrible years: about the horrors of the occupation, the burning and pillage of undefended villages, the famine which carried off more than 300,000 men, women and children, and the multitude of the homeless approaching in number the population of Athens and the Piraeus. Long before the end of the struggle with the Communists was in sight the destruction had become so manifest, so universal, that after a time one no longer marvelled. One came to accept the long lines of shattered rolling-stock stretching westwards from the walls of Salonica across the plain towards the muddy waters of the Vardar; the rusting carriages which lay strewn around the fair shores of Salamis. It was impossible to travel for any distance without encountering a dynamited bridge, a recently filled mine-crater, or the blackened ruins of an abandoned village. Every town of northern Greece was crowded with refugees, and even the suburbs of Salonica were liable to nocturnal bombardment.

Little attention, however, has as yet been given to the effect of ten years of all but unbroken warfare upon the life of the Church: to the breakdown of normal parochial organisation over large tracts of country for two or three years at a stretch, in consequence of the flight of the clergy together with their people from the villages; to the slaughter of the country parsons, and the destruction and looting of countless churches and monasteries which were to create such insuperable problems when the time came for the refugees to return to their homes; to the fate of those dioceses which were occupied by the Bulgars, who attempted to eradicate every trace of 'Hellenism' from those areas of eastern Macedonia and Thrace which fell to their lot; where the Greek bishops and their clergy were supplanted by Bulgars, the Greek service-books burned; where the very saints were de-Hellenised and had their names repainted in Slavonic characters. All who were able to do so fled from this region and took refuge in Salonica or in other towns to the west of the river Strymon, though some 40,000 were massacred. In the diocese of Drama no less than forty of the 112 parish churches were burned down, as well as the monastery of Eikosiphoinisses.

Elsewhere in Greece, and particularly in those areas traversed by important lines of communication, the number of the homeless mounted steadily as guerilla activity drew savage reprisals upon the villages. One had only to spend a few days in the mountains which lie to the westward of the Thessalian township of Kalambaka, for example, to see something of the effect of these reprisal raids. Church after church was gutted: mere empty shells with fragments of ancient paintings clinging to the tottering walls. In this diocese of Trikka and Staghi alone, twenty-four village churches were completely destroyed during the occupation and many others more or less seriously damaged. Nor did the towns escape the flood of destruction: Edessa, for example, which was set on fire by the Germans on September 12th, 1944, and where five churches perished in the ensuing conflagration, or Iannitsa which suffered a like fate two days later; Larissa, which had scarcely recovered from an earthquake when it was bombed by the Italians, and Kerkyra where more than sixty per cent. of the buildings were destroyed or damaged.

After the occupying troops had withdrawn from Greece in the autumn of 1944 and the Communist sedition had met with its first reverse, there ensued a period of comparative tranquillity. The refugees returned to their villages and some progress was made in repairing the damage wrought during the years of occupation. But a greater trial was still to come. From the autumn of 1946 onwards the full violence of the armed sedition which had slowly been gathering its energies since its temporary set-back of December, 1944, was let loose upon the country dioceses. It was utterly out of question for the Greek army, even with the assistance of the gendarmerie and the local militia, to garrison hundreds of isolated hamlets lying in mountainous districts where communications were of the most rudimentary kind. The defence of the northern frontiers presented problems enough and to spare. It was not long, therefore, before the country people were forced to flee from their lands and homes and to seek refuge in those centres which possessed a garrison. Large areas of northern and central Greece were soon abandoned to the roving Communist bands.

Some of the refugees found their way to Athens and Salonica, but the majority crowded with their surviving animals and such few possessions as they had been able to carry with them in their flight into the small country towns which serve as centres for the ecclesiastical administration. Here many of them remained for three years. Some, and those the most fortunate, were able to build themselves wooden houses or *kalyvai*; others were lodged in huts; multitudes, especially in Macedonia, lived (often twenty or twenty-five families together) in old Turkish houses; those who fared worst of all had to be content with hastily improvised shelters of mud and thatch, or even to pass the bitter months of winter in tents. By the end of 1948 the number of the refugees exceeded 700,000: for the second time within ten years a tenth part of the whole nation was homeless. The country towns were packed with refugees: not a ruined cottage or a stable but sheltered two or three families. Some words from Thomas Alcock's *Travels in Russia, Persia, Turkey and Greece in 1828-29* might well have been written 120 years later: "Nothing in Greece", says this traveller, "can more forcibly give an idea of the war that has been carried on, than finding on inquiry that not a third of the residents in any place are natives of it, but only sojourners there, till security is afforded them in their own birth-places."

The parish clergy fled with their people to the comparative security of the towns, but the priest was a marked man and many failed to make good their escape. No less than 239 priests and monks were done to death by the Communists alone, and seventy-seven by the Germans, while a further forty-seven died at the hands of Bulgars, Italians or Albanian moslems. Of the total number of 363 the majority (297 to be precise) were parish priests: no single category of the population sustained heavier casualties in the slaughter of these years than the village *papades.*

"I triumphed", says De Quincey, "but infer not, reader, a condition of joy or exultation." Not all of those who died were men of the quality of the heroic parish priest of the village of Megarchis, Papa George Skrekas, who was crucified by the Communists on Good Friday, 1947. Nor, needless to add, did every Christian who suffered for the faith during the first three centuries of our era embrace death with the ardour of an Ignatius or the serenity of a Polycarp. The Church of Greece has ever been rich in martyrs, and there are not a few names—unknown though they be to Christendom at large—which have been added during the last ten years to the roll of those who will be remembered in the mountain dioceses whenever the Church gathers for the eucharist:

"Thy Church, O Christ our God, in all the world is adorned with the blood of thy martyrs as with purple and fine linen."

But for every village *papas* who died, a dozen fled to the shelter of the nearest fortified post. Some went further afield, to live with relatives in Athens or the Piraeus, and in 1949 many bishops had, in addition to their catalogue of refugee clergy, a further list of those who were 'missing'—whose fate and whereabouts were unknown. Often a very large proportion of the clergy of a diocese were homeless: seventy-five of the ninety-three parish priests of the diocese of Grevena, for example, had been forced to abandon their parishes by the winter of 1948-49; while in the neighbouring see of Trikka and Staghi there were at that time no less than ninety-nine refugee clergy. The Lord Nikephoros, Metropolitan of Kastoria, told me that his sixty-three homeless *papades* included eighteen men, recently ordained after completing their training at the Kozani seminary, who had had no parochial experience under normal conditions. The economic situation of the refugee clergy was peculiarly difficult, deprived as they were of their fees as well as their lands.

It is doubtful whether anything—not even the carrying off of Greek children to territories beyond the iron curtain—did more to deprive the Communists of any vestige of sympathy in the country districts of Greece than their barbarous treatment of churches and clergy. The impassioned harangues of the Communist schoolmaster could avail but little, in the face of this desecration of holy things, to commend his cause to a people whose deepest loyalties had been outraged. What could be expected of men who burned down churches and defaced the eikons of the saints; who laid their infernal engines within the very sanctuary before the holy table; who crucified priests, and pillaged the monasteries where prayer had been offered for the whole state of Christ's Church from time immemorial? What could words avail the unhappy perpetrators of such terrible deeds? The 'Accursed of God' might burn and pillage and make fervent protestation of the surpassing excellence of their aims, they could not wipe out the impression created by their manifest hatred of the Church. As after the disclosure of the atrocities committed during the battle for Athens and the Piraeus in December, 1944, so in the face of these new horrors, there was a widespread reluctance to admit that Greeks could perpetrate such deeds. The men who did such things must be Slavs or Bulgars—no Greek could be capable of such crimes against God and against his own nation.

By the summer of 1950 it had become possible to gain some notion of the full extent of the material destruction which the Church had sustained since the beginning of the war; although with large tracts of northern Greece uninhabited until a few months before, the compiling of accurate statistics—never a simple matter—presented problems such as only one who had been in Greece during the last few years could hope to appreciate fully. I have already referred to the wholesale destruction of churches and monasteries. This, though serious enough, was perhaps most easily remedied. I remember one bishop who chuckled inordinately when I questioned him on this subject; "All that is necessary", he assured me, "is that I should go in person to the village with a spade and set to work, and then: *Panaghia!* in no time at all the whole village will turn out and a new church will be built before one can say a *kathisma* of psalms!"

More serious, perhaps, and not confined to those villages where the fabric of the church had been demolished, was the acute shortage of liturgical books, chalices, vestments, and other accessories of worship which could not be supplied from local resources. The dearth of service-books, in particular, was occasioning widespread difficulty. Old Venetian editions had been brought in from long-abandoned monasteries and remote hill-top chapels which had escaped pillage—though the antique characters in which many of them were printed, while intelligible enough to the experienced monk, made it difficult for the average *papas* (to say nothing of the village choir) to read the service with any facility.

I remarked in an earlier chapter that the metropolis is as a rule one of the most impressive and substantial buildings of a provincial town. In 1950, however, several bishops were homeless. The Metropolitan of Grevena was living in lodgings, having one room for his personal use and another which served as the diocesan office; the Lord Agathangellos of Nevrokopi was living in the most apostolic simplicity in two barely furnished rooms; nor, amongst the provincial 'saints', were such cases exceptional.

Faced by a catastrophe so complete and overwhelming, the first concern of the Church was to try to meet the urgent demand for the bare necessities of life: for food, clothing and shelter. Everywhere the response was the same: orphanages, homes for refugee children, centres for the distribution of food and clothing, clinics and hospitals, were created as it were out of nothing. Everywhere these institutions were hastily improvised in the face of desperate and clamorous necessity, and, more often than not, maintained with a heroic disregard for the universal lack of material resources, and a courage worthy of a St. Vincent de Paul.

In almost every diocese the bishop bore a heavy responsibility in this work of relief. Nearly always he exercised a close personal supervision over the various institutions which had come into being in response to the need of a people driven, for the second time within less than ten years, from their homes and lands; over the *estia* where for several years milk was distributed daily to thousands of refugee children; the *paidikos stathmos* where infants were cared for during the day; the distribution of clothing, black stuff for cassocks, soap, cocoa, macaroni, beans, sugar, boots and shoes—all the multiplicity of urgently needed supplies with which a host of relief organisations, societies, British and American towns and villages, and private benefactors sought to succour the people of Greece in their distress.

At Siderokastro, for example, the Metropolitan (who as assistant bishop of Salonica was an ardent supporter of the work of the Near East Foundation during the period between the wars), founded a small hospital where poor families could receive free medical attention, as well as a remarkable school of housekeeping for girls of marriageable age. Like all the Macedonian 'despots', the Bishop was president of the local branch of the national relief organisation known as P.I.K.P.A., and supervised the two centres from which milk and cocoa were issued daily to thousands of refugee children from the villages of his diocese.

At Edessa, in western Macedonia, the Metropolitan founded, shortly after the end of the occupation, an orphanage for twenty-five boys. This was originally situated in a house on the outskirts of the town, but during the heavy fighting at Epiphany, 1949—when Naoussa, a few kilometres to the southward, was sacked by the Communists and more than 600 of its inhabitants carried away captive to the mountains —this building was extensively damaged and rendered almost uninhabitable. The Bishop then established his orphans under the care of a monk in a dilapidated Turkish house next to the metropolis, and this was subsequently transformed into a permanent orphanage. Not content with this, the Bishop proceeded to found two further orphanages attached to nearby monasteries, as soon as the district was sufficiently tranquil to permit the monks and nuns—who had taken refuge in the town of Edessa—to return to their respective convents. A fourth orphanage was established a few miles away at Iannitsa.

So, all over Greece, there was heroic improvisation in the face of overwhelming material need; and, as at Edessa and Siderokastro, so in many another provincial town from the Peloponnese to the remotest fringes of northern Epirus and Thrace, the courage and initiative of the local 'despot' were factors of incalculable importance.

And yet, as I emphasised at the beginning of this chapter, pre-occupation with the material needs of her children did not cause the Church to neglect their spiritual welfare. The feeding and clothing of the homeless and the destitute, the distribution of soup and the creation of hospitals and orphanages, went hand in hand with the preaching of the Gospel. The Metropolitan of Siderokastro was not content with his hospital, his P.I.K.P.A. centres and his school of housekeeping. Even while the issue of the long struggle with the Communists was yet in the balance—and the Bulgarian frontier lies barely ten miles to the northward of the town—the Lord Basil was organising his "Guardians of Spiritual Enlightenment" and pressing ahead with the construction of a *Christianiki Estia*: a building comprising a large hall, library, class-rooms and offices, which should serve as a centre for the already vigorous Christian youth movements of the diocese and for training catechists and preachers. He needed, as every bishop did, cassocks for his clergy, food and clothing and medical supplies for his stricken people; but he was anxious above all to obtain Greek New Testaments for his catechetical schools, and a duplicator which would enable him to send a weekly sermon to every village *papas* in the diocese.

So it was elsewhere. Nothing that I saw in Greece impressed me more deeply than the fact that it was so often in precisely those districts where suffering had been most acute, where destruction and devastation were most evident, that the life of the Church seemed to burn most brightly. Suffering and desolation, which in a people less profoundly Christian than the Greeks might have brought forth nothing more creative than despair, have in Greece borne precious fruit. Deprived of all worldly security and riches, the Church has been forced back upon the Rock whereon she is founded; has learned anew that there can be no resurrection apart from the cross—the instrument of shameful death which is yet the throne of the victor. Through prolonged suffering she has come to know in her own life the truth of the apostle's words: "as having nothing, and yet possessing all things".

The notion of the kingdom of Christ which conceives of its coming in terms of the progressive and manifest overthrow of the powers of evil within this present world, and in the establishment of an earthly paradise, finds little support either in the New Testament or in the experience of the Church. The mystery of the redemptive work of Christ in His members cannot be measured in terms of worldly progress or success. The restoration of man to paradise is through incorporation in the humanity of the second Adam, in whom mankind, shattered and disintegrated by the fall, finds a new unity. For fallen man glory and humiliation are inextricably mingled, and every road that leads back to paradise, no matter whence it come, must pass through Calvary. Death and corruption have themselves become the way towards eternal life and the glory of the heavenly Sion, for the King of kings has united to Himself that humanity which in Adam fell beneath the dominion of Satan, and through death has overthrown death. But as in His own ineffable humiliation the royal purple was also the vesture of the servant, so likewise in His life in the members of His body, the glory and the strength are veiled and hid from the world's eyes: are revealed only to those who have themselves been baptised into the life-giving death of the incarnate Son of God; who have undergone that initiation which is already the beginning of our resurrection—the way out from the labyrinth of death, to use the expression of one of the Greek fathers.

One of the plainest lessons which history can teach us is that the Church thrives not on what the world accounts success, but on persecution and affliction. It is in the fires of tribulation and when the powers of evil are most nakedly manifested that her true glory shines most brightly—though the world discern it not. So it was during the first centuries of our era. So too in Greece to-day, as in other lands and in former ages, for those who have eyes to see there is revealed, beneath the outward semblance of failure and weakness, the lineaments of that glorious Church *not having spot or wrinkle or any such thing; but holy and without blemish.*

X

A MACEDONIAN DIOCESE

Wyd was his parisshe, and houses fer a-sonder.

A FEW paces from the gates of the University of Salonica, just south of the Via Ignatia where antique tramcars go clanging across the dusty waste that was once the Jewish cemetery, the daily papers, which play so important a part in Greek intellectual and social life, used to be publicly displayed every morning so that all men—poor scholars and unbeneficed clerks as well as prosperous merchants rich in this world's goods—might read of the heroic exploits of the armies which strove to drive the Accursed of God from the snowy heights of Pindos: a public-spirited gesture, worthy of a people who have ever set the pursuit of truth far beyond mere commercial advantage, and one of which I was often glad to avail myself on my way from the university library at midday.

One sunny forenoon in the spring of 1949 as I scanned the headlines of *Kathimerini* and *Akropolis* a photograph caught my eye. At first sight it seemed in no way remarkable: a group of country clergy gathered about their father in God—the latter an impressive figure wearing the *enkolpion*, or pectoral eikon, which is the mark of the higher clergy. Closer scrutiny, however, revealed that this was no ordinary clerical assembly, for every one of these reverend personages had a rifle slung across his shoulder. I turned in some astonishment to the accompanying paragraph and read that "in the war against the insurgents, the clergy of Grevena hastened to be enrolled under the banner of the movement for the deliverance of the Hellenic race. . . ." The photograph, it concluded, "shows the Metropolitan of Grevena with his armed priests".

I went to lunch with my curiosity whetted. Grevena, I knew, was a peculiarly isolated diocese and one that had suffered severely, first at the hands of the Germans and again in the present troubles. Further enquiries disclosed that the present Metropolitan, the Lord Theokletos, was a man renowned for his ardent patriotism and his immense stature.

During the weeks which followed I had occasion to correspond with this prelate as to the state of his diocese, and received a pressing invitation to come and see for myself the desperate conditions resulting from eight years of all but continuous warfare.

Some months went by before an opportunity presented itself, and then one morning in February, 1950, found me travelling westwards from Kozani in a jeep belonging to the 2nd Army Corps. When I had last come this way, the previous March, we had been constrained to travel in convoy: a seemingly endless line of heavy army trucks laden with provisions, fodder and ammunition for the outlying garrisons of northern Pindos. It had been the eve of the festival of the Annunciation —which is also the day on which Greece commemorates the raising of the standard of revolt by the Archbishop of Patras in 1821—and every vehicle was decked with evergreens and plastered with patriotic slogans:

ZHTΩ O BAΣIΛEYΣ
ZHTΩ TO EΘNOΣ
ZHTΩ O ΣTPATOΣ.

The wild, mountainous tract of country that lies south and west of Kozani is a desolate region at all times, and never more so than in early February when the outworks of the great fortress of Pindos are veiled in snow, and icy winds scour the exposed valley which leads westward away from the haunts of men. A mile or two from Siatista the road forked and we turned southwards out of the teeth of the wind, the lightly-laden jeep lurching and jolting over the deeply-scored, rock-strewn surface of a truly Hellenic road—"the worst road in all Macedonia", the driver assured me with emphasis.

At Grevena—set drab and cheerless amongst low hills, the gaunt ruin of the orphanage dark against the sky—boulders gave place to mud. It lapped about us as we turned out of the market, where I had a fleeting glimpse of whiskered *papades* in rusty cassocks sprawled round a table amidst the dull gleam of copper pans and cauldrons. A veritable sea of mud, churned by the wheels of heavy vehicles, stretched unbroken from the steps of the regimental headquarters towards the broken line of ramshackle dwellings beyond the river.

Here on the furthermost fringe of Macedonia the road was swallowed up in the muddy deeps; beyond the cottages lay the massive rampart of Pindos, traversed only by mule-tracks winding high among the snows, westwards towards Metsovo and Epirus. To the southward a few paths—impassable save on foot during the winter months—gave access to Kalambaka and the plains of Thessaly.

After paying my respects to the colonel in command of the garrison I plunged afresh into the inland sea and struck out for the metropolis: a simple cottage where the Bishop rented a couple of rooms. The Lord Theokletos—a monumental figure in an ungirt robe of indigo—looked strangely out of place in such a setting. The Friday fast was waived out of regard to the presence of a traveller, and when we had eaten the Metropolitan told me something of the state of his diocese. It was a gloomy picture that he outlined.

Owing to the remoteness of the district and its poor communications almost every village had been abandoned by its inhabitants from 1947 till the summer of 1949. Grevena itself, a comopolis with a pre-war population in the region of 3,500, had, for more than two years, sheltered five times that number of refugees. During the past six months it had been possible for the people to return to certain villages situated in the northern part of the diocese, but there were reputed to be more than 2,000 families still living in the great refugee camp on the southern fringes of the town, and sixty-four of the diocese's ninety-six villages were still, after three years, uninhabited. Many of the fugitives had fled southwards to Kalambaka, Trikkala and Larissa; others had sought refuge in Kozani.

The refugees had included seventy-five parish priests, only sixteen of whom had as yet been able to return to their villages. Two priests had been done to death by the Germans; three others, as well as three monks, murdered by the Communists. As recently as October, 1949, the solitary occupant of the monastery of St. Athanasius, close to the village of Trikomon, had returned home after two years' exile, despite the advice of the Bishop and others who counselled him to wait two or three months longer, only to be brutally murdered within the space of a few days. It was when matters were at their worst that the Bishop formed his clerical militia and drilled his venerable warriors in the square where stands the monument to his predecessor in the see of Grevena, the Metropolitan Aimilianos, who had suffered death at the hands of the Turks in 1911 and is revered in this region as a martyr. This redoubtable force had never been called upon to take the field against the Accursed of God, but, said the Lord Theokletos, it had served as an example.

As to the destruction of churches, it seemed that some months must

II   The church at Ziakas

III Byzantine Salonica

inevitably elapse before the Bishop could hope to be in a position to make a detailed statement. He instructed his secretary to provide me with a report embodying such information as had reached him. Grevena itself had suffered a heavy bombardment during the retreat of 1941 and the cathedral church of the Annunciation had been seriously damaged (the old cathedral of St. George had been destroyed by fire several years earlier). On the outskirts of the town lay a little church dedicated to St. Archelaos of Larissa. This had become the parish church of the refugees. Here, from 1947 onwards, the refugee clergy had assembled daily to sing mattins and evensong, and on Sundays and festivals to celebrate together the divine mysteries. This church, as I subsequently discovered, also served as a centre for the distribution of rations to the vast multitude of the homeless who dwelt in the nissen huts on the edge of the town. On my way back to the metropolis I ran into a large group of refugee clergy. They had got wind of my projected expedition and begged me to visit their villages and to bring back news of their condition after three years' abandonment.

I returned to the regimental headquarters at dusk, armed with my report, and spent an hour poring over maps with a young captain from Volos. We finally decided upon two itineraries, each of several days' duration. The first would enable me to see something of those parts of the diocese which were still uninhabited, and about which the Bishop had little information; the second, to visit several villages north and west of Grevena to which the refugees had lately returned. Arrangements having been made for a nine o'clock start the following morning, I returned to the metropolis for supper and discussed the Zoë movement and the architectural projects of the Metropolitan of Siatista with the Lord Theokletos until it was time for bed.

Saturday, February 4th, dawned fine and dry. The first stage of my journey was accomplished in a jeep driven by an *Epeirotes* who had concealed two British soldiers in his house at Iannina during the occupation. Less than five miles from Grevena the track which we were following gave up the ghost and further progress was impossible. At this point we were met by a sergeant and two soldiers, mounted on mules and leading a handsome bay mare caparisoned after the European manner. It took us an hour to climb to the village of Mavranaioi, which was strongly garrisoned (it had been partly inhabited since the previous October). After lunching with the officers of the garrison I resumed my journey with an escort of seven soldiers, and with a corporal of the gendarmerie as guide.

At three o'clock we reached Mavronoros, the 'Black Mountain'; a small village, quite deserted and in ruins. Somewhat surprisingly, the church (which was dedicated to St. Theodore) had survived the bombardment. A single projectile had apparently found its mark and a portion of the vault had collapsed, but the walls were sound enough and the paintings which covered them had not as yet suffered greatly from exposure to the elements. A chapel on the hill above the village was completely gutted and almost every house was in ruins. So complete was the destruction that we were unable to identify the remains of the school.

A brief halt and we set out towards Ziakas, where I was to spend the night. We followed a water-course for some distance before intercepting the mule track. The ground had thawed since morning and the going was laborious. On a ridge commanding a wide prospect of this abandoned countryside we met the relief escort from the Ziakas garrison, and I reluctantly relinquished my handsome mount for a mule saddled after the school of Macedonia. We crossed the Venetikos by an ancient bridge and reached the headquarters of the garrison, a kilometre below the ruins of the village, a little before sunset.

It was too late to see anything of Ziakas that day, but the isolated community was delighted to have a visitor and the evening passed merrily enough. The night was chilly and I slept fitfully. From the mountains, which rise to close on 5,000 feet above the village, came the howling of wolves and jackals. Two wolves had ventured into Mavranaioi itself a few nights earlier, and, despite the vigilance of the sentries, had attacked and killed one of the mules picketed amongst the cottages. There had been neither sheep nor goats in these mountains for more than three years.

The morning was cold and cheerless without trace of sun. I took leave of my hosts about half-past nine and was accompanied to the village by a young lieutenant from Salonica. Ziakas had not only been burned by the Germans; it had more than once been the scene of heavy fighting within the last three years. The church stood at the entrance to the village. It was completely ruined, but a few paintings still clung to the walls of the apse, and, amidst the waste and desolation wrought by man's sin, the Son of the Virgin, the Alpha and the Omega, raised His hands in blessing. The destruction of the village—one of the largest in the region—was complete and spectacular. The shattered walls were daubed with Communist slogans. We threaded our way amongst the ruined houses to a building on the farthest side of the village which had been roughly repaired to afford shelter for an advanced outpost, drank a glass of cognac whilst my escort laced up their boots and buckled on their equipment, and left for Spelaion and Trikomon shortly after eleven.

The paths were ice-bound and treacherous, the snow deep in places. Spelaion came into view after half an hour, set amongst towering cliffs. A long and laborious ascent between high rocks, the Venetikos murmuring through its gorge far below, the path clinging to precipitous cliffs rising from the dwarf oaks and myrtle to lose themselves in the grey mists that swirled about their summits, brought us to a point immediately below the village. After a stiff climb through massive fortifications of uncertain date, we suddenly found ourselves looking down upon a tiny Byzantine church with twin domes, sharply outlined against the untrodden snow; a sombre red jewel laid in a setting of purest white.

This proved to be the catholicon of a small monastery, dedicated to the Mother of God. The interior of the church was dark and silent as a tomb; within the sanctuary liturgical books, eikons and vestments were strewn in confusion. The book of the Gospels lay closed upon the holy table, between two reliquaries of tarnished silver. We found a few stumps of candle and lighted them before the eikons of the Lord and His Mother; the spluttering flames banished the darkness and disclosed the presence of a host of emaciated figures gazing down upon us from wall and eikonostasis. We said a prayer and withdrew.

Though the church was undamaged, the other buildings which enclosed three sides of the roughly quadrangular space occupied by the monastery were all in ruins. Below, in the centre of the village, we found a second church, dedicated to St. Athanasius. This too had escaped serious damage, though the windows were unglazed and dead leaves lay piled against the eikonostasis and rustled about the throne of the bishop. Inaccessible on the cliffs above the Venetikos, Spelaion seemed built to withstand a siege, and we were not surprised to find that it had apparently served as a base for the *katsapliades*. A large house in the centre of the village had evidently been the Communist headquarters, and party slogans were scrawled over every wall. When we returned to the monastery, where the animals had been tethered, the candles still flickered within the church. Leaving the saints to their solitary vigil we plunged deeper into the uninhabited wastes that stretched southward toward Metsovo and the Thebaid of Staghi.

During the course of the next four days we worked our way eastwards to Trikomon and Kipouryio, and then turned north towards Mavranaioi and Grevena, to complete the first part of my itinerary. At three of the villages on our route there were isolated garrisons: otherwise the whole district lay abandoned. We passed through hamlet after hamlet where every house was destroyed, where churches stood open to the skies and no living creature broke the three-year silence. At Kipouryio the chapel of St. Paraskeve—a saint whose apparent connexion with the sixth day of the week (in Greek, *paraskeve*, the day of preparation) has given rise to some very singular local cults in the country districts—had been stripped of its furnishings and turned into a hospital by the Communists: empty bottles and boxes which had contained medical supplies lay strewn about the building.

Upon our return to Grevena we encountered a vast multitude of ragged children straggling back towards the refugee camp, grasping huge slabs of bread and honey: more than 4,000 children were being fed daily at the *estia* outside the high school. We found the Lord Theokletos a little concerned lest I should have fallen into the hands of the *katsapliades*—communications in the mountains out beyond Mavranaioi were notoriously unreliable. I waded through the mud with my captain from Volos to call on the colonel of the local militia, under whose protection I should be travelling for the rest of my itinerary. There was no news to be had anywhere save of the forthcoming elections.

At ten o'clock the following morning we were making slow progress westwards through melting snow: four militiamen, the president of the village of Elatos and myself; a large American mule floundering astern with the baggage. Above the ruins of Doxaras we turned aside to view the pile of stones which was all that remained of the church of St. George. A few families had returned to this hamlet and were living in nissen huts on the hillside below the ruined church. The whole village had been destroyed.

An hour later we found ourselves among the newly built cottages of Elatos. Above a cluster of wretched *kalyvai* rose the fabric of an unfinished church. The village, the president told us, had been burned down in July, 1942, and reduced to ruins. The work of rebuilding was begun in 1945, but two years later the people fled to Grevena and all was left unfinished. Some fifty families had returned in November, 1949, and were now settled in their old houses. The church which was to replace that destroyed by the Germans stood roofless: the windows unglazed, the eikonostasis of rough-hewn timbers. There was a tiny chapel dedicated to the prophet Elias on the brow of the hill, half a mile beyond the village, where the holy mysteries had been celebrated for a time. Now the church which was in Elatos assembled Sunday by Sunday for the breaking of the bread in the half-finished structure which dominated the village.

Whilst we were within the church there was a murmuring amongst the crowd that had gathered in the snow outside: shouts of "Behold! He comes. Make haste, O Papa Iannis!" The parish priest had just returned from Grevena, having followed a more direct route than ourselves. He came scrambling up through the orchard below the church, a ragged figure clad in *kalymmafchion* and tattered overcoat, his boots heavy with mud, his cassock slung across his shoulder, clawing his way up the slope with the aid of a shepherd's staff. We all retired to the *taverna* for a glass of ouzo, and then, after despatching three of the escort with the baggage-mule, the rest of my party (together with two lads from the local militia and the indefatigable Papa Iannis, who, despite his seventy-three years, had already covered the best part of ten miles that morning), set out for the neighbouring village of Anavryta— a deserted hamlet set on the brink of a deep chasm where the inky thread of the Venetikos lay twisted in the pale sunlight. Far away against the towering ramparts of Pindos the ruins of Ziakas could be distinguished: a dark stain on the white vesture which enfolded the silent countryside.

The more enterprising of the Anavrytans had found lodging in the recently reoccupied village of Kallirachi (where we spent the following night) and were planning to return to their houses in the spring. The parish priest at Kallirachi had improvised a temporary oratory where he said the daily offices. The church lay in ruins, and the liturgy was celebrated in a tiny chapel dedicated to St. Demetrius of Thessalonica, a full kilometre from the village. I left my escort at Kallirachi and set out early with a couple of local guides for Megaron, the largest village of the district and, like Kallirachi, reoccupied by its inhabitants some two months earlier. Here I made but a brief stay, as I was anxious to reach Kydonies (which lay well outside the inhabited zone) and get back to a populated village before nightfall. The *kapetanios* of the local militia undertook to have an escort ready by noon, and in the meantime the parish priest carried me off to the refectory of the police station (where we broke our fast) and thence to see the parish church: an ancient structure roofed with corrugated iron, the walls bulging and sagging ominously at several points.

By one o'clock I was riding westwards on a handsome white mule, with an escort of local militia, armed to the teeth, in line ahead and astern, and all the mountains of Macedonia spread out around the horizon. Kydonies, where we arrived a little after three o'clock, was utterly deserted. It had been a large village (some 175 families, according to my escort), and the destruction was more restricted than in many villages of this region. The church, like that at Elatos, had apparently been left uncompleted when the people fled: a temporary chapel which occupied the position of the outer narthex was in a ruinous condition. Several eikons lay half buried amongst the fallen masonry. The whole building, like the ruined school-house adjoining it, was daubed with democratic slogans.

The parish priest of Kydonies, Papa Athanasius Toskas, had been murdered by the Germans who fell upon the village on July 7th, 1944. Papa Athanasius, despite his sixty-seven years, had gathered up his skirts and made for the forest as fast as his legs would carry him, in company with the curate of the neighbouring village of Ekklesia, Papa Nicolas Tsabiri. The latter succeeded in making good his escape, but Papa Athanasius was surrounded and captured. His body was found some days later, barbarously mutilated. His ears and hands had been cut off, his beard set on fire, and his chest and back slashed with knives. All about the village were little chapels: one which we passed, as we recrossed the stream at the foot of the hill and turned towards Rodia, had been burned down.

I lay that night at the house of George Sabbas: the house where his brother had been killed before his eyes three years earlier and whence he had fled into the darkness to blunder about the wooded hills all night before reaching Aghios Georgios and safety. The people of Rodia had returned home only two months earlier. The youngest of my host's three sons had married the daughter of the parish priest, and this young woman now kept house for her father-in-law. After supper who should appear but Father Athanasius, the *ephemerios*, who proved to be an old friend from the Kozani seminary. He had come home for the week-end. Conversation turned to the subject of the parish clergy; Papa Athanasi was a whole-hearted admirer of the new system; he was not one who could learn only from the Lord or rest content with a mere facility in turning the pages of the service-books:

"The divine liturgy, *Kyrie Petre*, can be gabbled through by a man who is all but illiterate: *we* are called to be shepherds, and a shepherd has need of great knowledge and wisdom."

Next morning Father Athanasius celebrated the holy mysteries in the village church. It was one of the Saturdays of all souls, and the priest's daughter was early astir, making preparations for the commemoration of departed relatives and friends. Before the service was ended I left for the neighbouring village of Sydendron, where the curate, Papa Constantinos, introduced himself as "the priest who bore the machine-gun in the sacred company of the despot". St. Nicolas, Sydendron, had been a fine church, apparently dating from the sixteenth century. It had survived the years of occupation only to be set on fire by the Communists on the night of July 25th, 1947. The ancient frescoes were slowly crumbling away, but sufficient remained to show something of the former splendour of the church.

I lunched at the presbytery and rode on to Amygdalies in the early afternoon. Most of the village's 200 children seemed to be dancing barefoot in the sun outside their newly opened school: a nissen hut erected on the site of the building destroyed by the Germans in July, 1943. A huge new church was in process of construction, but work was at a standstill through lack of funds, and the liturgy had to be celebrated in a brick chapel hastily constructed in 1946 within the walls of the unfinished church. Being anxious to reach Aghios Georgios before nightfall I resisted the efforts of the parish priest to persuade me to stay the night at Amygdalies, and as twilight deepened into darkness came clattering down the steep slopes to the stream where a few children still lingered, on a mule which I would have pitted even against Urquhart's Aristotle, and dismounted outside the house of the president.

Aghios Georgios was one of the only two villages in the diocese of Grevena where the population had remained throughout the troubled years which followed the end of the occupation, and had, moreover, afforded shelter to many refugees from other communities. The church—a massive structure dating from the middle of the nineteenth century—stood on rising ground in the centre of the village. The windows had been blocked with masonry and stones, and the church, thus barricaded and surrounded by an elaborate system of trenches, pill-boxes and barbed wire defences, transformed into a citadel. Here the greater part of the population had taken refuge while the militia, with a stiffening of gendarmerie, had fought off an assault on the village which raged for a night and a day on May 8th-9th, 1948. The fabric had suffered extensive damage from mortar and machine-gun fire, but the Communists had eventually been driven off. Earlier, the village had suffered grievously at the hands of the Germans. Though the church had been spared, the school and a large proportion of the houses had been destroyed. The school was now flourishing in a large nissen hut: formerly it had been housed in the nave of the church.

On Sunday morning there was great scrubbing and polishing of muddy boots, and at half-past eight I ventured forth, looking as spruce as three weeks of sleeping in my clothes would permit, in company with the *proedros*. The latter was anxious not to be too early at church, and, since the second bell had not yet sounded, we went first to inspect the new school. After smoking a cigarette with the *didaskalos* we proceeded to the church at the third bell, followed by all the children of the village. When the liturgy was ended the president climbed with great dignity to the top of one of the pill-boxes and made an impassioned oration welcoming the representative of Greece's great and traditional ally to their gallant and Christ-loving village, and dwelling at some length on the ties which, despite the infernal machinations of the Accursed of God, would surely bind together for all ages the Hellenic and British nations. The said representative thereupon made a brief, but it is to be hoped fitting, reply to this masterpiece of presidential rhetoric, and the whole company drifted away in high good humour to sip cognac and discuss the latest news which had arrived from Kozani.

After a visit to the family of a young theologian from Salonica I went to feast, first with the president and then—at the dictates of charity rather than of appetite—with the parish priest also. The influence of the Kozani seminary had made itself felt in this village, and the catechetical school was in full swing as I passed the new school-house on my way to the parsonage. There the wine that makes glad the heart of man flowed freely, and it was a drowsy traveller who rode across the hills to the neighbouring village of Kivotos later that afternoon. Communications having proved unreliable, I was constrained to accept the hospitality of one of the churchwardens. Shortly before noon the following day I rode into Vatolakkos with an escort of six militiamen and fell straight into the hands of the parish priest, who was sunning himself on a bench outside the gendarmerie station. This *papas* was a graduate of the Kozani seminary; his father had been a priest in Smyrna (like Kivotos, this was a refugee village). He spoke with pride of the catechetical school which had been flourishing in the village since the previous autumn.

Vatolakkos, like Aghios Georgios, had never been abandoned by its inhabitants. Owing to its important position—astride the main road from Grevena to Kozani—it had been strongly garrisoned throughout the troubles, and had offered sanctuary to the fugitives from no less than ten neighbouring communities, despite the fact that the greater number of the houses had been destroyed in the German advance of 1941—there were bomb craters all along the road from Kivotos southward. The parish priest had sheltered five refugee families in his house for more than two years. The church, which had never been completed, had, according to the Bishop's report, been pillaged by the Germans. It had moreover been damaged by mortar fire during an attack on the village by the Communists. A new school had just been opened to take the place of the one destroyed by the Germans.

From Vatolakkos I succeeded in telephoning to army headquarters at Grevena, and shortly after three o'clock I was picked up by my friend from Iannina. After attending the evensong of the refugee clergy, in company with the Bishop's deacon, and a long talk with the fugitive *ephemerioi* of Spelaion and Kosmati, I paid a final visit to the metropolis. The Bishop was unwell: he had been ill for some time past, and I took my leave early. Some months later, after a letter enclosing photographs of the ruined churches of the diocese had remained long unanswered, I saw from a notice in *Ekklesia* that the Lord Theokletos had passed to his rest.

Like Father Ioakeim, his deacon, he was a native of the Piraeus and had laboured there for thirty-three years as vicar of the parish of St. Constantine before being called to take charge of the see of Grevena in the third year of the occupation. The state of the diocese even in those days was serious enough, and had the new *despotes* been able to foresee the full extent of the catastrophe which was to overwhelm the widely scattered communities committed to his charge within the space of another five years, he might understandably have shrunk from the heavy burden of responsibility that he was called to bear.

From 1947 onwards the Lord Theokletos found himself the bishop of a vast multitude of displaced persons; the whole outward framework of diocesan administration disrupted; his parish clergy driven from their cures and scattered to far corners of Greece, or crowded together in the nissen huts on the margins of Grevena; the town itself threatened by the Communists. Called to face a truly desperate situation, the Metropolitan set an example worthy of his predecessor, the martyred Aimilianos, and of the great traditions of the Greek Church. Somehow, despite all material difficulties, food, shelter and clothing were provided for the innumerable refugees who descended upon Grevena during the fourth year of his episcopate, the philanthropic institutions of the battered township continued to function, and the Saint and Despot of Grevena, at the head of his 'sacred company' of refugee clergy, showed that the spirit of the warrior-prelates of the old wars was not yet extinct.

This alone was sufficient to ensure that the episcopate of the Metropolitan Theokletos of Grevena would long be remembered, not merely in western Macedonia but throughout the Church of Greece. But this was not all. I have said that it was often in those districts where devastation and suffering had left their deepest mark that the Church manifested most plainly the Source of her life. The episcopate of Theokletos of Grevena may well serve to illustrate this truth.

The late Metropolitan had not been long in residence (he had been forced to spend some months in Kozani before coming to his diocese) before he summoned to his assistance a priest-monk then working in Florina, the Archimandrite Augustine: a powerful preacher, an ardent evangelist noted for his adherence to the letter of the dominical counsels in such matters as personal property, and an outspoken rebuker of vice —even when manifested in high places. This last characteristic having apparently rendered Father Augustine's relations with a certain dignitary of the Church somewhat delicate, he established himself at Grevena during the third year of the Lord Theokletos' episcopate and threw himself into the task of building up a Christian movement among the young men and girls of the diocese.

Father Augustine's method was to gather round him a little band of potential leaders: a score of young catechists of both sexes, the majority drawn from the senior classes of the high school, who would in time be able to carry on the work which he had begun. Before long it had proved possible to organise catechetical schools for children of all ages, and (as the refugee camp became more and more swollen during the course of 1947) to draw into the new Christian Unions many hundreds of boys and girls from the remote hamlets of Pindos, few of whom had ever heard a sermon preached in their village churches, let alone received any systematic course of instruction in the faith such as was now offered them. Whilst the whole diocese lay desolate and the Communist bands roamed the mountains almost at will, there was slowly growing up amongst the young Christians crowded together in the mud and squalor of Grevena a movement which promised to transform the religious life of this barren region.

In 1949 Father Augustine left Grevena to take up new work as chaplain to the 2nd Army Corps at Kozani, but the Christian Unions continued to flourish. Their membership at the time of my visit was in the region of 1,600—and this figure did not include the hundreds of children who had recently returned to their villages. In order that these latter should not be lost to the movement, several young catechists were visiting the lately repopulated villages around Grevena every week-end, giving addresses either during the liturgy or else in the village square when the people came out of church, and labouring to build up catechetical schools in every village. The Metropolitan had given immense stimulus to this work by sending as many parish clergy as he could spare to study at Kozani seminary—men like Papa Athanasius from Rodia—who would be qualified to run their own catechetical schools when they returned home.

Outstanding among the catechists trained by Father Augustine was a young gendarme who, now that there was no regular *hierokeryx* attached to the metropolis, was himself acting as the diocesan preacher and assistant to the Metropolitan. It would have been hard to match the burning devotion and zeal of these young catechists; the enthusiasm and eagerness of their still younger pupils. The Bishop himself had no illusions as to the importance of the work that had been begun three years before: in the face of devastation such as I had seen with my own eyes during the course of the ten days I had spent in the diocese—material destruction on a scale equal to that sustained by any Greek diocese—it was his considered opinion that the most desperate need was not for clothing or food or medical supplies, not for animals to replace those slaughtered by the Germans or driven off to the mountains by the Communists, not for domestic or agricultural implements and tools, but for a properly equipped building to serve as a centre for the Christian Unions, for Greek New Testaments and other Christian literature, and for a magical *polygraphos* which would enable him to distribute every week a homily to be read by every *papas* in the diocese at the Sunday liturgy.

For the truly notable feature of his episcopate had been neither the destruction and pillage of the villages, nor the slaughter of his clergy and the flight of his people from their homes and lands; all this had but provided the setting for a flowering of new and vigorous spiritual life of untold power, which promised to spread, from the little band of catechists whom Father Augustine had gathered about him, to every village and hamlet of the diocese—to Spelaion, high amongst the towering rocks above the Venetikos, where the saints brooded over the dark church, to Samarina and the summer pastures of the Vlach shepherds, southward and westward to desolate Trikomon and the uninhabited wastes towards Metsovo—and to bring a deepened and more conscious sharing in the Christian mystery to a people who had, as it was, retained their hold upon the fundamental virtues of faith, hope and charity with a tenacity which is rare in the world to-day.

XI

THE FIRST STIRRINGS OF REVIVAL

The people have indeed a lively sense of religion in their
hearts, but because they have neither guides nor preachers,
nor pastors to lead them to the saving and life-giving truth,
they are sleeping the sleep of apathy and spiritual death.

Letter of FATHER EUSEBIUS
MATTHOPOULOS, dated 1879

We live in an Age that hath more need of good examples
than precepts.

GEORGE HERBERT

I HAVE dwelt at some length upon the recent history of a single
Macedonian diocese, for the *eparchia* of Grevena was as it were a micro-
cosm of the Greek Church as a whole; the essential features of its
history during the previous decade were writ large from the Peloponnese
to the northern frontiers of the kingdom. It was not only amongst the
overcrowded refugee *kalyvai* of Grevena that there sprang up within these
last few years a flowering of evangelical Christianity such as tempted
one to prophesy that the day might not be far distant when the Church
of Greece—poor and naked though she were in the world's eyes—
would again become a lamp whose bright beams would extend to every
corner of Christendom.

This widespread kindling of the smouldering embers of the Church's
life shone out the more brightly by reason of the unrelieved blackness
of its setting. We must not on this account forget the all-important,
though less spectacular, work of preparation that had been going on
for a century and more. The remarkable developments of the last few
years would have been unthinkable were it not for the devoted labours
of all those who had worked and prayed for the quickening of this
ancient Church during the course of three or four generations.

We do not lack abundant testimony to the wretched condition of the
Church of Greece during the first half of the nineteenth century.

Though the traditions which enshrine the saving truths of the Gospel had been handed down from generation to generation throughout the centuries of Turkish dominion, the life of the Church was nevertheless gravely threatened by corruption and decay. The ministry of the word had fallen into almost complete neglect even in Athens, while in the country districts sermons were all but unknown. The ordinary people were for the most part "ill instructed, or rather not taught at all, sermons and catechising rare amongst them, Masses and Divine Service hudled and run over in a cursory and negligent manner . . ."

The higher clergy, with few exceptions, paid but scanty heed to their pastoral responsibilities. By the eighteen-forties (owing to the long delay in the recognition of the autocephalous status of the Church of Greece by the Oecumenical Patriarch) the number of the bishops had declined until only four remained, and those well advanced in years. As to the parish clergy, one may read accounts of their ignorance that differ but little from those which Covel had set down 200 years earlier: "Most priests have no books by them, but only their Church Offices; and . . . all their Study is only to get them by Heart, which takes up so much of their time as they cannot attend to read or Study other learned books if they had them. . . . Their ordinary prayers and liturgies, like Parrots they commonly mumble and hurry over by heart, and use them very imperfectly, with strange variety and confusion."

As for the monasteries, though there remained many holy monks and learned even in the darkest days, all too many of the *kalogeroi* were worldly and ignorant; jealous of their privileges, content with a merely formal discharge of the duties belonging to their state; drowsing in sunny galleries, cultivating their vegetables and their pleasant vineyards.

It is against such a background that we have to view the labours of that little company of priests and laymen who laid the foundations of what, in our own time, has become a nation-wide movement. The initiative in the growing revival of evangelistic and missionary activity that has characterised the last 100 years of the history of the Greek Church has come, not from the hierarchy—though many bishops have been whole-hearted supporters of the new movements—but from individual churchmen: lay theologians, monks and clergy. It is only very recently that an official 'Home Mission' has come into being, with the foundation of the *Apostoliki Diakonia* of the Church of Greece (not to be confounded with a far older movement of the same name which still flourishes in Salonica and the northern dioceses).

The history of the revival begins in 1839 and for a generation centres upon the convent of Megaspelaion in the valley of Kalavryta: the greatest monastery of Old Greece. The initial impulse, however, came from elsewhere. In that year there arrived at Patras a certain Cosmas Phlamiatos: a layman who had been banished from the Ionian Protectorate on account of his reckless denunciations of Masonic propaganda. He began to travel about the Peloponnese, preaching in the towns and villages and rekindling the fires that had burned low for generations past. Before long a hermit from the vicinity of Kalavryta, Christophoros Panaghiotopoulos by name, was inspired by the example of this lay theologian to abandon his cell and to devote himself to similar apostolic labours. The biographer of Father Eusebius Matthopoulos justly observes of this hermit-evangelist that "throughout the Peloponnese tradition has preserved, even to the present day, the memory of the celebrated and most profitable activity of this unlettered but zealous missionary".

But the times were evil and neither of these two itinerant evangelists was able to resist the temptation to denounce the established régime. Their activities came to an abrupt termination: Phlamiatos died in prison in 1850 (after a renewed attack on the Masons) and the former hermit disappeared into exile, never to return. In the meantime, however, Phlamiatos had gained a further disciple in the person of a monk of Megaspelaion named Ignatius Lambropoulos, who now became the leader of the movement.

Father Ignatius, who was born in a village near Megalopolis in 1814, entered the famous monastery (then inhabited by some 200 monks) while scarcely more than a boy. He was ordained deacon at the age of twenty-five, and then priest. In 1842 he met Phlamiatos at Aigion and was greatly moved by the ardour and enthusiasm of the lay evangelist. For the next seven years Ignatius Lambropoulos laboured incessantly throughout the whole length and breadth of the Peloponnese, preaching and confessing the people. Like Phlamiatos, he also exercised a most fruitful ministry through the medium of correspondence (it is related of the lay theologian that it was his custom to divide the night into three equal portions: one for rest, one for prayer, and one for writing the hundreds of letters by means of which he kept in touch with those whom he had encountered during the course of his missionary journeys).

Unlike his fellow-evangelists, Father Ignatius never succumbed to the temptation to mingle the pure milk of the Gospel with denunciation of current abuses; but, in spite of his restraint, he was imprisoned for several months at the time of Phlamiatos' arrest and was afterwards confined to his monastery. He remained at Megaspelaion for twelve years, and, despite the curtailment of his missionary journeys, continued to exercise a most effectual ministry through correspondence; while, as the fame of his holiness and wisdom went abroad, there came to the monastery a constant stream of visitors. Father Ignatius continued to preach and to hear confessions, and at last, when H.M.S. *Scylla* had borne away to Venice the unfortunate Otho and his consort, he was free once more to resume his itinerant work. The story of the last seven years of his life is a record of strenuous missionary activity amongst the towns and villages of the Peloponnese. His work received the blessing of the hierarchy, and he gathered about him a little group of disciples which included both clergy and laymen, prominent amongst them the deacon Hierotheos Metropoulos, uncle of Eusebius Matthopoulos, himself a monk of Megaspelaion and a future Archbishop of Patras. In 1866 Father Ignatius declined the offer of the bishopric of Triphylia on the plea of ill-health, and three years later he died.

The life of this zealous monk had already exercised a most potent influence throughout the Peloponnese, and through the little company of disciples that gathered about him at Megaspelaion his labours were destined to bear fruit over a far wider field than that covered by his own missionary journeys. Until the advent of Cosmas Phlamiatos there had been but little preaching in the towns and villages of Old Greece, and the labours of this lay theologian had inaugurated a new era of missionary activity.

The pattern of the first phase of the revival—from the arrival in the Peloponnese of Phlamiatos down to the death of Father Ignatius—bears a curious resemblance to that of the period which ensues, and which culminates in the foundation of the Brotherhood of Theologians, Zöe. Again the original stimulus is provided by a layman whose effective ministry is terminated by a clash with authority, and again a monk of Megaspelaion is left to build upon another's foundation and to consolidate his work.

*

In 1866, three years before the death of Ignatius Lambropoulos,

IV   Abandoned Monastery of St. Nicolas, Meteora

V   St. Barlaam, Meteora

VI Eikon from Edessa in Macedonia

there came to Athens a certain Apostolos Makrakes, a lay philosopher from the Cyclades, who had studied in Constantinople and in Paris, and had already won a considerable renown through his writings against the Franks and on the true nature of the Church. Makrakes electrified the Athenians by his preaching in Omonoia Square and other public places in the city. To all who heard this Christian philosopher it was evident that a new spirit was abroad in Greece. Shortly before the death of Father Ignatius, Makrakes visited Megaspelaion and there encountered a young monk from Melissopetra named Eusebius Mattho-poulos. This meeting marks the beginning of a long association between the two men which, clouded though it was by the eccentricities of the layman's later years, was to prove of incalculable importance for the Greek Church.

Father Eusebius (who, with Apostolos Makrakes, dominates the history of the revival of missionary activity for the next half-century and more) seems to have been set apart for the monastic life almost from his cradle. Despite recurrent bouts of fever (which left him with a thorn in his flesh for the remainder of a long life of strenuous activity), his uncle, Hierotheos Metropoulos, secured his admission to his own convent at the age of fourteen, and during the next few years he became the closest and most ardent disciple of Father Ignatius. It was he who took up the mantle of the great preacher and confessor at the latter's death.

Early in the 'seventies we find Eusebius Matthopoulos (now a deacon) studying the holy scriptures and the ancient philosophers and divines in the Athens schools, and already launched upon his long and most fruitful ministry as a *hierokeryx*. The year 1876 is memorable for two events: the ordination of Father Eusebius to the priesthood, and the foundation of the School of the Logos.

Hitherto the missionary revival inaugurated by the preaching of Phlamiatos had been quite unorganised. Though the monastery of Megaspelaion had afforded a base for the labours of Ignatius Lambro-poulos and his fellow workers, there had been no question of any formal association or 'movement'. These itinerant preachers and confessors had but restored and extended that "pious and laudable institution" (so Dr. Covel) whereby certain monkish theologians—"Grave and Reverend Persons that had been bred up in their Monasteries to a strict and mortified life"—would be appointed by the bishops "to go to their respective Cities and Towns . . . to advise, direct and assist all good People . . . for the encouraging and encreasing of their Devotion, and for the better management of their Lives and Conversations". The foundation of the School of the Logos constitutes an important landmark; it inaugurates the era of the voluntary movements and establishes the essential features of a pattern of missionary activity which has held the field until our own day, and from which the foundation of an official Home Mission marks the first radical departure.

In September, 1876, Makrakes and his associates founded the School of the Logos which combined the functions of a private *gymnasium* with those of an evening school for adults. Father Eusebius (who had been ordained priest a month before) was appointed chaplain and *pneumatikos* of this remarkable institution—he also made himself responsible for the cleaning of the school (especially, it is related, "of its vilest places", τῶν εὐτελεστέρων τόπων αὐτῆς: a phrase charged with sinister meaning for anyone acquainted with the lamentable decline in the standards of Hellenic plumbing since the far-off days when King Minos flourished in his Cretan palace!) The outstanding qualities of this young priest were quickly discerned by those about him, and not a few who were many years his senior in age and experience came to rely upon him as counsellor and spiritual father. It was during this period that Father Eusebius began his experiments with the small groups (*omades*) which were to become so important a feature of the brotherhood which he founded some thirty years later.

But the School of the Logos was not destined to enjoy a long career. Scarcely two years had elapsed from its foundation when Makrakes and his associates became involved in a violent controversy with the authorities, which brought their educational and spiritual work in Athens to an abrupt conclusion and scattered the leaders of the movement to remote islands and monasteries. In 1875, as the result of a scandalous transaction involving payments to certain ministers of the State, three men succeeded in obtaining the vacant bishoprics of Patras, Messenia and Kephallenia. The facts became widely known and public opinion was deeply aroused. Makrakes and certain of his fellow-workers published fiery articles denouncing this flagrant violation of the holy canons. A trial ensued; the guilty ministers were imprisoned and fined, while the three simoniacal bishops were committed to the Holy Synod, which should then, according to the canons, have proceeded to a sentence of deposition.

The Synod, however, declined to take this step. Makrakes thereupon extended his attacks from the simoniacal bishops themselves to those whom he now accused of being their accomplices—the members of the Holy Synod and the Archbishop of Athens. A bitter controversy ensued. Makrakes (whose language had never been characterised by moderation) threw discretion to the winds and attacked the bishops, the prime minister, the government and the theological faculty of the university without discrimination and in the most violent terms. The Metropolitan of Athens and of all Greece he denounced as "Simon Magus: *Archegos* of the hateful-to-God heresy and Metropolitan of evil courses!" The national university was no longer the *panepistemion*, the home of all the sciences, but the *panskotisterion*, the abode of universal darkness.

The clergy who were associated with Makrakes were more restrained in their denunciations of the hierarchy. They felt bound, nevertheless, to cease to commemorate their diocesan at the divine liturgy. The Synod retaliated by publishing unfounded charges of heresy and false teaching, and warned the faithful to have nothing to do with the theologians associated with the School of the Logos. The school itself was suppressed in the autumn of 1878, though Makrakes continued to publish his journal. In February, 1879, six of the 'Makrakist' clergy (including the archimandrites Hierotheos Metropoulos and Elias Vlachopoulos, as well as Father Eusebius) were brought before the Synod and tried on charges of heresy and *kakodoxia*. Despite the accused clergy's profession of orthodoxy and the absence of any shred of evidence in support of the charges, all were found guilty and sentenced to periods of exile, ranging from eight to ten years, in isolated monasteries dispersed amongst the islands of the Aegean and Ionian seas.

Father Eusebius was sent to the monastery of Palaiokastriotissa in Corfu—a small convent inhabited by ten monks, five hours' journey from the town of Kerkyra—where, cheerfully accepting this enforced interruption of his apostolic labours amongst the Athenians, he gave himself unreservedly to prayer and self-examination, and to the study of the scriptures. It was not long before the abbot of the monastery realised that the character of the exiled priest had been grossly misrepresented by the ecclesiastical authorities, and, with the consent of the local bishop, Father Eusebius began to preach in the villages of the diocese and to confess the people. Hierotheos Metropoulos was meanwhile turning his banishment to good account by reorganising the monastery of Longovardas in the isle of Paros, where his influence has endured to the present day.

The scandal occasioned by the simoniacal bishops had not been silenced by the banishment of the 'Makrakist' clergy. On the contrary, there was a widespread feeling that a grave injustice had been committed; petitions were organised, the subject was raised again and again in parliament, and at last, after three years, the exiles were recalled and the case of the guilty prelates reopened before the Holy Synod. Father Eusebius had so endeared himself to the people of Kerkyra that they refused to let him go immediately and he continued his work of spiritual regeneration amongst them for a year longer. In 1883 the Synod suspended the simoniacs for three years, and shortly afterwards the director of the Rizareion School, the then Bishop of Platamon, was charged with the re-examination of the case of the clergy formerly associated with the School of the Logos. He reported that the accusations of heresy and *kakodoxia* were utterly without foundation, the six priests and deacons admitted their fault in ceasing to commemorate their diocesan at the liturgy, and a formal reconciliation was effected.

Makrakes, however, refused to admit that the action of the Synod of 1879 constituted not a heresy (which might be held to justify separation from the local bishop) but a crime (ἔγκλημα) which certainly did not, and continued obstinately in schism. The story of the later years of this gifted but unbalanced man makes melancholy reading. In 1879 he had founded the 'Panhellenic Society of Constantine the Great' and announced the approaching overthrow of Constantinople and the end of the 'Kingdom of the Antichrist Mohamed'. From this time onward oracles and prophetic visions occupy a prominent place in his writings. The Apocalypse and the dreams of an eccentric lawyer from Patras (much given to threatening his unbelieving fellow-townsmen with earthquakes) are pressed into service for his shrill polemics.

Father Eusebius and the other clergy who had formerly collaborated with this Christian philosopher tried hard to convince him of the folly of his ways, but without avail, and in 1884 they regretfully dissociated themselves from their old teacher. Three years later Makrakes was abandoned by most of his remaining supporters, two of whom, Constantine Dialesmas and a lawyer named Michael Galanos (who was subsequently to exercise a memorable ministry as a lay preacher in one of the churches of Athens) were responsible for the foundation of the movement known as *Anaplasis* (Regeneration) which continued the work of Makrakes while renouncing the eccentric ways into which he himself had fallen. Makrakes lived till 1905 and, despite the violence of his attacks on those who had formerly been his associates, never wholly forfeited their love and affection. Father Eusebius and his fellow-workers were well aware how great was the debt that they and the whole Church owed to this unhappy man.

The ending of the controversy about the simoniacal bishops opened up a new field of activity for Father Eusebius and those associated with him. He was appointed *hierokeryx* first of Missolonghi and then of Attica (where his uncle, Hierotheos Metropoulos, collaborated with him for a time) and in 1895 the Holy Synod commissioned him to extend his field of activity to include the whole of Greece. From 1884 till 1906 Eusebius Matthopoulos gave himself wholly to the preaching of the Gospel and the ministry of the itinerant confessor, while, like his spiritual father Ignatius Lambropoulos, he shepherded and guided hundreds of Christians drawn from every walk of life by means of correspondence.

And what a ministry it was! For twenty-two years Eusebius Matthopoulos preached Christ crucified in every town of Greece: preached with a fervour and a simplicity that was wholly new. He spoke of the divine truths with the conviction of one who lived from day to day in their power. Never free from bodily ailments and often in acute pain, he gloried, like the apostle of the Gentiles, in his infirmities that the power of Christ might rest upon him.

As a confessor and spiritual father he was unsurpassed. He was one who (as Archbishop Chrysostom wrote of him) "had confronted sin in all its nakedness and virtue in its resplendent brightness, who had witnessed man's falling into evil and his resurrection, who had plumbed both the manifest motives of sin and also its hidden springs"; one who led countless men and women to God through the mystery of confession and, above all, through the potent example of a life which spoke of the beauty of holiness more eloquently than any sermon.

In 1893 Hierotheos Metropoulos was elected to the see of Patras and Eleia, and his brief but memorable episcopate has left an indelible mark upon the life of the church in those regions. The metropolis became a notable centre of spiritual energy and enlightenment. The Bishop, aided by his nephew and his old colleague, the Archimandrite Elias Vlachopoulos, and by a staff of zealous preachers and *pneumatikoi* —both priests and laymen—showed how potent could be the example of a true pastor and father in God. Father Eusebius was often at

Patras during these years, and when his uncle died in 1902 there was a great and widespread desire that he should succeed him. On this occasion, however, as on every other, Father Eusebius declined all offers of ecclesiastical preferment. With the example of Hierotheos Metropoulos before his eyes he was in no danger of underestimating the influence that could be exercised by a bishop who was a saint in deed as well as in name; but he shrank from the heavy burden of administrative cares which would inevitably hinder the free exercise of that ministry of preaching and reconciliation to which God had called him.

After the death of Hierotheos Metropoulos, Father Eusebius spent a further five years in missionary journeys to every part of liberated Greece, and then, in 1907, came the foundation of the Brotherhood of Theologians, Zoë: a society organised on monastic lines which should, if God so willed, serve as a fit instrument for the continued regeneration of the Greek Church and for the extension of the work begun nearly seventy years before by Cosmas Phlamiatos and Ignatius Lambropoulos. A small house in an Athens suburb served as the headquarters of the new brotherhood; and here Father Eusebius gathered about him a little group of young theologians consisting of two priests and two laymen. In 1911 they commenced the publication of the journal Zoë, which was destined before long to extend the teaching of the movement to every diocese of the newly-liberated provinces of northern Greece.

From these modest beginnings there has sprung a movement which in the course of a little more than a generation has exercised a most powerful influence upon the life of the Greek Church. Through the preaching of the Zoë brothers and the many-sided activity of the movements which have grown up under their supervision, the religious life of many a town and village has been transformed beyond all recognition since the days when Apostolos Makrakes first preached in the public places of Athens, and the youthful Eusebius Matthopoulos pondered the writings of the ancient divines and swept the classrooms and corridors of the School of the Logos.

XII

THE BATTLE OF THE DEPTH

Η ΜΑΧΗ ΤΟΥ ΒΑΘΟΥΣ ΔΙΑ ΤΗΝ ΝΙΚΗΝ ΤΟΥ ΠΛΑΤΟΥΣ

MOTTO OF THE APOSTOLIC DIACONATE OF THESSALONICA

IT IS a good general rule in dealing with something that lies outside the experience of one's audience to attempt to describe it in terms of what is known and familiar. Father Michael Manousakes, Hierokeryx of the Sacred Metropolis of Drama, no doubt had some such maxim in mind when he introduced the present writer to an audience made up of members of his catechetical schools as "a *theologos* of the Oxford Movement: a movement which closely resembles out own Zoë Brotherhood". It must nevertheless be admitted that the compact, well-disciplined organisation into which the little brotherhood founded by Eusebius Matthopoulos in 1907 has since developed bears little apparent resemblance to the movement which was stirring in the Oriel S.C.R. during the eighteen-thirties.

The Brotherhood of Theologians, Zoë (to give the movement its proper title), now consists of some ninety men—all graduates, the great majority of the theological faculty of the University of Athens—about thirty of whom are in orders, the remainder laymen. The organisation of the brotherhood is monastic in character, though its members do not bind themselves by permanent vows and are at liberty to withdraw at any time. They must be unmarried—though a lay theologian who leaves the movement is free to marry—and property is held in common. The superior holds office for life (at the death of Father Eusebius in 1929 the Archimandrite Seraphim Papakostas was elected as his successor).

Seven priests and ten laymen were in the spring of 1950 resident in Athens, five other theologians in Salonica. At that time no less than twenty-seven members of the brotherhood (including seven priests) were serving as 'preachers' with the army, and another was acting as chaplain to the camp in Leros where boys who had fallen beneath the influence of the Communists were being given the opportunity to rediscover the fundamental loyalties within the setting of a Christian community. The remaining members of the brotherhood were dispersed amongst the dioceses of Greece, preaching, confessing the people, training young catechists and preachers, supervising seminaries for the country clergy, directing catechetical schools and youth movements: in these and many other ways building up the body of Christ in each village, town and diocese; seeking, above all, to follow in the steps of their founder by living in the power of the Holy Spirit that Christ might indeed be formed in them.

Every summer all the members of the brotherhood assemble for a period of retreat at Aghia Paraskevi (on the outskirts of Athens), and each is called upon to give an account of his labours during the previous year.

There can be little question that the most potent factor in the religious revival which has transformed the outward face of the Greek Church within the last 100 years has, under God, been the hidden life and apostolic labours of Eusebius Matthopoulos, and of the brotherhood he founded. The latter is still far the most important of the many missionary and evangelistic movements that have sprung up during the last two generations. The number and complexity of these movements is at first quite bewildering, and the visitor to Greece will need to spend a little time in Zoë circles before he can hope to avoid confounding $X.E.N.$ with $X.E.E.N.$, or to be able to distinguish with assurance between the spheres of activity appropriate to $X.M.O.$, $X.O.N.$, $X.\Phi.E.$, $X.E.E.$ and $X.E.E.\Lambda.$ respectively.

There are, on the one hand, all the movements more or less closely connected with the Zoë Brotherhood: some under the immediate supervision of the central organisation, others enjoying a measure of independence. On the other, there are several entirely separate movements which sprang up within the circle of clergy and laity who gathered about Apostolos Makrakes; and, finally, there are several vigorous organisations which have grown up in provincial centres such as Patras and Salonica and are still flourishing at the present time. A detailed account of all these movements would afford material for a substantial volume, and I propose to attempt no more within the limits of a single chapter than the most cursory description of their scope and general characteristics.

I have already referred to the movement known as *Anaplasis*. This was founded as early as 1887 by two lay disciples of Apostolos Makrakes: it is to the latter that it owes its primary characteristics. Its efforts were mainly directed to resisting, by means of preaching, lectures, and the publication of apologetic and philosophical writings, the spread of materialistic notions derived from western Europe. It was from the start a predominantly lay movement widely supported by theologians, philosophers, lawyers and university professors, as well as by many merchants and business men. Its journal formerly had a wide circulation in professional and academic circles and was issued, at first weekly and then fortnightly, right down to 1941.

During the eighteen-nineties the Anaplasis movement supported ten preachers who worked in the Athens-Piraeus region and also to some extent in the provinces. The Crown Prince Constantine was an honorary president, and amongst its most active members were the lawyer, John Skaltsounes (who is looked upon in Greece as a forerunner of the *Aktines* movement), and a Minister of Justice, Nicolas Demetrakopoulos, who, though not himself a trained theologian, was one of the first persons to devote his attention seriously to Christian apologetics. The real leader of the movement, however, was the lawyer and *hierokeryx*, Michael Galanos, and its final eclipse coincided with his death in 1948.

Father Eusebius and his associates collaborated with this movement for many years as preachers and contributors to its journal. Then came the foundation of the Zoë Brotherhood and the growth of a separate movement with its own periodical, and from this time onward the older association declined. It lingered on for many years: Archbishop Chrysostom Papadopoulos gave it his vigorous support from 1922 to 1938 (his brother was for a time its director), and it was not until quite recently that it was finally swallowed up in newer movements like *Aktines*, the home mission society known as *Apostolos Paulos*, and *Enoria*.

The Anaplasis movement was admirably equipped to meet the rationalist influence at work in Athens during the latter part of the nineteenth century; it was not able to adapt itself to the needs of a changing situation—hence its decline. From this pioneer association, however, there sprang two other movements, both of which have exercised a considerable influence during recent years. Both, it is interesting to note, were founded by parish priests. One (which is now under the direction of Father Angelos Nissiotes) has developed until it is second only to Zoë amongst the unofficial movements in the scope and importance of its activity. The other was the creation of a remarkable parish priest, Father George Makres, who was for many years in charge of the parish of St. Basil in the Piraeus. He it was who in the year 1896 first established catechetical schools (there had been earlier but unsuccessful attempts), and both in this field and in that of the formation of 'circles' or groups for the study of the Bible he was a distinguished pioneer. He also edited a religious journal bearing the title of *Anamorphosis* (Transformation). After his death in 1943 his work in the Piraeus was taken up by one of his numerous spiritual sons, the then Archimandrite Damaskenos Kotzias (now raised to the episcopate).

The second of these movements was founded in 1913 by Father Mark Tsaktanes and grew up about his parish church of St. Catherine. Like Father George, in the Piraeus, this married priest led the way in the organisation of catechetical schools (some schools which still flourish in our own day are his foundations), and of circles for the study of the Bible. When he died, his brother-in-law, Father Angelos Nissiotes, the priest in charge of the parish of the Life-Giving Source in the heart of Athens, carried on and greatly extended his work. The 'Orthodox Christian Unions' and catechetical schools under Father Angelos' direction are now extremely vigorous, and out of this movement have come some of the most interesting experiments of recent years.

An admirable example of the older movements which have grown up in the provincial towns of Greece is that known as the *'Apostoliki Diakonia* of Salonica', founded in 1928 by a lay theologian with the primary object of promoting the study of the holy scriptures among adults. In addition to this side of its work it had founded by 1949 some thirty-one catechetical schools, with a total membership of nearly 3,000 boys and girls. The teachers in these schools included students and professional men. From this movement there has sprung since the end of the occupation a smaller organisation of great interest. This is the 'School of Christ', the creation of the Archimandrite Timothy Papamichael. Its primary object is the training of preachers and lay evangelists. This task has been tackled with such energy that already by 1950 there were more than 120 members of the movement—mostly young men and women—at work in Salonica and the north of Greece.

This unofficial 'Apostolic Diaconate' has led the way in the creation of catechetical schools and small groups for Bible study in the northern dioceses, for it was not until 1936 that the Zoë Brotherhood established a centre in Salonica. The motto of this movement (which I have quoted at the head of this chapter), provides a key to much of the most notable work that is being done in Greece to-day; 'the victory of the width'—to give a literal translation of a phrase that cannot easily be put into English—ultimately depends upon the faithfulness and energy with which 'the battle of the depth' is waged. There can, in other words, be no fruitful outward activity that does not spring from a deepened interior life. It is only as the missioner himself is truly converted, only as he himself learns to dwell in Christ and as Christ is formed in him, that he can be used as an effective instrument for the conversion of others. Apart from this all his activity is in vain:

"As the branch cannot bear fruit of itself, except it abide in the vine; no more can ye, except ye abide in me. . . . If a man abide not in me, he is cast forth as a branch, and is withered; and men gather them, and cast them into the fire, and they are burned."

It augurs well for the future that the strenuous missionary activity now being undertaken in almost every town and diocese of Greece is so completely grounded in prayer and the study of the scriptures, finding its centre in the divine liturgy and the sacraments. The foundations are being well laid.

The full scope of the activity of the unofficial religious movements is perhaps most conveniently described if we consider in turn the chief instruments now being employed to bring about the regeneration of the Greek people in Christ. These include preaching, the mystery of confession, the organisation of catechetical schools, youth movements and study circles, the publication of Christian literature, and, finally, liturgical reform.

Preaching has from the outset been of primary importance. Cosmas Phlamiatos, Apostolos Makrakes and Eusebius Matthopoulos all relied upon the spoken *kerygma* as their most effective instrument. The theologian—whether cleric or layman—who serves on the staff of a provincial bishop is first and foremost the *hierokeryx*, the sacred herald, whose duty it is to assist the bishop in the ministry of the word. In the course of the last two generations there has been a tremendous revival of preaching—at any rate in the towns. Every parish church in Athens and the Piraeus now has a sermon at the Sunday liturgy—normally an exposition of the Gospel which immediately precedes it—

while in many churches and halls there are regular sermons at other times during the week.

In the country dioceses, owing to the shortage of qualified preachers, sermons are still all too rarely to be heard outside the cathedral towns. The bishop and the diocesan preacher, with such other assistants as can be mustered from local resources, will visit one or two villages every Sunday, but in a diocese of perhaps 100 scattered communities it may well be that months will pass without the majority of the people having the opportunity to hear a sermon. I remember one Macedonian 'saint', who had taken advantage of the cessation of fighting in his diocese from the spring of 1949 onwards to undertake an intensive preaching campaign, telling me that in some villages it was more than ten years since a sermon had last been heard.

An energetic *hierokeryx* will often perform wonders; take for instance this typical week-end itinerary of a lay theologian, a member of Zoë, who used to be stationed at Kozani; on Saturday afternoon by army truck to Amyntaion (a distance of about fifty-five kilometres) and thence to the village of Lechovo, an hour's journey to the westward towards Kastoria. Here he gives an evening address in the church, the greater part of the community present. On Sunday morning a sermon at the liturgy is followed by an address to the young men and women. After a hurried meal he sets off on foot to the neighbouring village of Skydro for an address, not this time in the church but in the square. Thence he climbs to the village of Nymphaion, high on the mountain-side, for two further addresses before nightfall—one in church, the other, for the young people, in the school. On Monday morning he proceeds by mule to Aetos and thence to Amyntaion and Kozani. The assistant *hierokeryx* of the diocese will in the meantime have set out for the *comopolis* of Servia to preach, from a cart standing in the midst of the square, to the crowds who have gathered there for the weekly market.

The Greek *hierokeryx* can in general assume in his hearers a knowledge of the fundamentals of the Christian faith such as can no longer be taken for granted in England, at any rate. He and they will speak a common language—even though many have forgotten the reality that lies behind the familiar phrases. The outward tokens of a Christian society have still survived to a remarkable degree—the fasts of the Church's year, for instance, are still observed as a matter of course by multitudes who would make no claim to piety above the average. In these circumstances it is understandable that contemporary preaching should (to accept the distinction now current in reforming circles) be practical rather than theoretical: should deal less with doctrine than with conduct.

Father Eusebius was wont to insist on the importance of ending every sermon with a clear and distinct conclusion, to bring home the particular moral and spiritual truth with which the preacher had been dealing to the conscience of his hearers, as well as on the need for preaching in a style suited to their condition. His example has been salutary, and in reforming circles to-day one never hears the type of homily still cultivated by a few eccentric saints who bewilder their silly sheep with florid discourses framed in the ornate periods of Psellos or Anna Comnena. I well recall a certain *hierokeryx*, a lovable if idiorrhythmic character, who modelled his festal homilies on the funeral orations of Bossuet (a much-thumbed volume that accompanied him everywhere). These triumphs of rhetoric, which must have left the Epirote peasantry groping in vain for any clear and distinct practical conclusion, would be composed months before the date of their delivery and constantly reworked and polished until they reached the requisite height of literary perfection. Such artistry would be frowned upon in the religious societies.

The work of the preacher is supplemented by that of the confessor. Although the mystery of confession has in practice fallen into sad neglect, owing to the shortage of qualified *pneumatikoi*, there has been no more effective instrument for the reawakening of the Greek Church; none that is more highly prized in reforming circles to-day. While east and west are at one as to the fundamental nature of this 'mystery', there is a certain difference of emphasis. Amongst the Greeks the element of 'ghostly counsel and advice' is far more prominent than is commonly the case amongst western Christians. So marked is this difference of emphasis that Dr. Covel—who is as immoderate in his assaults upon the Romish doctrine of auricular confession as upon any other of the 'seven pretended sacraments'—is yet moved to applaud the Greek practice as a pious and laudable institution: such a confession, he remarks, or rather (lest there should be any misunderstanding) "serious Conference or Discourse as this with a Ghostly Father, or discreet Minister, is justly observed and commended by our own Church".

In these circumstances it is natural that considerably more importance should be attached to the personal character and qualifications of the confessor amongst the Greeks than in the west. The power to bind and to loose is given by the laying on of hands: the grace of the wise director of souls is conferred only upon a few, and is normally the fruit of great personal holiness and wide experience. Throughout Orthodox Christendom there has been a tendency to demand a high degree of perfection before authorising a priest to exercise the ministry of the confessor: one must oneself become a *spirituel* before aspiring to the office of a *père spirituel*.

The number of confessors at work in Greece to-day is still very small. In the country districts, in particular, this sacrament is still largely neglected. The ministry of the *pneumatikos* is nevertheless a factor of the very greatest importance in the present revival, and one which is held in the highest estimation, within the voluntary movements and the official Apostoliki Diakonia alike.

While preaching and the mystery of confession have thus been restored to something approaching their rightful place within the life of the Greek Church after long years of neglect, the leaders of the new movements have forged other weapons to meet the peculiar needs of the time. Chief amongst them must be mentioned the catechetical schools and Christian unions which are now so prominent a feature of Greek church life.

The creation of catechetical schools was essayed as early as the eighteen-seventies, but unsuccessfully, and it was the married priests George Makres and Mark Tsaktanes who were the real pioneers in this field. By the late 'twenties there were many catechetical schools flourishing in Athens and the Piraeus, especially under the direction of Father Angelos Nissiotes, who had taken over the movement founded by Father Mark at the latter's death in 1924. The Zoë Brotherhood (which had by this time emerged triumphant from two further attacks by suspicious hierarchs, and had also survived the premature death of one of the first and most ardent disciples of its founder, the Archimandrite Dionysios Pharazoules), first turned its attention to the organisation of catechetical schools in 1926. From this time onward these schools begin to establish themselves until at the present day Zoë alone has well over 600 under its supervision, and the movement of Father Angelos some 350, not to mention hundreds of others now flourishing in every part of Greece.

These schools (which are directed almost entirely by lay men and women) afford a systematic course of instruction in Christian doctrine and practice for boys and girls between the ages of nine and twenty-two. These children have all, it must be borne in mind, been full communicant members of the Church since infancy. There are no confirmation classes in Greece, and, within the new movements at least, the period of adolescence, when so overwhelming a proportion of our own children lose all vital contact with the Church, is commonly that at which the young Greek Christian begins to play an active part in the life of his local community.

The size of the catechetical schools, even in the provincial towns of northern Greece (where such schools were not founded until the late 'thirties and had hardly established themselves when these districts were overwhelmed by foreign occupation and Communist sedition) is often quite staggering. The figures for the town of Kilkis—a few miles north of Salonica and the scene of some of the bloodiest massacres of the whole war—may serve as an illustration. During the year 1948–49, when the war with the Communists was at its height, membership of the catechetical schools was as follows:

	Boys	Girls
Junior schools	782	696
Middle schools	165	180
Senior schools	55	77
Young workers	123	293
	1125	1246

These are the figures for a Macedonian market town whose pre-war population scarcely exceeded 7,000. Even allowing for the fact that several hundreds of the children belonging to the catechetical schools in 1948–49 were refugees from the villages of the diocese, they show the astonishing development of these new Christian schools within a bare ten or eleven years.

Remarkable as these figures may seem they are by no means exceptional. All over Greece catechetical schools have sprung up as it were overnight and multiplied with incredible rapidity, despite the lack of trained leaders. At Kilkis the metropolitan had the assistance of one priest-theologian. In the adjoining diocese of Siderokastro, where the bishop had only a seminary-trained preacher to help him, and where catechetical schools were in September, 1949, quite a recent innovation, membership of the schools, in a town considerably smaller than Kilkis, had already risen to 957 and was increasing rapidly. In and around Salonica the number of catechetical schools under the supervision of the Zoë Brotherhood rose from less than thirty in 1942 to 170 in 1949.

The catechetical school normally meets every Sunday, and the teaching is based on one of the two courses now in circulation—the first issued by the Zoë Brotherhood, the second (only recently published) by the official Home Mission. While the parallels with our own Sunday Schools and 'catechisms' are evident, these Greek schools have a character which is all their own. Particularly impressive is the stimulus which is given to the active apostolate of the laity. The children are from their earliest days encouraged to pull their weight in the life of the local *ekklesia*. At Verroia, in the spring of 1950, boys of nine were visiting the townsfolk and delivering letters from the *hierokeryx* of the metropolis. At Salonica, where the catechetical schools under the auspices of the Apostoliki Diakonia were normally directed by a student of the theological faculty of the university, the teacher would at the end of a lesson despatch his pupils, two by two, to call at the homes of any who through sickness or for some other cause had been unable to be present that day. When the defaulter was run to earth he would be given a brief *résumé* of the afternoon's lesson.

The catechetical schools form the base of an impressive structure still in process of creation. In describing the Christian youth movements that now flourish in almost every diocese of Greece I will start with those connected with the Zoë Brotherhood, which are the most important. The reader will recall that as early as 1877 Father Eusebius (then chaplain to the School of the Logos) was experimenting with small groups of young people and adults, and such *omades* have played an important part in the extension of his teaching and influence.

First, then, the movement known as *X.M.O.* (*Christianikai Mathetikai Omades*). This is made up of selected members of the catechetical schools between the ages of fifteen and eighteen. Its members try to bring others to the catechetical schools, to spread sound sacramental teaching, to distribute Christian publications and generally to set a high standard of conduct by their example. Each group consists of from fifteen to twenty members, meets once or twice a week and is led by an undergraduate (at any rate in Athens and Salonica).

These student-leaders are drawn from another youth organisation known as the 'Christian Union of Students', or *X.Φ.E.* (*Christianiki Phoitetiki Enosis*), founded in 1933, membership of which is confined to undergraduates of the two universities. The movement is sub-divided into 'circles' which meet every week for Bible study. Members of this organisation often preach in village churches in the vicinity of Athens and Salonica, and teams of students undertake missions in the country dioceses. About 1946 there was created a further youth movement, the 'Christian Union of Young Workers' (*Christianiki Enosis Ergazomenon Neon*, or *X.E.E.N.*) This had spread to most of the chief towns of Greece within three years of its foundation and is growing fast. It is organised in factories and workshops much as *X.Φ.E.* in the universities, in 'circles'—one would be tempted to say 'cells' had the word not acquired associations which would be misleading in the present context. The age limits for this movement are seventeen to twenty-five. Many of its members are at present serving in the army.

These three youth movements, *X.M.O.*, *X.Φ.E.*, and *X.E.E.N.*, are all under the direction of the Zoë Brotherhood. Amongst other organisations for young men and girls, too numerous to describe in detail, several demand special mention. I have already referred to the 'Christian Union of Young People' (*X.O.N.*) that flourishes in the Piraeus. From the movement of Father Angelos Nissiotes there has sprung up in recent years a 'Student Christian Association' which meets every week under the guidance of Professor Bratsiotes, for the study of the Bible. Membership of this extremely lively group is confined to university men and women: it includes some of the ablest of the younger theologians, and has taken the lead in co-operating with the Oecumenical Institute in Switzerland and with the World Student Christian Federation.

Other vigorous youth organisations are to be found attached to several parish churches in Athens—notably at the church of the Prophet Elias, Pankrati, where the then Archimandrite Timothy Matthaiakes (now assistant bishop of Salonica) built up an extremely interesting movement—while many a provincial town has become a centre for similar activities.

It would, however, be a mistake to suppose that membership of the voluntary movements is confined to young men and girls. Their scope is far wider. As a lay theologian of the Zoë Brotherhood once said to me, it is scarcely an exaggeration to claim that the various Christian unions now make provision for every man or woman from the cradle to the grave. Many of the youth movements have in fact sprung from older associations which were intended in the first place for adults. This was so in the case of the Apostoliki Diakonia of Salonica, for instance, and it was not until nearly twenty years after its foundation that Zoë turned its attention to the development of catechetical schools.

So far as Zoë organisations are concerned, the young man or woman who outgrows $X.\Phi.E.$ or $X.E.E.N.$ may pass to one of the three movements known collectively as $\Sigma.X.\Sigma.$ (*Synergazomena Christianika Somateia*) One of these is for parents, another for teachers. The third, the 'Christian Union of Scientists' ($X.E.E.$) founded in 1935, membership of which is open to all sorts of professional men, is of considerable importance. This is the movement responsible for the publication of the fortnightly journal *Aktines*, and, moreover, for the remarkable volume entitled *Towards a Christian Civilisation* which was published in Greek and English in 1947. It is in Aktines circles that the pioneer labours of Makrakes and his associates who founded the Anaplasis movement have come to fruition.

Until quite recently $X.E.E.$ was confined to Athens. Now, however, there is a lively branch in Salonica and little groups of professional men are being formed in many provincial towns of Greece. One such town, which I visited early in 1950, had a 'circle' whose members included the mayor, the doctor, the dentist, the commanding officer of the gendarmerie and two lawyers. All these would meet once a week, together with the preacher of the metropolis (a priest of the Zoë Brotherhood), to study the Bible and to discuss the bearing of their faith upon the life of their community. Such a movement abounds in promise. Not the least interesting feature of the Aktines wing of the Zoë organisation is the prominent part that many distinguished professors of the science faculties of the universities have played in the leadership of this Christian movement.

Apart from the Christianika Somateia there are several other movements which have grown up under the supervision of the Zoë Brotherhood: the home mission association known as *Apostolos Paulos*, which was founded three years before the death of Father Eusebius and has an admirable centre in the very heart of Athens; the *Eusebeia* sisterhood, which organises catechetical schools, trains certain of its members as nurses, and publishes a periodical for children. There are, besides, several educational establishments in Athens and the Piraeus, hostels for university students in Athens and Salonica, and a Young Workers' centre at Agrinion which includes an orphanage, a hospital (where the nurses are members of the Eusebeia sisterhood), and a group of workshops. All this has sprung from the little brotherhood which Father Eusebius gathered about him in 1907.

I have made no mention of many other voluntary movements which now flourish in Athens and its suburbs: movements like the 'Christian Corner', the 'Christian Social Union' and the association known as the 'Three Hierarchs'. All these were founded by lay people and have remained wholly lay in character. Their members include many distinguished men and women; their activities are both evangelistic and philanthropic.

No account of the evangelistic activity of recent years can ignore the part played by Christian literature, both periodicals and books. Almost every movement has at least one periodical of its own, and the circulation of these weekly and fortnightly papers is astonishingly large for a country where most of the inhabitants devote little time to reading, and where (even in the universities) oral instruction still predominates. The periodical *Zoë*, for example, which has been issued weekly since 1911, now has more than 100,000 subscribers. Several of the provincial movements publish excellent periodicals which circulate all over Greece; such for instance is the journal *Apolytrosis*, published every month by the Apostoliki Diakonia of Thessaloniki, which has a circulation of about 12,000 copies. The 'School of Christ' in the same city also publishes monthly papers, devoted to scriptural exegesis, which are used by many preachers. Both Zoë and the Christian Unions of Father Nissiotes publish periodicals for children.

In the field of book production, as elsewhere, the Zoë Brotherhood has led the way, and the exhibition held in Athens in January, 1950, was an impressive monument to the diligence with which the written word has been cultivated in recent years. Father Eusebius himself wrote many books during the last twenty years of his life, and his *magnum opus*, *The Destiny of Man*, has exercised untold influence. Amidst a wealth of books covering almost every field of Christian literature I would pay special tribute to the work of the brotherhood in publishing the text of the New Testament and the Septuagint in moderately-priced editions well printed on good paper. The Zoë pocket edition of the New Testament has had an enormous circulation.

Of liturgical reform I have already had occasion to speak. Its primary object is to enable the laity to participate more fully and intelligently in the eucharistic action, through more frequent communion (Father Eusebius was himself in the habit of celebrating daily), and through a greater 'openness' in the manner of celebrating the holy mysteries. In Athens and Salonica many people now follow the services in the little manual of the Archimandrite Seraphim Papakostas—the popularity of which may be judged by the fact that it had reached its fifth edition by 1950. In general, where the new movements have exercised an effective influence, a high standard of liturgical propriety prevails, though it must be confessed that certain musical innovations of recent years have been unfortunate, to say the least.

*

All the movements of which I have been speaking have remained quite unofficial in character, though they have always carried out their work with the blessing of the ecclesiastical authorities and under the general supervision of the local bishop. There has of late, however, been a development of a rather different nature, so important as to demand brief consideration. This is what amounts to the refounding of a body known as the 'Apostolic Diaconate of the Church of Greece', which came into being as long ago as 1930. I do not propose to dwell upon its fortunes prior to its virtual reconstitution: suffice it to say that although great potentialities were latent in this organisation from the outset, its actual activity during the first fifteen years of its life was on a very small scale. It is directed by a council of members of the Holy Synod and professors of the theological faculty of the University of Athens under the presidency of the Archbishop, with Professor Basil Vellas as general director.

The aim of this official organisation is to systematise and co-ordinate the many-sided missionary activity now being undertaken throughout the length and breadth of Greece. In addition to its headquarters at Moni Petraki in Athens it has a local office in every diocese, and is assured of a basis of material resources by a system of annual diocesan contributions.

The possibilities inherent in such a venture are without question very great, and already much has been accomplished. A theological hostel and a school for preachers and confessors have been established at Moni Petraki: the latter promises to be of the greatest service in the training of men for work in the provinces. The new movement has taken up and extended almost every type of evangelistic work developed by the voluntary associations. Its activity in the field of publishing has been particularly notable, and has been greatly extended by the setting up of a modern printing press at Moni Petraki in December, 1951. The official journal of the Church of Greece as well as new periodicals for the parish clergy and for the family are printed on this press.

Amongst the projects which the Apostoliki Diakonia hopes to carry out within the next few years is the creation of a 'spiritual centre' just outside Athens, which will include a training college for deaconesses, a hostel for girls studying in the theological faculty of the university, and a model high school, all grouped about a church. Other model schools are to be set up in Tenos and Patras. Like the voluntary movements, the official Apostolic Diaconate supports preachers working in the country dioceses and organises catechetical schools. It seems probable that many of the smaller voluntary movements that flourish in the provinces will before long be absorbed by the official Home Mission with its centralised organisation and unrivalled material resources.

In the case of the more important voluntary associations, however, the position is rather different. The Zoë Brotherhood, above all, now has a highly developed organisation peculiar to itself, and while the movement's ultimate aims are in no sense incompatible with those of the official Home Mission, it has acquired a very marked spirit and tradition of its own. Though the days when members of the brotherhood could be tried for false teaching and *kakodoxia* are long since past, and its preachers and confessors stand high in the estimation of the ordinary people, Zoë still has many bitter opponents. The brotherhood is still young and it would be surprising had it escaped altogether from the growing pains of youth. Not all of its members have been endowed with the surpassing gentleness and mature discretion of its founder; in denouncing the evils of the times they have sometimes shown a spirit that recalls Apostolos Makrakes rather than Father Eusebius.

The voluntary movements have, it must be confessed, borrowed somewhat unwarily from the west. Their influence in the field of eikonography, for example, has been deplorable: the wonderful traditions of the Greek Church have been utterly abandoned in favour of feeble imitations of the effete and secularised religious art of Latin Christendom. Here, at least, the Apostoliki Diakonia has set a most courageous example and one can only hope that the work of Photis Kontoglou, somewhat mannered though it is, may mark the beginnings of return to a tradition that had not wholly perished in the remoter provinces of Greece when the dominion of the Turk was overthrown.

When all is said, however, the fact remains that the Zoë Brotherhood has, under God, been the most potent factor in the spiritual awakening of the Greek people during the last two generations, and the traveller who would form a just estimate of the present situation will, if he is wise, take the trouble to gain a first-hand acquaintance with the labours of this remarkable movement and to enter into its spirit before he pays heed to the strictures of its critics.

One can readily understand the desire of the ecclesiastical authorities to systematise and co-ordinate the evangelistic activity of the voluntary associations: even in reforming circles to-day one is frequently reminded of the saying 'every Greek a *kapetanios!*' It is, however, no less important to remember that the marvellous work of these unofficial bodies has sprung from the consecrated life and example of a handful of men who had given themselves wholly to God that His power might be manifested in them, and it may well be that the new Home Mission will have to learn by bitter experience the lesson that 'the victory of the width' is given only to those who have fought 'the battle of the depth' and have prevailed: the regeneration of the Greek people in Christ will not be brought about through legislation and centralised planning alone.

XIII

TRAINING FOR THE MINISTRY

> For a priest ought not only to be pure, as being honoured
> with so great a ministry. He should also be very intelligent,
> and experienced in many affairs, and even equally skilful in
> all secular business with those who are engaged in it, while
> he must yet be more entirely detached from the love of it
> than anchorites who resort to the mountains.
>
> ST. JOHN CHRYSOSTOM

> Let mariners learn astronomy; merchants' factors study
> arithmetic; surveyors get them geometry; spectacle-makers
> optic; landleapers geography; town-clerks rhetoric; what
> should he do with a spade, that hath no ground to dig;
> or they with learning that have no use of it?
>
> ROBERT BURTON
> *The Anatomy of Melancholy*

IN THE many-sided activity of the voluntary movements the
parish clergy, with two or three distinguished exceptions, have as yet
played little part. The whole weight of the burden has been borne by
the laity and the celibate clergy. To-day, however, it is widely realised
that the incalculable spiritual gains of the last two generations or so
can be consolidated and made available for the whole of the Greek
Church only through the patient labours of an enlightened and devoted
parochial ministry: the function of the itinerant confessor, the lay
theologian and the catechist is essentially complementary to that of the
parish priest; it is upon the latter that the responsibility for the building
up of the local church must ultimately rest. Hence the concern for
the raising of the prevailing standards of clerical education which one
finds among those who are most deeply concerned with the strengthening
and purifying of Greek church life at the present time.

For it is not only in the westernised circles of Kolonaki and Kephissia
that the word *papas* is liable to evoke a faintly contemptuous smile,
nor is it the hostile critic of the Greek Church who most vehemently

bewails the ignorance of her parish clergy. In 1920 only 805 married priests, out of a total number of nearly 4,500, had received any education beyond that afforded by the elementary schools; and although matters have somewhat improved during the course of a generation, it must be admitted that, in the urban parishes at any rate, the level of clerical education has not risen in the same degree as among the generality of the people. The average parish priest is lamentably ill-equipped for meeting the assaults of rationalism or for coming to the aid of a young man troubled by intellectual difficulties: "But as for the Bulk of their Clergy", says Covel, ". . . I do positively assert that they are in general profoundly ignorant in these points; and not one of a thousand amongst the ordinary *Papas*, or common Priests, knows any thing of the matter." It is not, alas, always possible to conjure up at will a learned monk or lay theologian well grounded in the science of the schools.

It is possible, indeed, to exaggerate the evils of the prevailing system. In a country where small rural communities still predominate there is not a little to be said in favour of a priesthood of peasant-farmers and craftsmen. Whatever the deficiencies of his intellectual equipment, the Greek country parson is not separated from the people to whom he ministers by a different cultural background—as is so frequently the case in western Europe to-day.

Provided always that the priest's education is at least as good as that of the people to whom he is called to minister, the less it differs from theirs as to its general characteristics the better—at any rate in a country where Christianity is still a living tradition and education has not been secularised. During the long centuries of Turkish dominion, when "the ancient Structures and Colleges of Athens were become ruinous, and only a fit habitation for its own Owle, and all Greece poor and illiterate", the faith was preserved less through the learning of its champions (though even in the darkest days of oppression there were always a few theologians and monks to keep alive the traditions of Hellenic scholarship) than through the passionate devotion of a people, ill-instructed enough, but for whom all that was requisite to salvation was mysteriously set forth in the Church's liturgy, in the recurring cycle of feast and fast. "It is admirable", wrote Rycaut, "to see and consider with what Constancy, Resolution, and Simplicity, ignorant and poor men keep their Faith."

Notwithstanding considerations such as these, however, the fact remains that the provision of a more adequate training for the parish clergy is perhaps the most urgent problem which the Greek Church has to face at the present time. Great efforts are already being made. Nobody who was in touch with ecclesiastical affairs during the years which followed the occupation could fail to be impressed by the energy with which the founding of new seminaries for the country clergy was pursued. The courage with which the problem was then tackled is already beginning to bear fruit in the mountain dioceses of Macedonia and elsewhere, but a vast amount of work remains to be done.

The reader will recall that the Greek parish priest must be at least thirty years of age at his ordination. There is much to be said in support of this rule; it does, however, together with the canons relating to clerical marriage, raise very grave practical problems as to the training of the clergy. These are particularly acute in the case of the so-called 'Hieratic Schools', seven of which were flourishing in 1950. These ecclesiastical boarding schools, normally with a priest-monk as director assisted by three or four lay theologians, are open to boys who have completed their course at an ordinary elementary school. A boy will normally remain at the hieratic school until he is eighteen or nineteen, but only a very small proportion of those who stay the course are eventually ordained. A few will decide against marriage and will be made deacons shortly after completing their studies—perhaps going on to the theological school at Athens or Salonica. These, however, form a small minority, and very few of the remaining students will be ordained. Some will marry, and become teachers of theology or the classics in secondary schools; some will attach themselves to episcopal households as secretaries or lay preachers. Far the greater number, however, drift into more or less secular occupations, and while it is doubtless admirable that there should be tobacco merchants and bank clerks who are not merely well grounded in theology but can quote Chrysostom and Nazianzen with as great a facility as any clerk in holy orders, it is understandable that the bishops should lament the fact that so few of those educated at the ecclesiastical secondary schools offer themselves for ordination.

It would seem that if the parish priest is to be given any theological education over and above that which every Greek boy acquires in his village school and in his home, he must be sent back to school after following some secular calling for twelve years or more, or even after having been in orders for many years. Hence the establishment of the

'Ecclesiastical Seminaries' (*Ekklesiastika Phrontisteria*) some fourteen of which are now in existence. One of these, the Rizareion Ecclesiastical School at Athens, stands apart from the rest; it celebrated its centenary during the occupation and was for many years the sole institution of its kind in all Greece. Most of these seminaries, however, were founded within the last twenty years. The dioceses of Old Greece are now served by seminaries at Corinth, Patras and Pyrgos, in the Peloponnese, and at Lamia, Larissa and Volos. Crete has its own seminary. At Ioannina there is another older foundation, the *Hierodidaskaleion Vellas* (of which the present Archbishop of Athens was once director) which serves the whole of Epirus. The parish clergy of Thrace and eastern Macedonia can now attend courses at Xanthi (founded in 1945), at Aghia Anastasis in the Chalkidiki peninsula, or at Salonica, where there is a 'higher' seminary. Another post-war foundation at Kozani, in western Macedonia, may serve to illustrate the general characteristics of these training schools for country clergy. This seminary was subsequently transferred to Florina.

The Lower Ecclesiastical Seminary of the Metropolis of Kozani, as it was known locally, was founded in 1946, during the lull which followed the Varkiza agreement. The director was a lay theologian, a member of the Zoë Brotherhood, and the seminary was under the immediate supervision of the Metropolitan of Servia and Kozani. During the first few months after its foundation there were no fewer than ninety students in residence, drawn from several different dioceses. Many had to leave, however, as fighting became general during the course of the following year and the refugees again flocked to the towns. By the winter of 1948–49, when the situation in the country dioceses was at its worst and the whole parochial organisation threatened to collapse, only twenty-five students remained. With the suppression of the Communist sedition, and the return of some measure of security, the number slowly increased again, and by March, 1950 (when I last visited the seminary), it had risen to thirty-five.

Only three of these students were laymen, sent by their bishops to the seminary for a pre-ordination course—all three were over thirty years of age. The rest were parish clergy, some of whom had been in orders for many years. They had come not only from the diocese of Kozani but from many different districts of northern Greece. The dioceses along the western fringes of Macedonia —Grevena, Kastoria and Florina—were particularly well represented, but there were other students from places as far distant as Drama and Katerini. A candidate for the two-year course which the seminary provided must have reached the fourth class of his elementary school: an event which in the case of certain of the more venerable amongst these bewhiskered scholars must have been more than a generation remote from their reappearance *in statu pupillari*.

The programme of studies, as at all these lower seminaries, was eminently practical and was related at every point to the peculiar circumstances within which the Greek country parson exercises his priestly ministry. It was grounded, as is fitting, "in the Book of books, the store-house and magazine of life and comfort, the Holy Scriptures," and, in particular, in the study of the text of the Gospels. The director was assisted by another lay theologian, the preacher of the diocese. Their lectures on the Bible, doctrine, catechising, the holy canons and liturgical matters, were supplemented by instruction in the ecclesiastical chant (given by the chief singer of the metropolis), and by talks on the rudiments of first-aid from a local doctor: for the country parson does not merely "condescend to the knowledge of tillage and pasturage"; he desires to be all to his parish, and "not only a pastor but also a physician". A little medical knowledge does indeed constitute an invaluable addition to the skills of a country priest in a region where the only known medicaments are aspirins and ouzo, and doctors are as rare as dissenters.

The seminary at Kozani was housed in a rambling, somewhat dilapidated building adjoining the church of SS. Cosmas and Damian. Its furnishing and equipment were simple in the extreme. Twice a day the lecture-room was transformed into a refectory. The students slept seven or eight to a room on straw mattresses laid on the bare boards, and St. Benedict's maxim: *stramenta . . . sufficiant matta, sagum et lena et capitale*, was observed by all alike.

The liturgical life of the seminary was centred in the church which lies on the other side of the courtyard. The whole community assembled twice daily to sing the divine office, and on Sundays and holy days the liturgy was celebrated. Those amongst the students who lived within easy distance of Kozani used to go home every Saturday and return on Monday morning after celebrating the holy mysteries in their own parish churches. They used also to go to their villages for the great festivals. In other cases some temporary provision would be made for the parishes concerned: the late Metropolitan of Grevena, for example, would allow only one parish priest from each group of three inhabited villages to be away from his flock at any given time. In such circumstances it was not always possible for a priest to complete the full course at the seminary, and many had to be content with twelve months at Kozani.

Despite all these difficulties, however, the seminary had already, by the spring of 1950, established itself as a real centre of pastoral and liturgical teaching in the dioceses of western Macedonia, and its influence could be detected in several score of parishes dispersed throughout this barren region. In remote hamlets of northern Pindos, catechetical schools were flourishing for the first time under the direction of a priest trained at Kozani. The holy sacrifice was being offered week by week with renewed fervour in many a village church; and there were not a few country parsons (not all of them young men) who had gone back to their parishes after spending two years at the seminary with a quickened realisation of the high dignity of their calling.

Not all the clergy, it is hardly necessary to add, are as yet fully convinced of the utility of the new training school. I well recall meeting one old gentleman who was highly indignant at his metropolitan's suggestion that he might profitably spend a year or two at Kozani, and who maintained with some heat that after thirty-three years in the sacred ministry he could learn only "from the Lord". There has been much hilarity in many a rural tavern that some grave *papas* should have been sent back to school for a couple of years. It will doubtless be a long time before these seminaries for parish clergy (which are still something of an innovation) win universal acceptance and approval, and it would be idle to pretend that they offer a wholly satisfactory solution to the problem of how best to train married priests not ordained till many years after they have completed their ordinary schooling.

The seminaries do, nevertheless, meet an urgent need, and it is to be hoped that they will exert an ever increasing influence upon the country dioceses of Greece, and will send forth into the villages a steady stream of true pastors—men who are not "witty, or learned, or eloquent, but *holy*"—for in Greece, as in other countries, that is perhaps the greatest need of all.

*

As I stressed in an earlier chapter, the Greek clergy fall into two sharply defined categories: on the one hand the married *papades*, on the other the celibate clergy from whose ranks the chief ministers of the Church are normally chosen. In the training of the former book-learning plays but little part. The seminaries aim at providing no more than an elementary grounding in pastoralia for a race of craftsmen and peasant-farmers who, with few exceptions, are more at home with a plough than a pen, and are wholly unequipped for academic pursuits. The higher clergy, however, are almost invariably graduates, well versed in the disputations of the schools.

While the married clergy receive their training in the seminaries, the potential bishop is fashioned in the theological schools of the universities of Athens and Salonica. The theological faculty of the northern university was established only a few years ago. In former days many of the higher Greek clergy went to the theological academy at Halki, near Constantinople: a celebrated institution which, in the days of its prosperity, attracted students from every part of the Orthodox world. After the first world war, however, this sank to the level of a provincial seminary, and it is only in recent years (under the guiding hand of a new Oecumenical Patriarch) that it has regained something of its old prestige. Thus, the great majority of the present Greek bishops and archimandrites are graduates of the University of Athens.

In considering the place occupied by the theological schools of the universities within the framework of training for the ministry, it must not be forgotten that the clergy account for only a small proportion of the students of these faculties, far the greater number of whom are lay men and women (there are quite a few girls amongst the theological students of Athens and Salonica, and their number is steadily increasing). In the universities, moreover, as in the seminaries and the ecclesiastical schools, the majority of the teaching staff are laymen. The only cleric among the Athens professors—the Archimandrite B. Stephanides (whose *Ecclesiastical History* seems likely to be a standard work for every Greek student for many years to come)—retired in 1950 and was succeeded by a layman; while at Salonica likewise, only the professor of ecclesiastical history—an archimandrite who was formerly in charge of the Greek church in Paris—is in orders. Although the lay theologian has a long and distinguished ancestry in eastern Christendom and is often a man of deep spirituality, it can nevertheless be a trifle startling to hear a layman lecturing, to an audience which includes experienced priests and *pneumatikoi*, on the mystery of confession.

The university course normally lasts four years. The theology of the schools is characterised for the most part by a somewhat arid academic-ism. During the nineteenth century a theologian who went abroad for post-graduate studies went almost as a matter of course to Germany; and, although this is no longer so, the shadow of Harnack still lies across the threshold of the theological school at Athens. "Berlin, Leipzig, Jena, Halle, etc.", wrote Dr. Adrian Fortescue in 1907, "are full of Greek students, who with the versatility of their race, very soon learn to talk German perfectly, and to think and argue about theological questions like German higher critics!"

Greek academic theology, though distinguished by great technical competence and erudition, and considerable familiarity with the critical work which one associates with the German schools of the latter part of last century, is largely deficient in those qualities which have made the work of certain Russian theologians of the diaspora of such absorbing interest for the western Christian. The Greek theologian, while he has benefited incalculably by his scientific training in the schools of Germany, has scarcely as yet been forced back upon his own proper tradition by the pressure of an alien environment. With few exceptions, moreover, he is curiously out of touch with recent tendencies in western theological thinking: often he seems to be a generation behind the times, unaware that critical theories no longer hold the field in the schools of Paris and Oxford—not to mention Geneva.

How long this state of affairs will last it is difficult to say. The present isolation is not hard to understand if one takes into account the effect of the war years and the lack of contact—even on the in-tellectual level—between the Greek professors and those Roman Catholic scholars whose work has been so important for the west during the past decade, and whose exchanges with certain Russian theologians have proved so mutually rewarding. It may well be that the links now being forged between Athens and Paris—and in particular with the Russian Academy of St. Sergius—are of crucial importance for the future. At present, it must be confessed, the transition from the theological climate of Orthodox Paris to that of the Athenian schools is apt to be somewhat disappointing to the Frankish *theologos* to whom a first glimpse of the wholeness of Orthodoxy has come as the revelation of a long-forgotten realm. The theology of the schools seems to be earthbound and wholly academic: a theology of the manuals which bears little relation to holy living.

The theoretical character of much contemporary Greek theology has had regrettable consequences for the development of the new movements, with which the theological schools have, in general, little vital connexion—although more than one professor of the theological faculty at Athens has played an important rôle in their work and organisation. In many quarters—and especially, perhaps, within Zoë circles—a sense of the apparent irrelevance of this theoretical science to practical piety has given rise to an impatience with all theological questions. We must, it is said, be *practical*—and this theology of the schools is not practical; it is a theoretical science wholly unrelated to the urgent problems which are the daily concern of the preacher and the confessor. Such an attitude cannot but strike one as curiously out of place in an Orthodox *milieu* and is not without its dangers.

A few of the clergy go abroad to continue their studies after graduating from the Greek theological schools. Many a young layman is sent to western Europe or America for post-graduate study in the hope that upon his return to Greece he will offer himself for ordination; but a first acquaintance with ecclesiastical conditions very different from those to which he has been accustomed (particularly in the matter of the status of the married clergy and their field of activity) can easily have an unsettling effect upon the potential *despotes*, and it is not unknown for a young graduate, not conscious of a very definite call to the celibate life, to waver in his first resolve of becoming a priest, after two or three years in England or America.

Apart from the minority who go abroad after leaving the university, the celibate clergy normally pass immediately to an episcopal household without further study. Until quite recently there was nothing in Greece comparable to the English theological college. Since the war, however, there has been opened in Athens an establishment which approximates in some measure to the English institution. This is the 'School for Preachers' which is housed in the hostel of the Apostoliki Diakonia: a fine modern building occupying two sides of the quadrangle at Moni Petraki and overlooking the garden of the British School of Archaeology. Though completed some years ago, it was long requisitioned as a military hospital, and it was not until the early part of 1950 that the whole building was made available to the Church.

The School for Preachers provides a two-year course of study (primarily of a pastoral character) for men who have already graduated from the theological school of the university. In 1950 a considerable number of the students were experienced preachers and confessors from the provinces, but in the years to come they will normally consist in the main of young graduates of the theological school. The primary aim of this school is to equip priests (and lay theologians) for work in the dioceses, and it promises to be of the greatest service to the Church of Greece.

The same building serves as a hostel for theological students who live at some distance from Athens and who would otherwise be dispersed in lodgings (though some find a home in one of the hostels of the Zoë Brotherhood). All the inhabitants—theological students as well as those belonging to the School for Preachers—share a common life, with morning and evening prayers, and meals taken together in the refectory on the coenobitic pattern. Now that the theological faculty of the university is attracting students from Ethiopia and America, as well as from the autocephalous Church of Cyprus, and the Apostoliki Diakonia is offering generous hospitality to occasional Frankish visitors and a student or two from the Russian Academy in Paris, this community is fast acquiring an oecumenical character such as belonged to Halki in the day of its fame.

The theological faculty at Salonica, as I mentioned earlier, is of recent foundation. Despite the difficulties of the times, however, it is now in full vigour and holds out very great promise to the sorely-tried and understaffed dioceses of northern Greece. It is greatly to be hoped that it will prove possible before long to set up at Salonica an institution similar to that now flourishing in Athens, and combining the functions of a post-graduate theological college and a hostel for theological students from the outlying provinces. Many of these students at present have some difficulty in maintaining themselves for the period of their studies, and comparatively few can be accommodated in the new hostel of the Zoë Brotherhood or in the little hostel maintained for several years in the face of tremendous material difficulties by the Apostoliki Diakonia of Salonica.

At present there is an acute shortage of educated clergy in these the more remote provinces of Greece. Few dioceses have more than one priest-theologian and in some *eparchiai* the metropolitan is single-handed. In such circumstances preaching and the mystery of penance are inevitably much neglected. Not a few amongst the bishops of these northern dioceses are advocates of some kind of 'direction' of the educated clergy which would counteract the prevailing current which sweeps away so inordinate a number of archimandrites to Athens and its suburbs, leaving the mountain dioceses wretchedly short of trained theologians.

It is interesting to note that the present Archbishop of Athens has recently been moved by the continuing shortage of clergy of all classes in the outlying districts of Greece to conscript from amongst the clergy of the Athens-Piraeus area a 'Sacred Company', consisting of fifty archimandrites, for a 'Spiritual Campaign' (*Pneumatike Ekstrateia*) of a month's duration and covering the dioceses of Didymoteichon, Maroneia (Comotini), Drama, Serres, Siderokastro, Kilkis, Verroia, Edessa, Florina, Kastoria, Grevena and Naupaktos: 393 parishes in these dioceses were without a priest in September, 1951. It may well be that similar campaigns, and perhaps some kind of clerical conscription of a more permanent character, will be forced upon the Church if many of her children are not to be left without adequate spiritual guidance.

It is perhaps needless to add that the reader would be greatly deceived if he should suppose for one moment that Athens and its suburbs afford a refuge for idle drones of archimandrites who have from time to time to be dragged forth from their retreats by a stern archbishop, and packed off to the barren mountain dioceses of Macedonia for a month's hard work. Nothing could be farther from the truth: were there three times the present number of educated clergy in the Athens-Piraeus area there would yet be urgent tasks left undone for want of priests capable of tackling them. The Athenian archimandrite is the busiest of men, constantly in demand, not merely to serve on committees, but for preaching and confessing and real spiritual work.

In the country dioceses, nevertheless, the present situation is still more serious; the shortage of educated clergy is even more acute. True, the position is slightly better now than it was in 1949, when many a diocesan *hierckeryx* was somehow contriving to combine his already arduous duties with those of an army chaplain, and others had had to abandon their dioceses for a time in order to minister to isolated mountain outposts, but it remains sufficiently disturbing. Many a provincial 'saint' is acutely conscious of vital work still neglected, which could be undertaken could he but command the services of a single priest-theologian.

The Metropolitan of Kilkis, for example, charged with the care of 140 scattered communities, had only one priest qualified to assist him in the work of preaching and confessing the people; a priest already

burdened with the spiritual care of more than 2,000 children belonging
to the newly organised Christian Unions of the diocese and a score of
isolated garrisons, yet contriving somehow to find time to train a group
of young men and women to take charge of the village catechetical
schools when the time came for the refugees to return to their homes.

Is it any wonder that in such circumstances the shepherd of one of
these mountain flocks will sometimes persuade himself that the populous
cities of the south have more than their rightful share of the educated
clergy, and picture them as a pleasant haven from the chill blasts that
sweep his own desolate pastures; a place where university men "tarry
out their time, wither away as a flower ungathered in a garden, and are
never used; or, as so many candles, illuminate themselves alone, ob-
scuring one another's light . . . the least of which, translated to a dark
room, or to some country benefice, where it might shine apart, would
give a fair light and be seen over all."

Much will depend upon the success of the strenuous efforts now being
made to raise the prevailing standards of education among the country
clergy and to increase the number of priest-theologians available for
work in urban parishes and as assistants to the provincial metropolitans.
So far as the village clergy are concerned, the lower seminaries do, on
the whole, meet the needs of the present situation tolerably well. The
system whereby the pastor of a small rural community is normally
chosen by the village elders ensures that the mountain *papas* is a man of
good character and reputation, often the natural leader of the community.
The Greek country parson has little need of book-learning, and a lengthy
academic training would be wasted upon him.

With the parish clergy of the towns the position is less satisfactory.
The urban parish priest does not always command that universal respect
and affection normally enjoyed by his rural colleague. This is not to say
that the clergy of the towns are credited with any of the more spectacular
vices. The Greek bishop is not compelled to exercise an unsleeping
vigilance to ensure that his priests and deacons do not "being drunk
bellow in the streets; or what is worse, in their drink whoop and hollow
in the church; or read the church service in a double tone . . . that their
upper dress though plain be clean, and not one black and another red;
that they walk not in a dronish lazy manner, nor lie down to sleep in the
streets; nor tipple in brandy houses and alehouses, nor boast the strength
of their heads in drinking at entertainments." Such deplorable failings
(though apparently regrettably prevalent in the Russia of Peter the

Great) cannot be said to characterise the Greek clergy of the present day.

It is, however, frequently asserted that the town clergy are for the most part ill-educated, worldly, idle, more concerned with fees than with spiritual things; and, while there are, happily, many and notable exceptions to such generalisations, it must be confessed that there is some truth in these charges. The education of many of the urban pastors is woefully inadequate, and a lamentably small proportion of those educated in the ecclesiastical schools—and to whom, one might suppose, the Church would turn in recruiting her ministry for the urban parishes —seem ready to offer themselves for ordination.

This leakage is in part explained by the late canonical age for ordination, but the reluctance of many well-educated men to become parish priests is also due in no small measure to the precarious economic situation of the clergy. "Our diocese", a Greek bishop wrote to me in 1949, "lacks educated clergy . . . no eagerness is to be observed on the part of the laity to attain to the priestly office, on account of the poor, indeed ridiculous stipend which is at present paid to the clergy." Other causes of this lack of eagerness may be discerned in the style of dress, the untrimmed hair and beard, and general manner of life which custom continues to demand of the clergy (and which are often thoroughly distasteful to the young graduate of the ecclesiastical school), as well as in the abundant opportunities open to the lay theologian. It is, perhaps, hardly surprising that the provision of educated priests to serve in the urban parishes of Greece is a matter which in the eyes of the ecclesiastical authorities is of absolutely primary importance at the present time, and which is receiving the most serious consideration.

XIV

THE HISTORY OF A COUNTRY PARSON

So great was his sanctity while a shepherd, that he was
thought worthy of being made a pastor of men: and having
been assigned the bishopric of one of the cities in Cyprus
. . . on account of his extreme humility he continued to feed
his sheep during his incumbency of the bishopric.

SOCRATES
Ecclesiastical History, I, xii

IN 1892, scarcely more than a decade since the day when the blue and
white ensign of the Kingdom of the Hellenes had replaced the crescent
of the infidel over the citadel at Trikkala, the wife of the village
carpenter in an obscure hamlet amongst the mountains to the westward
of Kalambaka gave birth to a son. The carpenter and his family dwelt
in a substantial stone house a few paces beyond the village square, where
a great plane tree overshadowed the church, dedicated in honour of the
Egyptian anchorite Bessarion. Like many families in northern Pindos
they spoke not only Greek but also the language of the Tsintsars, the
Koutso-Vlachs who come down from the high pastures every autumn
with their flocks and herds to winter in the Thessalian plain.

Like their neighbours at Palaiochori the Photis family (for so the
carpenter was named) was virtually independent of the world that lay
beyond the mountains. They owned a few sheep and goats; the *Kyria*
Photis and her daughters spun their own yarn and wove the strong
indigo cloth which was made up into *sarka* and *palto* for men and women
alike. There was home-baked bread, goats' milk cheese and *yiaourti*, and
an occasional lamb roasted on a spit to celebrate a festival; an abundance
of rough red wine and the fiery ouzo which gladdens the heart of the
traveller when the snow lies deep in Pindos. From time to time the
carpenter would saddle his pack-animals and make an expedition to
Trikkala, returning with an axe or a set of chisels, and dried figs for the
children.

Constantinos, as the carpenter's son was duly christened, began to
go to the village school when he was seven. Long before this time,

however, he was familiar with the mysterious drama which was enacted week by week in the little church of St. Bessarion. Sunday by Sunday, festival by festival, the people of Palaiochori—the carpenter (who had a fine voice and was also the chief *psaltes*); his wife and daughters; Makroiannis, who presided over the tavern; the *Kyria* Andromache, who always stood before the royal doors when Papa Athanasi read the gospel of the resurrection at the end of mattins; Papa Demosthenes, who had fought in the old wars and had seen innumerable wonders, had been to America and visited the holy mountain of Athos—all were caught up for a brief space into the life of the heavenly Jerusalem and joined their praises to those of the saints who looked down on them from wall and eikonostasis.

The carpenter's son learned by heart many of the great psalms and hymns of the Church: long passages from the Gospels and from the Old Testament prophecies which were read on the eves of great festivals and during Holy Week. As he grew older and learned to read he would stand among the singers who crowded round the two lecterns every Sunday, and sometimes the parish priest would allow him to climb up the steps of the bishop's throne that stood on the south side of the church and sing the Epistle from a tattered volume printed at Venice towards the end of the eighteenth century. On the eve of a festival he would come running from the saw-mill or his father's workshop when Papa Athanasi clanged the two bells which hung in the branches of the plane tree beside the church, to take his place among the singers. He learned to find his way about the complicated service-books and to sing the ecclesiastical chant with a confidence which rivalled that of the chief *psaltes* himself.

When Costas left school he went to work with his father. He was already well versed in the rudiments of his trade, and by the time he was called to the colours in 1913 he was a proficient craftsman. He served in the army for three years and had two further spells of soldiering— from 1917 to 1919, and again, in the disastrous campaign in Asia Minor, from 1921 to 1923—before, released from the army at last, he came home to Palaiochori and married a girl from the neighbouring village of Krania. The marriage was blessed with three children: two boys, born in 1924 and 1934, who were christened Leonidas and Athanasius respectively, and a daughter born in 1931.

Meanwhile there was work enough for the village carpenter besides begetting children; even when he was not at his bench there was ground to be tilled and seed to be sown and a score of sheep to be cared for, as well as an occasional expedition to Trikkala. Fourteen years slipped by: there were good harvests and bad; once a blight fell on the vineyards and once the bishop rode out from Trikkala and preached in the village church where, since the death of his father, Constantinos Photis had been the chief singer. The people of Palaiochori heard few sermons; they worked and prayed, sinned and repented; danced in the square on warm Sunday afternoons and argued about the doings of the great world beyond the mountains as they sipped their ouzo in the village tavern.

In 1937 the parish priest died. The elders of the village debated the question of a worthy successor—and who more suitable than the carpenter, Constantinos Photis? A man universally respected among his fellows for his uprightness and integrity; who knew the intricacies of the Venetian service-books with a familiarity such as could come only from long experience. Polycarp, Metropolitan of Trikka and Staghi, willingly acquiesced in the village's choice of a pastor, and Constantinos Photis, the carpenter, went off one day to Trikkala (after a short stay in a nearby monastery) and returned clad in black gown and *kalymmafchion* as 'Papa Costas'. Back in Palaiochori, life went on much as before. The village priest now wore a cassock of the same indigo homespun in which he had been clad from infancy. There was the same pattern of feast and fast, of eucharist and office; and though an occasional wedding or funeral now broke the regular rhythm of the carpenter's life and the former *psaltes* had a different liturgy to perform on Sundays and holy days, it was one with whose least detail he had long been familiar. The tools in the workshop were not permitted to rust, and the vegetables and the vines, the twenty sheep and the pigs, needed no less attention now that their owner wore a cassock and addressed his wife as *Papadia*.

Early in 1941 the Germans poured into Greece. For many months the mountain villages of Pindos, remote from the lines of communication, were scarcely affected by the occupation which, even at that period, brought such acute suffering and privation to the townsfolk and to the villages of the plains. As guerrilla activity became increasingly widespread, however, German and Italian troops were employed in a series of reprisal raids upon the undefended villages lying north and south of a road which connects the Thessalian plain with Epirus by way of the Metsovo pass.

One day early in November, 1943, several hundred soldiers descended upon Palaiochori. The people fled to the forest and watched helplessly while the invaders set fire to their homes and slaughtered their animals. When at length they withdrew the whole valley was shrouded in smoke: the incendiaries had done their work only too thoroughly. The church of St. Bessarion—the most prominent building in the village—had been amongst the first to be set on fire. When Papa Costas and a few companions ventured down from the mountainside to make a cautious reconnaissance they found nothing save the blackened walls and a great pile of charred timbers. The school, just below the parish church, was likewise completely gutted, and more than forty of the village's seventy-odd houses were irreparably damaged. The parsonage, a somewhat more substantial edifice than most of its neighbours—a monument to the professional skill of its builder—had resisted the first attempts of the incendiaries, and before the flames had thoroughly obtained a hold Papa Costas and his sons had come scrambling down from amongst the trees, and the building—though badly damaged—was not utterly destroyed. Amongst the smoking ruins of another cottage was found the body of an old woman who had been unable to make good her escape. Every animal in the village had been slaughtered.

After this catastrophe the people of Palaiochori took refuge in Kalambaka—already crammed with refugees from a score of similarly stricken villages—and there, in the shadow of the great rocks, they remained until 1945. In January and February of that year they went back to the village that had become a wilderness. During the first few months after their return home there was tremendous activity at the sawmill and in Papa Costas' workshop. No sooner had a sufficient number of cottages been rendered habitable than the parish priest turned his attention to the church. With the assistance of his elder son and a score of willing if unskilled helpers, the requisite timber was cut and shaped; and soon—though the church was without vestments and Papa Costas had with difficulty been able to procure copies of a few of the most indispensable liturgical books—there was at least a roof to the building and it was no longer necessary for the people to stand for long hours without protection against wind and snow whilst the holy mysteries were celebrated. Then the school was re-roofed, and as summer gave place to autumn the regular pattern of village life began to reassert itself—though Papa Costas no longer had twenty sheep and there were no more than three pack-animals available for the whole community.

But security was short-lived. The following year brought wandering bands of *andartai* and rumours of terrible deeds wrought in the darkness of long winter nights. In August, 1946, the parish priest of Palaiochori received warning that the Communists planned to murder him as a 'traitor'. Papa Costas fled for the second time within less than three years to Kalambaka. There, at the foot of the limestone cliffs crowned by the hermitages of the ascetics of Staghi, he built a little *kalyva*: a wooden cottage consisting of a single room and a large porch.

Before many months had passed, the whole village was back in the comparative security of Kalambaka, and the mountains were given over to the Accursed of God. Papa Costas and his family (all except Leonidas, who had gone off to the wars) settled down in their new house and the younger boy began to attend the overcrowded school. There were many other refugee clergy in the town: not from the diocese of Trikka and Staghi alone but also from many of the villages lying to the north and west of Kalambaka towards the *comopolis* of Grevena.

The second period of exile lasted until October, 1949. As a refugee priest, Papa Costas was entitled to a monthly stipend of 175,000 dr. (the equivalent of a little more than four pounds sterling) and the usual refugee rations of flour, sugar, etc.; but there was no ground to be tilled, no sheep or goats, no fees from baptisms or weddings to supplement the meagre wages of a 'fourth-class priest'. There was, however, some slight measure of security in Kalambaka, with its garrison and its communications, and Papa Costas' wife and daughter wove gaily coloured rugs, and adorned the little house with lace and tins of basil until any craftsman might have rejoiced in his handiwork.

*

The defeat of the Communists at Florina early in 1949 marked the turning point in the seemingly interminable struggle against an enemy who, when defeated, could always withdraw beyond the northern frontiers of Greece to lick his wounds and build up his strength for another assault. During the summer months the wild region that lies to the westwards of Kalambaka was laboriously combed by units of the Greek army, and in October Papa Costas led the first party of returning refugees back to Palaiochori. His daughter and his younger son remained behind, however, in order that the boy might complete his studies at the high school, and it was in Kalambaka in January, 1950, that we first encountered our country parson.

VII   Constantinos Photis

VIII   The phelonion

He had set out from Palaiochori at half-past two that morning, and with the moon often obscured by clouds and with drifts of snow lying deep in places, it was well past ten before he reached the town. We had taken refuge from the bitter winds that scoured the valley of the Peneios and brought sudden flurries of snow down the pass from the mountains above Metsovo, in one of the dimly lighted taverns that open off the main street, and were deep in conversation with the president and schoolmaster from a village away to the north-eastward of Kalambaka when Papa Costas arrived. We shared a further bottle of ouzo and he invited us to lunch in his cottage.

He had come down, he told us, to do some shopping, and was off to Trikkala the next morning. He would return to Palaiochori early the following day. Why did we not come with him and see with our own eyes the ruined villages of Pindos? Mitsos—a cousin, we subsequently discovered—would be in Kalambaka with the remaining animals the next evening and there would be mounts to spare if we would come. We were not afraid of *katsapliades*? We fairly jumped at the suggestion —*katsapliades* indeed! I sat down there and then and addressed a hasty note to the Lord Theokletos, Metropolitan of Grevena, which was carried off by Athanasi and put aboard the afternoon bus to Trikkala, informing him that I should be several days later in reaching his diocese on the fringes of Macedonia than I had supposed. We laid our plans for the journey, and the light was failing as we set out to climb to the monastery of St. Stephen where we were expected that evening.

Two days later we left the monastery at daybreak: all the monks were ill, and, since Basil was away in Trikkala, we had ourselves to unbar the massive doors that open on to the encompassing abyss. Forty minutes after leaving St. Stephen we were breaking our fast at Papa Costas' cottage: scraps of pork, bread soaked in oil, cognac and retsina. Our priest-carpenter had brought back from Trikkala a great saw, and a pig to be fattened against the following winter. The pig, despite loud protestations, was tied up in a sack and slung from his owner's saddle:

"He has a splendid voice—we must make a *psaltes* of him when we get him back to Palaiochori."

We led our horses out along the Metsovo road. Papa Costas' niece, Katina, had been staying at the 'town-house' for the festival and was returning with her uncle to Palaiochori. On the outskirts of Kalambaka we overtook a party of homeward-bound refugees, their beasts heavy-laden with bedding and great copper pans. A little way out of the town we abandoned the road and struck across the valley towards the river Peneios. The water lapped about our horses' bellies as we forded the swiftly flowing stream, and the potential *psaltes* had a ducking and screeched in muffled protest. Amongst the low hills beyond the river the going was far from easy, and several times we were obliged to dismount and lead our slithering beasts across some particularly difficult stretch of terrain.

About eleven o'clock—soon after we had left the dilapidated cottages and recently rebuilt church of Vanakoulia to our left—we halted outside what had evidently once been a substantial stone house, but which had been burned down and only lately repaired by means of rough-hewn timbers supporting sheets of corrugated iron thrown across the ruins. Here lived Father Constantinos' godparents: well advanced in years and in wisdom, with four sons serving in the army. We broached the cognac and warmed ourselves at the hearth, while the old lady opened one of the wooden chests that lined the tottering walls and brought out walnuts and the golden apples in which this part of Thessaly abounds.

Setting out again a little before noon we descended from the ridge crowned by the ruins of Vanakoulia, and turned eastwards up the boulder-strewn bed of the Aspropotamos. Throughout the rest of the day we journeyed in a desolate landscape of bleached plane trees and white stones, ground and polished by the melting snows; picking our way amongst the boulders of water courses or leading our beasts delicately along narrow paths—mere scratches in the face of the rock— winding high above the torrents and the frozen pools, the long snowy ridges of Pindos far above us.

It was nearly dark when we reached Palaiochori. Mitsos stabled the tired beasts, and the exhausted *psaltes*—long past speech or feeling— was tipped out of his sack into a pile of straw where he lay motionless. Papa Costas led the way upstairs to the living quarters of his parsonage where we were welcomed by his *papadia* and the schoolmistress, a young girl lately come from Ioannina. We supped sitting tailor-wise before the fire, and soon afterwards the women brought in piles of rugs, Papa Costas divested himself of his outer *rason*, and, commending ourselves to the protection of the all-merciful God and of His saints, we all lay down on the floor and were asleep in a twinkling.

In the morning, after breaking our fast with a glass of cognac and a few walnuts, we went to see the church of St. Bessarion. Papa Costas, Mitsos and the churchwardens accompanied us. The interior of the little church was a melancholy sight: the stone eikonostasis had survived the fire but every trace of woodwork had perished. Our priest-carpenter had just completed two new lecterns for the singers and an episcopal throne: there was plenty of work to be done as soon as Leonidas—who had been discharged from the army with wounds in both hands—was home again and fit to return to his trade.

We went on to the school where sixty-four ragged children were huddled round a smoking stove. There had been no teacher in the village between the first and second periods of exile; the schoolmaster, we were told, had disappeared in 1946 and nothing had been heard of him since. Had he gone to the mountains, we asked? Nobody knew— he had disappeared. Kleoniki Zambra, the girl we had met the previous evening, had just been sent to reopen the village school. The windows of the building—roughly re-roofed by the priest and his sons—were blocked with stones and cardboard from packing cases which had contained powdered milk; light was an altogether secondary considera- tion when warmth was in question.

"Last Friday", the *didaskalissa* assured us, "it was so cold that the children cried aloud and we were obliged to give up." There seemed to be no books or slates or paper—there was indeed no equipment of any description save for the stove and a few wooden benches—but the school was again performing its liturgy, and the whole village was conscious that an important step had been taken along the road that led back from the anarchy and insecurity of a decade of war towards the halcyon days which none of the children who crowded the school- house that January morning was capable of recalling.

Time and time again as I travelled about the ruined villages of Pindos during that terrible winter of 1949–50 it was brought home to me how essential an element the school constitutes in the pattern of Greek village life. Almost invariably the first thought of the returning refugees, once they had succeeded in improvising some temporary shelter from wind and snow, was for the church and the school. They would rest content with the most wretched living quarters, provided only that the house of God were decently furnished and their children were re- ceiving regular instruction; but a village without a priest and a school- master was a village only in name.

Urquhart arrived in Metsovo astride the sagacious Aristotle, in the summer of the year 1830, to find that mountain township in a state of the utmost panic and alarm: the houses barricaded, the sheep, cattle and horses dispersed and hidden among the rocks; the town occupied by the troops of "a Turkish Binbashi". And yet, amidst all this martial activity and excitement the good people of Metsovo were occupied with repairing one of their schools. "It is incredible", comments this traveller, "how ardent and universal among the Greeks is the desire of instruction . . . even in the wildest spots that man has chosen for a habitation or a refuge." The universal destruction of the village schools during the recent troubled years has done nothing to abate this passionate desire for instruction, which may still be reckoned one of the most striking and attractive features of the Greek character.

We did not linger long in Palaiochori. Mitsos was returning to Kalambaka for supplies with a train of pack-animals, and before the sun was fairly round to the south side of the parsonage (where the *psaltes* lay late abed, reflecting upon his astonishing deliverance from the perils to which travellers are subject) the horses were saddled and we were ready to depart.

Some four miles down the valley, where the waters of the Aspropotamos divided, lay the cottage of Nicolas Kokoravas—the *geros*, as he was known in the villages round about. An ancient personage with a great reputation for wisdom, it was whispered that he spoke no less than seven languages. We had made the acquaintance of this venerable polyglot the previous evening, and had paused for a few moments outside his dwelling while one of his numerous grandchildren, a fair girl clad in Vlach costume with two children clinging to her voluminous skirts, had brought us apples as we sat astride our beasts, and Papa Costas had scribbled a hasty note addressed to the president of the village of Chrysomelia (an hour's journey to the eastward) to warn him of our impending visit and asking that an escort might be sent to meet us the following day at the cottage of the *geros*.

"Mitsos will leave you at the house of Papa Nicolas, where the waters divide", explained our priest-carpenter; "there you will await the animals from Chrysomelia."

"At what hour will they come?"

"At twelve, without doubt."

The schoolmistress borrowed Boris' camera and took our *eikon* as we perched upon our high wooden saddles. The children peered out at the door and through the chinks in the United Nations' packing cases. Mitsos led the way down the path between the high drifts of snow towards the bleached plane trees and the polished boulders of the

torrent bed, and we followed while Papa Costas and Spyridon Oikonomides, the *epitropos*, stood beneath the great tree in the village square
and waved farewell:

"*Kalo taxeidi; o Theos mazi sas!*"

A good journey; may God go with you.

At dusk we rode into Chrysomelia—a large village lying at 900 metres
—after a journey which will long linger in my memory. For the best
part of an hour Antony the Zealot (our guide) had questioned me
relentlessly as to the constitutions and canons ecclesiastical concerning
marriage with a deceased wife's sister within the jurisdiction of the
metropolites of Canterbury, whilst the mules floundered in deep snow as
we climbed laboriously towards the village, the buildings of an abandoned monastery far below among the pines. We had been delayed at
the cottage of Papa Nicolas, the *geros*, till it was close on three o'clock.
There had been a misunderstanding as to the rendezvous, arising,
apparently, from the fact that the curate of the neighbouring hamlet
of Aidona was also a Papa Costas.

It was the eve of the feast of St. Antony, and the Zealot was preparing
to celebrate his name-day. In a tiny chapel on the outskirts of the
shattered village vespers was drawing to a close. The village church,
dating from 1580 and dedicated to St. George, was a total ruin. We
stayed for the liturgy next morning and all the men and boys of the
village accompanied us to church. After a distribution of the blessed
bread Papa Athanasius Tsergoulas, the pastor of this mountain flock,
took us to see his dwelling—a tiny cell of mud bricks set amidst the
ruins of the house which he had built some thirty years earlier—and
there we sat around a table in the pale sunlight outside the newly-opened
tavern and sipped ouzo with the village elders, while crowds of wild,
ragged children played amongst the ruins of the church—there were
nearly 300 of them and it was eight years since the school had ceased
to perform its liturgy.

Chrysomelia had been one of the most important villages of this
region, with a population of 1,050. It had suffered at the hands of the
Germans at the same time as Palaiochori. The people had begun to
return in October. Scarcely a house in the whole village had escaped
destruction.

The devastation was no less widespread at the hamlet of Kato
Perlangion, where we slept the following night, wrapped in rugs on the

floor of the village president's cottage with a great fire burning at our feet. The parish priest had been awaiting us in the square, and after I had photographed the ruins of the church he rang the great bell which hung from the branches of a plane tree and the whole community gathered to sing the first vespers of the feast of St. Athanasius the Great, in a chapel which had been disused for generations and had only been repaired since the return of the refugees the previous autumn. No more than forty families had as yet found their way back to the village and the destruction was very great. The next morning it was raining heavily and the mud lay so deep in the tiny chapel that planks had to be laid down to facilitate the movements of the celebrant.

Papa Georgios Papageorgiou was himself a native of Chrysomelia. He had been ordained in the early days of the war after living for a time in the monastery of St. Stephen on the windy heights above Kalambaka. His first parish had been wiped out of existence by the Germans, and now the Lord Cherubim, Metropolitan of Trikka and Staghi, had sent him to this ruined hamlet, deep in the folds of Pindos. He lived with his 'priestess' and their four children in a wretched hovel roofed with corrugated iron a little way below the church and, in the absence of a schoolmaster, was himself acting as a temporary *didaskalos*.

We spent a night at the village of Vanakoulia on our way back to Kalambaka. When we arrived the whole population seemed to be engaged in the task of setting up a school in the narthex of the church: a severe structure only lately completed. Over the doorway was set a rough inscription in rustic Greek commemorating the destruction of the church by the Germans and its subsequent rebuilding by the inhabitants—aided, as we later discovered, by generous gifts from relatives in America.

DESTROYED BY GERMANS

1943

REBUILT

AT THE EXPENSE OF THE INHABITANTS

JUNE 1949

ΥΠΕΡΠΟΛΙΘΗ ΑΝΗΓΕΡΘΗ
ΥΠΟ ΜΕ ΔΑΠΑΝΗ
ΓΕΡΜΑΝΟΝ ΤΟΝ.ΚΑΤΟΙΚΟΝ
1943 ΙΟΥΝΙΟΥ:1949

About eighty of the 200-odd houses in the village had been destroyed. The old school-house was a total ruin and would have, in due course, to be rebuilt from its very foundations. The church of St. Menas had been reopened, and the desks and benches which had arrived a few days earlier had been stacked in the narthex. There was tremendous excitement in the village at the prospect of the reopening of the school. The schoolmaster, who was directing operations when we arrived, had just been released from the army. He proved to be the son of the proprietor of the largest store in Kalambaka. Needless to say, the unexpected advent of the *xenoi* caused all work to be abandoned for the afternoon, and half the village accompanied us to the church. The priest, a young man named Antony, was in a sanatorium near Athens. For the time being his place had been taken by a refugee *papas* from the diocese of Grevena.

The evening brought torrents of rain. We slept at the house of one of the churchwardens and set out for Kalambaka the following morning. The *epitropoi* insisted on accompanying us as far as the river, as they feared lest the Peneios, swollen by the heavy rains, should prove difficult to ford. Fortunately, their anxieties were excessive, and shortly after midday on the feast of St. Euthymius the Great we rode briskly into Kalambaka. My mule, smarting under a sense of outraged propriety at its Frankish rider's use of an umbrella (borrowed from the village president at Vanakoulia) as an instrument of coercion, eyed the inhabitants malevolently. As we dismounted outside the cottage of Papa Costas we were greeted by a score of old friends headed by Basil the resourceful, just descended from Aghios Stephanos and bound for Trikkala to negotiate some delicate piece of monkish diplomacy. Papa Costas' daughter and two cousins from Trikkala were bent over their sewing, and a dish of bean soup simmered on the stove.

Boris bade us farewell that afternoon and set out for Larissa, whence he would travel southwards the following day to sunny Attica and the populous cities: back to that strange, mad world where men spent their days poring over antique folios and writing solemn dissertations; effeminate creatures who slept at night between linen sheets and pillowed in soft down, clad in ridiculous garments fit only for infidels: not indiscriminately, men and women together, upon the hard earth, snugly rolled in warm rugs beside a roaring fire; a pampered and degenerate race.

As the sun went to his rest that evening amongst the snows of Pindos I sat for the last time amidst the ascetics of the Thebaid of Staghi and related the strange and terrible things that we had seen during the past few days, while Father Anthimos boiled some eggs in an empty salmon tin, the stylite cats lurked in the shadows, and old Papa Iannis stroked his venerable beard and murmured an occasional *Kyrie eleison!*

*

The country parson of Pindos, writes an early nineteenth-century traveller, displays a truly primitive simplicity. He is at once the director, adviser, friend and companion of those who till the same fields or pursue the same occupations as himself. The unaspiring *papas*, endued, as it were,

> . . . in spite of his ignorance with an evangelical instinct, sympathised with the sorrows and shared in the joys of his people, and abandoning himself to them, made up for any deficiency of ecclesiastical dignity by a fraternal affection which was rendered doubly dear by the misfortunes and misery of those on whom it was bestowed. In the evening, when the labours of the day were finished, the pastor of the mountain assembled with his parishioners at one of their unadorned chapels on the hills. . . . On the festival and the feast, when

the service of the morning was concluded, he joined with enthusiasm in all their gaiety and rejoicings; he had his seat at their festive board and his place in the evening dance, nor did his hilarity and mirth render him less dear, or less venerated in the eyes of those who had yet to learn that cheerfulness was sin, and that ascetic melancholy alone was suited to the dignified sobriety of Christianity!

Several years have passed since Papa Costas and Spyridon Oikonomides, the *epitropos*, stood in the village square and waved farewell; the isolated hamlets of northern Pindos have suffered prolonged and untold hardship, for the process of reconstruction and recovery is inevitably a slow one. Occasional letters reveal the continuing scarcity of the bare necessities of life and the unremitting struggle to restore a disrupted economy. At Palaiochori the ground is again under cultivation, Leonidas is back at his bench, and the church of St. Bessarion bears eloquent witness to the skill of the village carpenter and his elder son.

The passage of time has done little to efface the memory of that journey to the silent depths of Pindos: the chapel at Kato Perlangion, the whole community gathered for the evening office, the candles hissing and spluttering as the rain dripped from the roughly patched roof; Papa Athanasius, the parish priest of Chrysomelia with its golden fruit and shattered dwellings, beside the desecrated altar where for a quarter of a century he had pleaded the one perfect and sufficient sacrifice for the sins of the whole world, a silent multitude of men and boys bare-headed in the snow; Nicolas Kokoravas the many-tongued, like one of the patriarchs of the old dispensation, amongst his children and his children's children in their dilapidated dwelling in the midst of the rushing torrents and the frozen pools; the whitewashed cottage beneath the towering cliffs of Staghi, with its tins of sweet basil and its gay Vlach rugs, a lamp burning in a corner before the eikons of the Lord Christ and His saints; and Papa Costas—village carpenter and minister of the holy and ineffable mysteries—at the head of a winding column of pack animals, threading his way amidst the polished boulders.

XV

GRAVE AND DIFFERENT GARMENTS

The true, ancient, and flourishing Churches of Christ,
being ever desirous that their Prelacy and Clergy might be
had as well in outward reverence, as otherwise regarded for
the worthiness of their ministry, did think it fit, by a pre-
script form of decent and comely apparel, to have them
known to the people, and thereby to receive the honour and
estimation due to the special Messengers and Ministers
of Almighty God.

Canons of 1604

The parson's apparel . . . plain but reverend, and clean,
without spots, or dust, or smell.

GEORGE HERBERT

CAVALLA, the ancient Neapolis, where St. Paul first set foot on
European soil, is a flourishing port, the chief centre for exporting the
tobacco grown on the rich coastal plains of Thrace and Macedonia
east of the river Strymon, the gateway to the Plain of Gold which
stretches from the marshes of Philippi to the mountains to the northward of Drama. Great stone warehouses surround the harbour and give
an air of solid commercial prosperity to the town, which boasts, moreover, two cinemas, a restaurant with plate-glass windows and chromium
fittings, and a remarkable town hall in Hungarian baroque, apart from
lesser amenities. Yet the pedestrian who pauses for breath after scrambling up the steps which give access to the metropolis, or who through
some narrow break in the line of warehouses gazes out across the busy
harbour and the waters of the Aegean, may observe—faint and barely
discernible at midday, sharper and more clearly defined at dawn and
towards sunset—a distant triangle rising from beyond the sea's rim:
Aghion Oros, the holy mountain of Athos, "that is so highe, that the
Schadewe of hym rechethe to Lempne, that is an Ile; and it is lxxvi
Myle betwene".

Thence, as from another world, come occasional caiques manned by
singular bearded figures in black gowns and tall cylindrical caps;

168

mingling strangely with the merchants and tobacco-workers who throng the quays and sip ouzo outside the taverns which sprawl against the low cliff below the old Turkish quarter of the town. Here, under the canvas awnings, one may meet the visitors at close quarters; one may discern the strange aroma, redolent of incense, garlic, fish, tar, resin, the smoke of candles and the salt Aegean, which clings to their garments and persons, defying analysis. Here too the careful observer may note the unwonted mingling of ecclesiastical and nautical attire which characterises these monastic seafarers: a black gown parted to reveal a rope-girt cassock and sea-boots; the cuff of the seaman's jersey peeping from beneath the monkish robe. These seafaring monks from Athos are a race apart, rarely to be seen among ordinary mortals save on the wind-swept quay at Salonica, supervising the discharge of a cargo of timber, or munching sour herbs soaked in lemon in the harbourside taverns at Cavalla.

To the casual beholder, however, the ordinary Greek ecclesiastic is no less plainly a man set apart from other men. Whatever may have come to be sanctioned in the outward garb of Orthodox clergy ministering to congregations in America or western Europe, a rigid conservatism prevails throughout the length and breadth of Greece. Here, at least, far from the corrupting influence of the Frank, the holy canons are faithfully observed. This is true above all of those which relate to the use of (or, rather, abstinence from) razor and scissors: the notion lingers on that in the divine economy there is some mysterious connexion between the orthodoxy of an ecclesiastical personage and the length of his beard; a beardless bishop would be unthinkable. "All the Greek Ecclesiasticks", observes a seventeenth-century traveller, "count it a great Glory to have store of Hair on their Crown, and all about their Ears, as well as on their Beards; and many old Monks, Hermits, and Anchorets, have I seen at Athos and elsewhere with their Hair both very thick and very long." And Mandeville tells us that "the Grekis also seye, that wee synne dedly, in schavynge oure Berdes. For the Berd is tokene of a Man, and gifte of oure Lord." This fidelity to the letter of the canons and to immemorial custom gives the Greek cleric a sufficiently distinctive appearance. The *papas* with his straggling beard, his hair gathered up in a bun and his tall *kalymmafchion*, is a familiar and accepted figure in all strata of Greek society.

The outdoor habit of all the clergy, from the "Prelates and topping

Ministers" down to the simple monk, is substantially identical. It consists of an inner *rason* (corresponding to the western cassock), very long and with narrow sleeves, often—but not invariably—belted at the waist. This is essentially an undergarment, and this it was that the metropolitan of a Macedonian diocese presumably had in mind when he returned some patterns of heavy black serge, which had been sent to him for inspection, with the comment that the cloth would be most suitable for making "warm winter underwear" for his clergy. Over it is worn a fuller gown with wide sleeves: the outer *rason*. The latter is always of black stuff but the inner *rason* may be of various colours. Purple and dark blue are often favoured by the higher clergy, while in the monasteries a grey cassock made of very light material is frequently worn. One abbot of my acquaintance (a resourceful and many-sided character) is accustomed to appear on Sundays and holy days decked in the purest crimson—a splendid sight for eyes grown weary of the joylessness of English clerical attire—while on lesser days he wears a fur-lined outer *rason* (if the season be chill) over a cassock of russet. Among a nation of individualists it would indeed be remarkable if one did not from time to time stumble upon minor sartorial eccentricities on the part of the clergy. These divergences from the norm of unchanging custom are never, however, of so radical a nature as to obscure the ecclesiastical character of their author. In Greece the priest and the monk are marked men, instantly recognisable to all.

I have already referred to the distinctive form of headgear in use among the Greek clergy. This is simply a cylinder of stiffened cloth about nine inches in height, most commonly known as the *kalymmafchion*. That worn by the married clergy is *surmounted* by a narrow brim, but the monastic form, sometimes called a *skouphos*, is brimless. In Greece all the bishops as well as monastic clergy not actually residing in a regular community, wear the former type of *kalymmafchion*. Over this, on formal occasions, a bishop or an archimandrite will wear a long black veil known as the *epanokalymmafchion*. This, however, forms part of the monastic habit, and consequently is never worn by the secular clergy. In the monasteries a soft cap often takes the place of the more formal *kalymmafchion*, though, unlike the Russians, the Greek monks do not venture abroad thus attired. Dr. Covel notes, somewhere in his journals, that on Athos the priests and deacons knit their own caps.

An English visitor to the monastery of Megaspelaion in 1829, the *milordos* Thomas Alcock, comments unfavourably on the attire of the monks: "the want of neatness in the persons of these people", he remarks, "is too conspicuous", a failing our traveller denounces as one of the sure consequences of "an unnatural and unsocial life". Thomas Alcock, it is hardly necessary to add, found the mode of life and habits of Greek monks "little agreeable". "They flatter themselves", he writes, "that their recluse life places them out of the way of the vanities and vices of the world; but it may be doubtful if this retirement does not produce even more disgusting effects than any it may remove." Whatever may have been the condition of the monks of Megaspelaion in 1829, certainly to-day the great poverty which afflicts many of the surviving communities is sufficient explanation of some want of neatness in their members.

The costume which I have thus briefly described, inner and outer *rason* and the appropriate form of *kalymmafchion*, is the customary outdoor dress of the Greek ecclesiastic, regardless of his status or office: of the aspiring archimandrite, in silken gown and with rolled umbrella and brief-case, who hovers discreetly about the chambers of the Holy Synod, as of the village *papas* who labours at his plot of ground, or, with a train of pack-animals picks his way along the boulder-strewn bed of some water-course in trackless Pindos.

Within doors, though the parish priest may put off his tall hat and outer garment, he is seldom to be seen less formally apparelled. And in the mountain villages what more appropriate night-attire for an ecclesiastical person than a thick homespun *rason*: though holy tradition be silent and the Greek country parson abed be subject to no such irksome canonical prohibitions as his brother, tending his flock beneath the vigilant eye of His Beatitude the Archbishop of Canterbury, who is strictly charged that in the interests of decency, gravity and order, he shall not wear "any Coif or wrought Night-cap, but only plain Night-caps of black silk, satin, or velvet".

It is not my intention to embark upon a detailed description of the liturgical vestments of the Greek clergy. "It would be impossible", asserts Dr. King, "to give a description of the habits of the clergy . . . to an English reader without the assistance of figures: for as we have none which resemble them so we have no names in our language to express them by." The reader who would learn to distinguish an *epigonation* from an *epitrachelion* or would comprehend the mystical signification of the stripes of red and white which adorn an episcopal *mandyas* and are called *pomata and potama*, may with great profit refer to the delightful engravings which illuminate that learned writer's discussion of these matters in his work on *The Rites and Ceremonies of the Greek Church in Russia*.

I will but refer briefly to the vestment known as the *phelonion*, which is of primary importance so far as the ordinary parish church is concerned. It is always worn by the celebrant at the liturgy and in its general appearance somewhat resembles the western cope, being of far more ample cut than the chasuble to which it in fact corresponds.

Dr. Covel (who has some diverting observations on this topic) connects it with the 'cloke' (*phailones*) which the Apostle asks Timothy to bring him from Troas (II Timothy, iv. 13), and with the ancient *penula* which was made in such fashion that "when the Head is put through the Top, all the rest hangs down round on all Sides, sloping like the Top of a round Tower or the Roof of a house . . . *Penula* was worn both by Men and Women in Winter upon their Journeys . . . purely to fence off Rain or cold Winter-like Weather. . . . *Tully* takes notice that it was a *peaceable* Garment (and so much more becoming *St. Paul* and a *Greek* Priest), for he was excuseth *Milo* from being guilty of Murder from having it on: *cum Penula irretitus, when he was wrapt up in his winter Peticoat, what could be less prepared or fit for fighting?* For a man cannot handle a Sword or any Weapon under it, either to assault another or to defend himself." The *phelonion*, he continues, is "something like a Woman's Petticoat, with only a hole at the top to put their Heads through, and the rest of it hangs down round about their thighs to their ankles. It is richly wrought with Gold and Silver; and the poorest Parish Priest hath such a one, though of a meaner making".

So much for the *phelonion*. Of the other vestures worn by the clergy at their various offices I will only observe that in former days every church would normally possess a complete set, while a large urban parish where several clergy might concelebrate on a Sunday or a festival would as a rule be suitably furnished with the appropriate vestments. The Greek Church has no scheme of liturgical colours: if a church possesses more than one vestment, the best will be brought out on high days without any regard to colour. The *kalymmafchion* is worn in church, as well as forming part of the outdoor attire of the clergy.

To-day, alas, it can no longer be affirmed with any confidence of the *phelonion* that "the poorest Parish Priest hath such a one"—of however mean a making—or that the other "Garments and Accoutrements" of the clergy are "very Glorious and different". The widespread devastation of the last few years has left many a village church denuded of its liturgical vestments and other furnishings.

The dioceses of Thrace and eastern Macedonia suffered particularly heavily in this respect at the hands of the Bulgarian bishops and clergy who swarmed into these unhappy provinces in the wake of the German armies. Thus, in the diocese of Alexandroupolis, all the episcopal vestments used by the Metropolitan, the Lord Ioakeim, were stolen by the Bulgarian Metropolitan of Philippopolis; while the cathedral church of St. Nicolas, the church of the Dormition in the Isle of Samothrace, and many village churches, were looted by the Bulgarian clergy. Other dioceses in this part of New Greece suffered no less heavily: the cathedral churches at Siderokastro and Serres (to take two examples at random) being plundered of all their liturgical vestments, as well as the important monasteries of Eikosiphoinisses, in the diocese of Drama, and that of the Prodromos near Serres, to the pillage of which I have already referred.

During the winter of 1949–50, when many of the refugee clergy were returning to their villages after an interval of three years or more, to minister in churches which had been wholly destroyed, or looted and perhaps turned into stables or field-hospitals by the Communists, the Archbishop of Athens appealed to all those parishes of Greece which still possessed anything over and above their essential requirements in liturgical books, vessels, vestments, etc., to come to the aid of those who had been less fortunate than themselves.

The need was great indeed. To the ordinary Greek Christian who worships Sunday by Sunday in his parish church it is but fitting that those who minister in the house of God—which is in truth a heaven upon earth—should be adorned with raiment of a finer and costlier making than suffices for the mere performance of one's daily liturgy, and the absence of the usual accessories of liturgical worship inevitably induces a more acute sense of deprivation than would be felt in similar circumstances by Christians of other traditions.

In this point [says Dr. Covel] they look askue even upon us English, for not being so Gaudy, Stately and Ceremonious in our Offices as themselves; though we are Episcopally Ordained, and have grave and different Garments for all sorts of our Clergy in their various

degrees, from the Primates and Metropolites down to the lowest
Order of Deacons . . . and if we English Churchmen are lookt upon
by the Easterlings in this Point, but as Mongrels or half primitive
Clergy-men at the best, how odious and abominable must the
Calvinists appear to them, when they shall be told . . . that there is
no such outward Pomp, or any reverend or decent Garments used in
their divine Offices amongst them; their Ministers are not Episcopally ordain'd, and they wear only a common black Cloak and a Coat
or Jump.

The Greek Church has never known a vestiarian controversy. The
phelonion, richly wrought with gold and silver though it be, has never,
like the western vestment and the comely surplice, served to kindle
polemical ardour. It is evident to all men that the earthly ministers of
Christ should be clothed in such apparel as becomes their high calling:
to celebrate the divine mysteries in a common black cloak or Calvinistic
"jump" would be indecent, a breach of good manners—like going to a
formal banquet in one's workaday clothes.

It is not a little startling to turn from the controversies about vestments and lights and incense which continue to agitate many western
Christians, to a church where these things are used quite simply and
naturally and without occasioning the slightest comment. The Greek
attitude towards the liturgical use of incense does indeed afford a
peculiarly striking instance of the dangers awaiting the Frankish
controversialist who seeks to bolster up his tottering defences with
unwary borrowings from beyond the Adriatic shores. Amongst the
Greeks incense is used at every service, from the most elaborate of
pontifical liturgies to a simple ceremony such as the blessing of a house.
To do otherwise would be thought irreverent: if any custom can claim
to be evangelical it is surely this. Did not the Lord God Himself
command Moses his servant:

Take unto thee sweet spices, stacte, and onycha, and galbanum;
these sweet spices with pure frankincense: of each shall there be
a like weight. And thou shalt make it a perfume, a confection
after the art of the apothecary, tempered together, pure and holy.
And thou shalt beat some of it very small, and put of it before
the testimony in the tabernacle of the congregation where I will
meet with thee: it shall be unto you most holy.

To worship without incense is commonly regarded as one of the innovations of the Catholics. There is a story of an English churchman who was catechised by some Orthodox monks (I fancy that they were Serbs) as to the practice of the *Ecclesia Anglicana*.

"Do you, in your divine worship", they demanded, "invariably offer incense?"

The Englishman confessed that this evangelical custom was not observed at every service within the territories of the Metropolitan of Canterbury.

"Ah!" said the monks, shaking their heads at this irrefutable testimony to the spread of popery: "We knew that you were tainted with Catholicism!"

Let not the western Protestant be dismayed if his refusal to burn incense in his churches is interpreted by the Orthodox not as a sign of his adherence to evangelical tradition but, on the contrary, as a badge of popery. I have always suspected that my Greek friends must find it extraordinarily difficult to enter into the history of the 'ritualistic' controversies of the latter part of the nineteenth century, since the issues at stake are so remote from their own experience. What *can* one make of muddle-headed *barbaroi* who are so perverse as to regard the observance of evangelical customs as evidence of the continuing influence of the Arch-Protestant?

XVI

EPILOGUE

THE WATERS OF MARAH

Thou only art more excellent than all the forests of cedars;
whereon hung the Life of the world, whereon Christ
triumphed and through death overcame death for
evermore.

AMONGST the miscellaneous papers of Dr. Covel which now
repose in the British Museum, there is a letter addressed to the Doctor
from "The Coach Office" on December 21st, 1714, by one Humfrey
Wanley. Covel—still industriously accumulating "Brick, Stone and
Timber" for his book on the state of the Greek Church—had apparently
asked this correspondent whether he had ever sounded Arsenius,
Metropolitan of Thebais, with whom he had had some association
since the latter's arrival in England, about his belief in the matter of
transubstantiation.

Mr. Wanley replies, somewhat irritably, to the effect that on the
previous Monday he had succeeded in extracting a highly unsatisfactory
profession of faith, "craftily worded", from the Metropolitan and his
archimandrite. "I told them", he goes on, "I believed it was taken
from some book I had heretofore read: They replied it is taken from
the Liturgies of Basil and Chrysostome. I told 'em roundly, the Question
was not about what Chrysostome or Basil believed, but about what they
themselves believed; They answered, They believe as those saints did."

Poor Arsenius! He must have had a trying time of it in this country,
what with his constant financial difficulties (rendered all the greater by
the necessity of providing for an oddly assorted following that included
"Gennadius, a Cypriot and Archimandrite, and Kathegumenos of
Alexandria, with four Deacons, an Anagnostes, a Cook and an Inter-
preter,"—who, says Wanley, "consume all") and his inability to enter
into the subtle disputations of the English divines. Nobody seems to
have known what to do with these jolly Easterlings; the universities
would not be pestered with them and the Bishop of London tried to

persuade them that they must quickly be gone. "The poor Archbishop", it is related, "cried out like a child when my Lord of London told him he must Depart." Clearly, the Metropolitan of Thebais was no theologian and felt himself quite out of his depth in controversies about the 'grand Dogma'. Nor was it otherwise with the majority of his contemporaries: "From a Native Greek or Easterling", writes Covel, "who never was out of his country, (though he was there a Man of some Dignity) I never could meet with any tolerable reasoning or answer towards the clearing of this point. Many of my acquaintance would avoid any set discourse about these matters, desiring rather to be quiet and not to embarrass themselves about these, φρικτὰ μυστήρια (as they called them) dreadfull or hidden mysteries."

For all his want of book-learning, however, the bishop's instincts were sound. In transcribing Chrysostom and Basil ("a copie . . . badly spelt and badly accented", says Humfrey Wanley) rather than hazarding a personal opinion, he and Gennadius were appealing not to the private views of two theologians, but to the common faith of all Orthodox Christians; Chrysostom and Basil did but bear witness to this common tradition.

From the day when darkness fell upon the empire of Constantine down to our own time, the Greek Christian has held fast with remarkable tenacity to the faith committed to his charge. He has, for the most part, been little capable of expounding this faith—certainly not in a manner likely to carry conviction with the western theologian. Nevertheless, throughout the dark night of Turkish dominion he has continued to cling at any rate to the outward forms of sound doctrine, and to live to the best of his power in the liturgical tradition inherited from an earlier and more creative epoch. This was no time for unprofitable speculation and the subtleties of the vanished schools, but for striving to preserve the royal treasure entrusted to his keeping.

Now, in our own day, the faithfulness with which through long centuries of oppression a host of unremembered parish priests and simple Christians held fast the traditions of the fathers is beginning to bear fruit. The Greek theologian, furnished once more with a scientific equipment not inferior to that of his western colleague, is rediscovering the marvellous riches of the incomparable treasure locked away these many centuries, and entering into his proper heritage. Unlike the Russian theologian of the diaspora—upon whom enforced contact with western ways of thought has already acted as a powerful stimulus—the

Greek is as yet only beginning to awake to the full significance of the discovery, and it may well be some years before Athens and Salonica are in a position to make that contribution to the life and thought of Christendom as a whole of which they are potentially capable. Yet from out of the depths of suffering and desolation there has come the rebirth of a Christian nation. The Church of Greece has emerged from her fiery trial purified, and conscious, as perhaps never before, of her mission. What may be the ultimate consequences of such a regeneration none can say: the possibilities are infinite.

★

In June, 1948, on the festival of the holy apostles Peter and Paul, the Christian Union of Professional Men of Greece published a stencilled typescript of a draft entitled *Towards a Christian Civilisation*—since issued in book form by the Damascus Press. These pages, as the authors remarked in the original preface to the work, came from a country wherein the agitation, the uncertainty and sometimes the agony of the world had been concentrated; from a land often referred to by her friends as "this unhappy country". And yet, they went on, "we know that our happiness (or unhappiness) depends not on the outcome of external political events, but on whether the Christian and spiritual foundations of our life are firmly established or not". Their voice, they concluded, was not the despairing voice of a nation crying out to the world: *morituri te salutamus*; rather it was that of a people who, even from the depth of their present agony, sought to echo our Lord's words: "If a man keep my saying, he shall never see death." That is the spirit that is abroad in Greece to-day.

If I were asked for a single picture to epitomise the present state of the Greek Church, I would turn once more to the Macedonian township of Edessa, set amidst streams and cherry orchards on the summit of the cliff that bars the way from Salonica to the frontier metropolis of Florina. In the early hours of the morning of the feast of the Epiphany in the year 1949, while the Metropolitan of Edessa and Pella, the Lord Panteleimon, with his deacon, Father Gabriel, two or three refugee monks, his mother, the boys from the orphanage and a handful of lay people, were singing the long vigil-service in the chapel of the metropolis, this already battered town was attacked by a Communist force. By dawn the place was encircled.

EPILOGUE

At the accustomed hour (despite the violence of the bombardment) the bells were rung and the Bishop went with his clergy to the ancient basilica, which stands on the very brink of the cliff, and began to celebrate the liturgy. Before the great blessing of the waters was reached, however, the din had become so appalling, the whole fabric of the church shook so violently, that it became necessary to move to the upper part of the town to the church of Saint Demetrius of Thessalonica. Here the service was resumed and at last the moment when the Bishop would plunge the cross into the waters drew near. Standing in the midst of his people and attended by his deacon, the Lord Panteleimon began to recite in a loud voice the Poem of Sophronius, Patriarch of Jerusalem. Without, the bombardment raged; but above the clamour of the artillery and the rattle of small arms fire the voice of the Saint of Edessa rang out exultant:

To-day the offences of men are washed away in the waters of Jordan;
To-day Paradise is opened to men and the Son of Righteousness has
  shed on us His light;
To-day the bitter water of the people of Moses becomes most sweet
  from the presence of the Lord;
To-day are we released from our ancient lamenting, and as a new Israel
  we find salvation;
To-day are we redeemed from darkness, and illumined by the knowledge
  of God;
To-day the gloom of the world is done away in the Epiphany of our
  God. . . .
To-day we have been purchased for the Kingdom of Heaven, for of the
  Kingdom of the Lord there shall be no end.

GLOSSARY

agamos (adj.) unmarried.

aghios saint—commonly used of a bishop.

ambon pulpit.

anagnostes reader.

andartes insurgent, rebel. Commonly applied to Communists, who were also known as *katsapliades* and *symmoritai.*

antidoron the blessed bread distributed at end of liturgy.

archegos leader, chief.

artos bread.

azymos unleavened bread.

basilissa queen.

caloyer see *kalogeros.*

catholicon principal church of a monastery.

coenobium, koinobion monastery of the common life.

comopolis a large village.

despotes (pl. *despotades*) master—commonly used of a bishop.

didaskalos (f. *didaskalissa*) teacher in a primary school (the first syllable is commonly omitted).

eikonostasis the screen which supports the holy *eikons.*

ekphonesis something pronounced aloud.

eparchia district, province; often used of a diocese.

ephemerios curate, parish priest.

epitropos one to whom a charge is entrusted, a guardian; commonly used of a churchwarden.

estia literally, a hearth or home; *Christianike estia* is the name often given to the headquarters of the Christian movements of a diocese.

geros old man, ancient.

gymnasion secondary school.

hegoumenos abbot, superior of a monastery (f. *hegoumenissa*).

hierarchia the Holy Synod of the Hierarchy

hierokeryx preacher (lit. 'sacred herald').

hieromonachos monk in holy orders.

igoumenos, igoumenissa see *hegoumenos.*

GLOSSARY

kakodoxia heterodoxy

kalogeros monk; literally 'good old man'.

'kalos orisete' welcome!

'kalo taxeidi' bon voyage!

kalymmafchion clerical hat

kalyva cottage or hut.

kapetanios one who leads (the English 'captain' fails to convey the full meaning of the word).

kathisma in general, a seat or chair. In particular: (*a*) a cell attached to a monastery; (*b*) a division of the psalter—a group of psalms for which one sits down.

katsapliades see *andartes*.

koritsi a young girl.

ktopodi (κτωπόδι) *oktapodi* octopus.

kyrios lord; colloquially Sir, Mr. (f. *kyria*).

latreia worship, service.

lavra a monastery organised somewhat less rigidly than a *coenobium*.

mesochori open space in centre of village.

mesonyktikon the midnight office, mattins.

metanoia, metagnia a prostration.

metousiosis approximate equivalent of transubstantiation.

oikoumene the inhabited world, the Byzantine empire.

orthros the office of the dawn, lauds.

ouzo a white spirit.

paidikos stathmos a sort of day nursery.

paidoupolis institution for children evacuated from dangerous areas during the Communist sedition.

palto overcoat.

Panaghia 'The All-holy': the Virgin Mary.

Pantocrator 'He who governs all things': the Almighty.

papadia priest's wife.

papas married priest (pl. *papades*).

paradosis teaching, tradition.

parekklesion chapel.

phakais (φακαίς) lentils.

phrontisterion training school for clergy, seminary.

pneumatikos spiritual father, confessor.

Prodromos   St. John the Baptist, 'the Forerunner'.

proedros   president

proskynesis   worship.

prosphora   eucharistic loaves.

prothesis   the preparation of the elements before the liturgy; the chapel on the north of the church where this takes place.

protosyngellos   bishop's chaplain.

psaltes   singer, cantor.

retsina   resinated wine.

sarka   long coat with loose sleeves.

semandron   a piece of wood (more rarely, of iron) suspended and beaten with a mallet to summon monks to church.

skete   dependent monastery.

skouphos   monastic cap

symmoritai   see *andartes*.

synodikos   member of the Holy Synod.

Taxiarchai   the Archangels (a common dedication for a church).

Theotokos   the Mother of God.

xenos   stranger *or* guest: there is no distinction in Greek.

INDEX

INDEX

Monasteries—*cont.*
35-6, 81-4, 168-70 and *passim*; Palaiokastriotissa (Corfu), 121; Panaghia Olympiotissa, 87; Prodromos (near Serres), 86-7, 173; Zavordas, 87; confiscation of lands of, 32, 88

Monastic life, importance of for Greek Church, 79, 83; character of, 79-83; decay of, 68-70, 88-90; effects of war upon, 77, 84-8

NEALE, J. M., 4, 62
Neapolis, 19, 29, 168
Nevrokopi, 29, 41-5, 50
Nissiotes, Angelos, 127-8, 132, 135, 137

OFFERTORY, 45, 60-1
Oxford Movement, 125

PANAGHIOTOPOULOS, CHRISTOPHER, 117
Panteleimon, Metropolitan of Salonica, 19, 97-8, 178-9
Papakostas, Seraphim, 7, 125, 138
Patras, 25, 27, 118, 122-4, 126
Pearson, Bishop, 1, 2
Pharazoules, Dionysios, 132
Phelonion, 172
Phlamiatos, Cosmas, 117-18, 124, 129
Photis, Constantine, 154-67
Preaching: the responsibility of the bishop, 30; in the new movements, 129-31; neglect of in early nineteenth century, 116, 118; revival of, 117-20
Prince of Kiev, Envoys of, 16, 51
Purvey, John, 63

RIZAREION, 122, 144
Roman Catholicism, Greek View of, 11-12, 24-5

Rousseau, Dom Olivier, 53
Routh, Dr., 3
Rycaut, Paul, 2, 7, 21, 40, 66, 73, 142

ST. ANTONY, 80
St. Augustine, 46, 54
St. Basil, 22, 79-81, 176-7
St. Benedict, 80, 82, 145
St. John Chrysostom, 16, 51, 63, 82, 91, 141, 176-7
St. John Climacos, 36, 81
St. Michon, Abbé de, 3, 27, 59, 87
St. Paul, 18-19, 45, 168, 172
St. Theodore of Studium, 80-1
Salonica, 11, 18-19, 22, 27, 29, 33-6, 44, 55, 89, 125-6, 128 and *passim.*
Schlumberger, 63
School for Preachers, 138-9, 149-50
School of Logos, 119-24
School of Christ, Salonica, 128, 137
Seminaries for Parish Clergy, 95, 108, 110-13, 144-7, 152
Serres, 29, 86
Siderokastro, 30, 97, 133-4
Skaltsounes, John, 127
Smith, Thomas, 2, 59
Solovyov, Vladimir, 6
Srawley, Dr., 61
Standing, normal attitude for prayer, 19, 57
Synodical Tome, 18

THEOKLETOS, METROPOLITAN OF GREVENA, 100-114, 145, 159
Timothy, Assistant Bishop of Salonica, 34, 135
Trikkala, 66-7, 70, 72, 74-5, 78, 95, 102, 154 and *passim.*
Transubstantiation, doctrine of, 1, 176-7
Tsaktanes, Mark, 120, 132

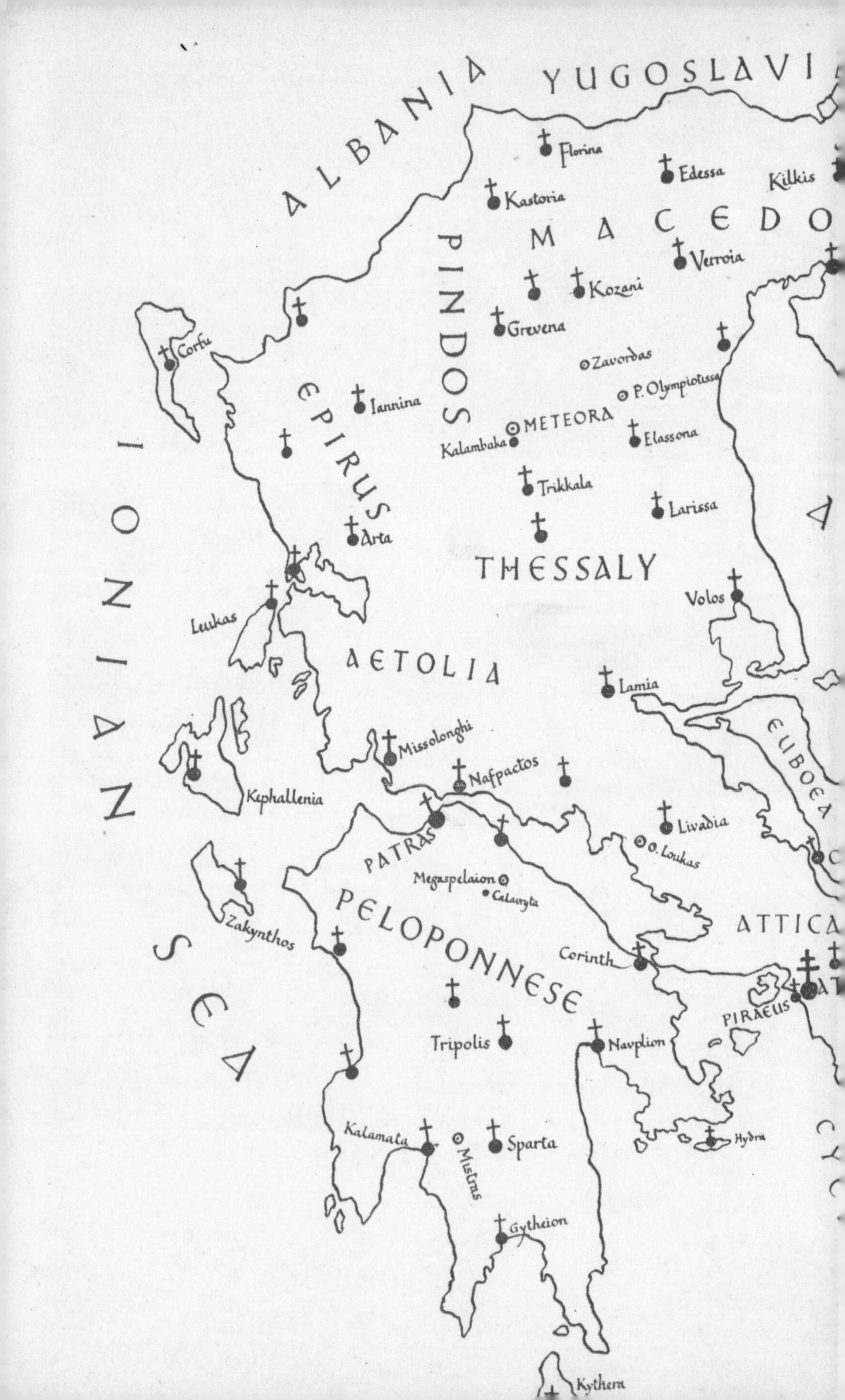
ALBANIA
YUGOSLAVI
Florina
Edessa
Kilkis
Kastoria
MACEDO
PINDOS
Verroia
Kozani
Grevena
Corfu
Zavordas
P. Olympiotissa
EPIRUS
Iannina
METEORA
Kalambaka
Elassona
Trikkala
Larissa
IONIAN SEA
Arta
THESSALY
Volos
Leukas
AETOLIA
Lamia
EUBOEA
Missolonghi
Nafpactos
Kephallenia
Livadia
PATRAS
O. Loukas
Megaspelaion
Calavryta
PELOPONNESE
Zakynthos
ATTICA
Corinth
PIRAEUS
Tripolis
Navplion
Kalamata
Mistras
Sparta
Hydra
Gytheion
Kythera